Mediation Career Guide

Mediation Career Guide

A STRATEGIC APPROACH
TO BUILDING A
SUCCESSFUL PRACTICE

Forrest S. Mosten

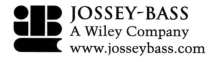

JOSSEY-BASS
A Wiley Company
www.josseybass.com

Published by Jossey-Bass
A Wiley Imprint
989 Market Street, San Francisco, CA 94103-1741   www.josseybass.com

Jossey-Bass books and products are available through most bookstores. To contact Jossey-Bass directly call our Customer Care Department within the U.S. at 800-956-7739, outside the U.S. at 317-572-3986, or fax 317-572-4002.

Jossey-Bass also publishes its books in a variety of electronic formats. Some content that appears in print may not be available in electronic books.

Library of Congress Cataloging-in-Publication Data

Mosten, Forrest S., 1947-
  Mediation career guide : a strategic approach to building a successful practice / Forrest S. Mosten.— 1st ed.
      p. cm.
Includes bibliographical references and index.
  ISBN 0-7879-5703-8 (alk. paper)
  1. Conflict management—Vocational guidance. 2. Mediation—Vocational guidance. 3. Negotiation—Vocational guidance. I. Title.
  HD42 .M673 2001
  303.6'9'02373—dc21

2001002463

Printed in the United States of America
FIRST EDITION
PB Printing   10 9 8 7 6 5

CONTENTS

PREFACE

I am a mediator. My background is as a lawyer. Over twenty years ago, I wanted to make peacemaking my day job. At that time, mediation was in its infancy and was often confused with meditation. It was an uphill climb to build my mediation practice. This book is my effort to help you avoid many of the costly mistakes I made along the way.

Everything in this book is self-taught from a mediator's perspective. Although modern mediation is still rather young, it has developed a flourishing literature contributed by pioneers who have both heavyweight academic credentials and the courage to forge a new profession. The names Jay Folberg, Frank Sander, Bill Ury, John Haynes, Christopher Moore, Michael Lang, Bernie Mayer, John Wade, and many others will long be remembered for the foundation that they have laid for generations of future conflict resolution professionals.

This book is built on their shoulders. I have taken their legacy and used mediation values and strategies to help others build satisfying conflict resolution careers and profitable practices. Bringing talented peacemakers into the field and having them make a living from their mediation craft are important for two reasons.

First, I cannot think of a more noble and worthwhile profession than being a mediator. If talented and committed people want to do this work, I want to help them live out their dreams. Second, and equally important, millions of people suffer from unresolved conflict and are underserved by the mediation profession. I want mediation to be the first stop on the conflict resolution highway and would like enough trained and experienced mediators available to meet this need.

The initial mediation pioneers were special in their willingness and ability to make such major contributions without adequate financial rewards. However, if the profession is going to expand to meet the needs of citizens in conflict, mediators must be able to earn a living.

As mediators, our skill and ultimate value is determined by how effective we are at the mediation table. Yet if we cannot pay our rent, few of us could afford to keep our round tables open for business. This book integrates mediation skills with practice building to provide a strategic approach that I hope will contribute to turning a growing pool of peacemakers into mediators who not only love the work but can make mediation their successful day job.

ACKNOWLEDGMENTS

Visit any meeting or conference of mediators, and you will hear robust dialogue peppered with laughter and play. This book is a product of the generosity and collaboration of my friends and colleagues developed over twenty years in the field.

I owe a debt of gratitude to my talented colleagues of the vibrant organizations in the field: Academy of Family Mediators, Society for Professionals in Dispute Resolution (now merged into the Association for Conflict Resolution), Association of Family and Conciliation Courts, American Bar Association, Beverly Hills Bar, Los Angeles County Bar, and the Southern California Mediation Association. The programs, committee meetings, and outreach projects provide a structure and emotional support for all of our work. My particular appreciation goes to Dan Bowling, Ann Milne, Peter Salem, Susan Bulfinch, Jeff Krivis, Jack Hanna, Neal Blacker, and Jeff Kichaven.

Outside formal organizations, mediators have shared their thinking and materials with me and others in the field. My colleagues at Mosten Mediation Centers—in particular, Sharon Kianfar and James Macpherson—daily test out and refine many of my theories of practice development. For nine years, my mediation study group met once a month in my living room, and my appreciation extends to Angus Strachan, Pam White, David Waller, Frank Garfield, Fred Glassman, and other lawyer-mediator colleagues. I extend special gratitude to my close friend John Wade of Australia for our talks and walks on both sides of the Pacific and to Mary Lund, my co-trainer, co-mediator, and close friend who has imprinted her style and approach in my work.

Much of my interest in mediation career development comes from my days in the training room working with mediators on all levels. I thank the motivated participants who have journeyed to Los Angeles to improve their craft and share their career aspirations. Their training was enhanced by my co-trainers, coaches, and course administrators in both Los Angeles and elsewhere. I am particularly grateful to Judge Dorothy Nelson of the Western Justice Center and Professor Andrew Schepard of Hofstra University for their support in making my dream a reality in the seminar and publication of *Training Mediators for the 21st Century*.

Over the past twenty years, I have been indebted to Steve Sorell for modeling how profitability can contribute to peacemaking. Steve's thinking is present throughout this book, but Chapter Eleven truly bears his blueprint.

The appendixes are largely a collection of information that has been provided by the generosity of Adele Boskey and Robert Collins of the *Alternative Newsletter,* (www.medate.com/tan), Heidi Burgess of CRINFO.com, and Jim Melamed and John Heile of mediate.com. The unselfish cooperation of all these mediators has saved me hundreds of hours and provided needed resources for this book.

I am also very appreciative of the entire family at Jossey-Bass for producing a book that enhances the content inside. Jossey-Bass was my publishing house of choice, and I am proud to be part of a book catalogue that features many of my conflict resolution heroes and friends. My special thanks go to Alan Rinzler, who is single-handedly assembling a world-recognized body of conflict resolution scholarship, and to Amy Scott for her careful editing and wise suggestions that improved the book. Editing a book together gives colleagues an opportunity to share differing perspectives, and I am particularly proud of the way we blended our views.

Finally, I must give tribute to the legacy and influence of my friend and mentor Louis M. Brown (1909–1996), whose photograph hangs in my training room, whose name is engraved in our firm's client library, and whose inspiration touches me every day.

Forrest S. Mosten
Los Angeles

To Jody . . . my beacon.

Mediation Career Guide

Is Mediation
Right for You?

Can Mediation Be Your Day Job?

I have always been a dreamer.

One of my boyhood dreams was that I could one day support myself and my family with a job that could help people and might stimulate me every day.

Some dreams come true. For over twenty years, I have gotten up in the morning eager to get to the office. Every aspect of my work is consistent with my core life values and the strengths of my personality. The work is intellectually challenging and requires conceptual and strategic thinking. I help people, and what I do makes a difference to the people whom I touch and to many whom I will never see.

I am a professional mediator and hope to continue working at my craft until either conflict becomes obsolete or I can function no longer. This bullish view seems to be shared by others who have already chosen to build careers as mediators. You can visit any conference of mediators, mediation Web site, or local mediation firm or group, and you will be impressed by the mediators as people and by their positive outlook toward themselves as professionals and their lives outside the office. The spring in the step of mediators is in contrast to the burnout and stress that many lawyers experience with the legal system (and often with their adversarial colleagues), the frustration that mental health professionals feel toward the intrusive stranglehold of managed care, the depression of public school teachers, and the unhappiness and lack of control that pervade so many in corporate life.

One of the joys of my own professional life as a trainer of other mediators is to witness the infusion of optimism and energy in graduates of mediation training courses. Instead of being asked to sell products that do not work or could actually be harmful, training graduates are thrilled at the prospect of delivering peace and conflict resolution to their future customers. They reach back to their basic values and motivations and realize that they can spend their days helping people and doing good for society. They can increase their control over their workday and feel hopeful about making their mark in a growing profession with plenty of room for innovation and new players.

THE CHALLENGES OF A CAREER IN MEDIATION

There are challenges to becoming a mediator. At nearly the same warp speed that "born-again mediators" embrace the peacemaking profession, many abandon it and return to dreary jobs that pay the bills. Since mediation is not yet a fully understood or a widely accepted way of handling conflict, teaching the public about collaborative problem solving is much like teaching people to eat soup with a spoon. It makes sense but seems strange at first. Many beginning mediators are frustrated at the time, expense, and hard work that it takes to make a living in a new profession.

This frustration translates to many mediators' jumping into, but then crawling out of, this profession. It is remarkable to see the number of new faces at the Southern California Mediation Association's Annual Conference each November. This influx of fresh blood is heartening. But where did all the familiar faces go?

The world's largest stand-alone mediator organization, the Association for Conflict Resolution (ACR), reflected this issue when it printed two contrasting perspectives on the cover of its winter–spring 2000 newsletter (actually, it was the newsletter of Society of Professionals in Dispute Resolution, one of the former organizations merged into ACR). The first article, which I wrote, is entitled, "Peacemaking Can Be Your Day Job." The other article, by respected mediator David Plimpton of South Portland, Maine, was titled, "Ethical Duties of Mediation Trainers in the Promotion of Training Programs." Plimpton argued that after luring training participants into expensive programs by feeding on the glow of a lucrative future as a professional mediator, the reality is that after the training (perhaps many trainings), there are few jobs and realistic practice building opportunities.

Mediators are dressed up with nowhere to go. Supporting his concern, he quoted noted mediation authority Kathy Birt's 1994 article, "Is It Ethical to Offer Graduate Degrees in Mediation When There Are So Few Jobs in Dispute Resolution": "Although overall interest in the ADR field is growing exponentially, actual jobs in the field are few. At the same time, the number of people requesting and receiving training in ADR is increasing each year. . . . Some believe the field is becoming glutted and question whether the profession ought to encourage the continued training of yet more mediators." Plimpton notes that the situation had not changed since Birt's article was published.

M. Scott Peck begins his transformational book, *The Road Less Traveled,* with the words, "Life is difficult." The journey to a day job in mediation is no exception. It took me from 1979, when I started practicing mediation, until 1986 before the income from my mediation work exceeded my expenses on an annual basis. During those seven years, I invested major capital and time (lost opportunity costs). Fifteen years later, in 1994 (the same year as Kathy Birt's article appeared), I was still investing over $15,000 in out-of-pocket costs and over a thousand hours (twenty-five work weeks) per year to build my mediation practice.

I am not alone. Ask any mediator who has a successful career, and you will learn that every one of them has made huge investments of time and money to follow their dreams. Nina Meirding, president of the Academy of Family Mediators, emptied out her teacher's retirement account to launch her mediation practice in the mid-1980s. Jim Melamed, cofounder of the world's largest mediation site, www.mediate.com, gave up a beautiful office in a modern office building in Eugene, Oregon, moved into his home office, and has spent countless days at exhibitor tables seeking to build his peacemaking business.

Perhaps the most poignant story is that of Tom Altobelli of Sydney, Australia. After establishing a successful law practice but feeling unfulfilled, Tom completed a master's degree in conflict resolution at night and on weekends. He attended every mediation conference, volunteered in community programs, coached for free in mediation training programs, and wrote articles for anyone who would publish them. When his mediation practice still hadn't taken off, Tom felt he needed more training to go to the next level. So with his wife and toddler son, Tom left his practice for six months and took courses in Los Angeles with me; in Boulder, Colorado, at Collaborative Decisions and Resources (CDR); at the Harvard Program on Negotiation in Boston; and at other programs in the United States, London, and Hong

Kong. Today, he practices mediation half-time, teaches mediation the other half, and is one of the most satisfied people you will ever meet.

I am not suggesting that you must copy Tom Altobelli in order to make mediation your day job. It may not be necessary for you to give up six months of income and another tens of thousands in out-of-pocket expenses as Tom did. But if you want to enter this profession and it is a distinct profession from your current day job, it will require a major investment and time commitment. And as with everything else in life, there are no guarantees.

If you want to enter this profession and it is a distinct profession from your current day job, it will require major investment and time commitment.

Despite the lack of guarantees, from everything I can see, the future of mediation looks so bright that I would lay a large wager on a successful career in mediation. In truth, I have! By investing in my training institute and national network of mediation centers, I have bet large amounts of capital, taken out major loans (secured by my house), and devoted countless hours based on my assessment that society will need more and more trained mediators.

THE RESEARCH YOU CAN DO

In deciding whether to start your journey toward a mediation career, it's a good idea to do your own field research on the field and its potential to support future mediators. Don't rely on any one source. Talk to individuals in the following segments of our population, compile your own data, and make your own decision.

People Who Have Gone Through Litigation

Find people who have been through the court system. Ask them:

- If they were pleased with the result.
- If they were satisfied with the process.
- If they found that the money they spent was worth it.
- If they considered mediation as an alternative while litigating. Why or why not?

Litigation Attorneys

If you do not personally know any litigators, ask some friends or call a few lawyers listed in the Yellow Pages. Ask them:

- If their clients are satisfied with the results, process, and costs of litigation.
- If they, as litigation professionals, are satisfied with the predictability of outcome, speed of result, and the quality of the finished product.
- If they are satisfied with the financial return on the litigation services they offer. As a subquestion, ask them if they get paid fully at their agreed prices for the work they do, even when the results are favorable.
- What the conflict and stress of litigation do to them.
- What their perceptions are of and experiences with mediation.

Judges and Court Staff

Take a field trip to your local courthouse and see if you can chat a bit with some of the sitting judges, court clerks, and bailiffs. Ask them:

- If the citizens who use these taxpayer-supported institutions seem satisfied with the results and how they are treated by court personnel and their lawyers.
- How they believe litigation serves the values, goals, and needs of the court itself.
- What their perceptions are of and experiences with mediation.

Corporations and Small Businesses

Make an appointment with an executive or high-level manager of a large corporation and another with at least one small business owner. Ask them:

- If they are satisfied with the litigation process as a way of recovering losses due to conflict and disputes.
- To try to quantify the financial internal and public relations costs to their companies in dealing with conflict and diverting positive and valuable business resources to dwell on past conflicts for months or years in litigation.
- What their perceptions are of and experiences with mediation.

Public Agencies and Nonprofits

In completing your field research, talk to someone who works for a local, state, or government agency, school system, or branch of government. Also, talk to someone who devotes his or her career to helping people through a career in a charity, public interest organization, or other not-for-profit activity. Ask them:

- How their institutions or their beneficiaries (taxpayers, clients, other agencies) are currently resolving conflicts and disputes and whether what they are doing is working?
- How litigation affects their basic mission and limited budgetary resources.
- What their perceptions of and experiences with mediation are.

WHAT TO DO WITH YOUR RESEARCH RESULTS

In compiling your findings and conclusions from your own field research, compare and contrast them with the results of the Comprehensive Legal Needs Survey completed by the American Bar Association in 1994 and the Report of Self Represented Litigants published by the American Bar Association in 1993:

- Over two-thirds of identified legal needs do not get handled by lawyers because of perceived high costs.
- When people use lawyers prior to litigation, satisfaction is very high. When the matter enters the litigation process, satisfaction levels with both the court system and lawyers drop dramatically, regardless of the results.
- In Arizona, over 62 percent of divorce litigants have no lawyers at all, and 88 percent of the cases only have one lawyer. Of those people who choose to self-represent without lawyers, over 50 percent could afford some legal help but chose not to pay for it because many see lawyers as deal breakers and conflict escalators.

Also consider the following selected findings from a 1998 report to the Massachusetts legislature demonstrating the high satisfaction, quality results, and cost-effectiveness of mediation:[1]

- Parties find it easier to express themselves in mediation.
- Parties appreciate increased privacy.
- Attorneys bill significantly fewer hours when a case is in mediation.

- Attorneys as well as parties express a high level of satisfaction.
- Seventy-two percent of attorneys report that mediation is less costly for their clients.
- The range of solutions is far wider in mediation.
- Over 90 percent of cases referred to mediation result in written agreements.
- Over 80 percent of the disputants are satisfied with the terms of the mediated agreement.
- Ninety percent of mediation participants felt that the mediation process was clear, the mediator had good ideas, and they had been listened to.
- Parties are more likely to abide by the terms of a mediation agreement.
- Mediating cases ends disputes faster.
- Parties save significant attorney fees, expert witness fees, and other costs.
- Overall costs of mediated agreements are 40 percent less than matters resolved through litigation.
- Plaintiffs are more likely to receive part of the claim in mediated cases than in nonmediated cases.
- Over 50 percent of participants felt they changed the way they handled conflicts from their mediation experience, and 70 percent of family members reported less arguing and fighting in the months following the mediation.
- Nearly 60 percent of participants report that they better understood the other person's point of view following the mediation.
- Ninety percent of participants felt the mediation process was good. Quicker settlements increase satisfaction levels for both clients and attorneys.
- Seventy-seven percent of participants expressed extreme satisfaction with the mediation process. A substantial portion of those who failed to reach an agreement in mediation believed mediation was useful and would recommend it to others.

Your own field study, bolstered by the research findings, should lead you to the conclusion that the current method for resolving disputes, litigation, is not working and produces low satisfaction by both its users and providers. The public and professionals have a need and demand for a better product. This is the key to any new market change: people do not like what they're being offered and want something different and better.

THE FUTURE OF MEDIATION

If mediation has proven demand and is increasingly available, what does the future look like?

The Rand Institute, an internationally acclaimed think tank, published a report in 1997 finding that only 7 percent of civil cases were then using private mediation.[2] Few would doubt that the use of mediation is on the rise. What would happen if 20 percent of civil cases used private mediation? Using 1997 as a baseline, if only one of every five court filings used private mediation, society would need three times the number of mediators to handle this increase. This 300 percent increase in consumer demand actually seems low (but we'll live with it for now), especially if you factor in the increased need for mediators for problems and claims that never hit the court system. For example, many use mediation to resolve workplace, family, and consumer problems long before litigation is ever contemplated, let alone used. Also, mediation is on the rise in the forming of family and business relationships; premarital financial and blended family mediation and construction industry preventive mediation are just two growing examples. If the trend continues, the 300 percent increase of mediation use might seem distortively low.

The growth of mediation in Australia is a positive indicator of what may happen within the next few years elsewhere in the world. For example, Australia has made significant changes in the language for mediation. In the United States, ADR stands for *alternative dispute resolution,* including mediation. In Australia, however, litigation and arbitration are the second-line options, while primary dispute resolution (PDR) endorses mediation, conciliation, and negotiation as the first option in its system. This change, promulgated by the Australian Family Court, has produced a cultural shift in the use and growth of mediation in that jurisdiction.

Another Australian institutional change has produced a rapid increase in demand. In the Australian state of Victoria, all civil cases in the court system must be referred out for private mediation. The litigants select their own mediator from the private sector at market prices at their own cost. Special provisions are made for litigants who lack the financial means to pay.

This change alone has so taxed the supply of qualified mediators in the private sector that there is a societal need to train more mediators, which has produced a deluge of interest in mediation training programs. In Melbourne, people who want mediation training often have to pay for a seat in the training room just for the opportunity to observe other future mediators being trained!

If similar court initiatives occur in this and other countries, the price of training will go up to meet demand, as will the need and price of mediation services in the marketplace. If I were starting my mediation career now, I would feel confident embarking on a field with this type of promise.

ESSENTIAL QUALITIES FOR MAKING
MEDIATION YOUR DAY JOB

There is no recipe for increasing your own chances of career success; however, beyond dumb luck and being at the right place at the right time (which is entirely possible), I have found that many successful mediators in the field today have the following:

- Commitment to peacemaking
- Commitment to the skills and craft of mediation
- Commitment to making a living through mediation work
- Strategic planning and implementation of their mediation career
- Reflection and continual reevaluation
- Successful models and mentors

Let's look at each of these elements more closely.

Commitment to Peacemaking

Several years ago, a friend told me he was thinking of shutting down his law practice and buying a tree trimming business. He was excited about the bargain price he could negotiate, the high-profile customer list, the profit margin on the books, and the willingness of the current owner, who was retiring, to coordinate the transition with the customers, suppliers, and working crews.

I asked my friend one question: "Do you love tree trimming?"

He stood dead in his tracks and shot back, "What does that have to do with it? It's a money machine—and certainly better than working the long hours under fluorescent lights for people who aren't happy with what I do and don't pay their bills."

He bought the business—and it cost him his life savings, his credit, his father-in-law's retirement, and his marriage. It is impossible to say whether the same disaster could have been prevented had he loved tree trimming, but at least he would have staked his money, time, trust, relationships, and dreams for a goal in which he believed and enjoyed.

The lesson here is simple: don't jump into a growing but still uncertain field like mediation unless you eat, breathe, and dream about creating peace and resolving conflict and are willing to risk everything to make it happen. If you are dissatisfied with your position or even your entire career path, it may be easier for you to make a small correction (another job, slight retraining, or jump to another similarly established field) rather than leap into mediation. Mediation is a distinct profession requiring its own intense training and practice.

Don't jump into a growing but still uncertain field like mediation unless you eat, breathe, and dream about creating peace and resolving conflict and are willing to risk everything to make it happen.

If you would like to further your awareness and commitment as a peacemaker, the place to start is *The Third Side: Why We Fight and How We Can Stop* by William Ury.[3] This brilliant, readable book by a master mediator is a primer in establishing a commitment to peace in your own life and for others. Ury, the coauthor of the negotiation classic *Getting to Yes,* uses numerous examples of creating a culture of peace as modeled by him, President Jimmy Carter, and other leaders in the field.[4]

Commitment to the Skills and Craft of Mediation

Quality pays off in every product and service. It is no less true in the field of mediation—and perhaps even more so.

One of the reasons that so many rush into the mediation field and then exit just as quickly is that there is no regulation or licensing monitoring minimal competency for entry into the field. Although there are certification programs that reward competency, mediators, unlike lawyers, mental health practitioners, or housing contractors, do not need a license to practice. This can lead to consumer abuse that hurts the entire field. Opponents of regulation point to the lack of traditional regulation and the freedom of the marketplace as being responsible for the growth of mediation, the variety of models, and the high satisfaction rate. Yet even critics of regulation concede that the future of the profession and its ability to escape regulation require that we keep our own house in order through self-regulated standards that include a high bar of mediation competency.

Consumers of mediation services are smart and discerning. At Mosten Mediation Centers, where mediation participants select their mediator from competing profiles on the Web, clients are articulate about their respect for mediators with extensive training and experience. Clients have an instinctual sense of calibrating a mediator's fee with competence; charlatans are not suffered gladly.

Regardless of the future of regulation and licensing, your key to success is a commitment to constantly improving your own quality through training, consultation, and supervision. Take a look at the mediation standards of professional organizations set out in Appendix Two. These voluntary and aspirational standards set out training and quality expectations that should be your *minimum* goals.

*Your key to success is a commitment
to constantly improving your own quality
through training, consultation, and supervision.*

The best mediators I know are continually in training. When they attend conferences, they are front and center in the presentations and workshops put on by their peers. They are current in mediation literature and can discuss new theories and techniques on a high level. They are knowledgeable about pending legislation and model rules, and they write articles, practice materials, and other contributions to the field. They consult with colleagues in difficult cases and seek out new approaches in situations that the less motivated would consider routine. They are learners both inside and outside the mediation room.

If you are considering a career in this profession, you should emulate the learning approaches and actions of successful practitioners. With the understanding that your mediation training is never over, you should always be seeking out new courses, books, and opportunities to improve your competence. The Japanese call this approach *kaisen*—that is, an approach of ongoing improvement. Try to incorporate *kaisen* in every aspect of your evolving competence. *Kaisen* is not only continually stimulating, but it will never let you settle for the known and familiar. Ultimately, regardless of your marketing or your practice management, your success in the field will be how effective you are at mediating.

Commitment to Making Your Living Through Mediation Work

When I entered the field in the late 1970s, many mediators and critics of mediation alike were in agreement on one point: unlike other professionals who charged fees, there seemed to be something wrong about mediators' charging money for their services. Critics saw mediators who charged fees as being opportunistic and just a bit fraudulent to the public. Their reasoning? If the service is so useful, it should be given freely and for free. Many mediators shared this view, but for very different reasons: because mediation is so important for the participants and rewarding for the provider, charging a living wage might hinder some of this important transformative experience and might deprive mediators of the opportunity to fully practice their mission in life.

This approach lives on today. Many judges and legislators eschew programs that pay mediators. Their view is that there is an ample supply of volunteers—and, after all, mediation is God's work. Mediators, particularly those born again after inspirational trainings or transformational experiences around the mediation table, often buy into this attitude and will work for free.

No wonder there are so many mediators who are talented and committed peacemakers but leave the field because they can't earn a living. Mediators who will think nothing of giving away their services would never expect the same of dentists or ice cream store owners. By not insisting that mediators be paid for their efforts and contributions, many mediators contribute to the large number of peacemakers who are leaving the field, thus depriving the public of their conflict resolution services.

The first step in making your mediation work to provide you a living is your affirmative decision to do so. Many mediators truly enjoy their peacemaking work as an avocation. They enjoy attending training sessions and conferences to improve their skills and then enjoy providing services on a volunteer or part-time basis. They work in community mediation centers or for nonprofit groups, or they fill in as needed for professional mediation groups. These mediators make an invaluable contribution to the resolution of conflict in their communities; many might lose their peacemaking zest if they did it full time, day in and day out, and depended on those skills either to attract clients or keep a job.

I fully understand and support this choice of part-time peacemaking. When I was a boy, my mother spent every evening on the sofa knitting elegant clothing for all members of our extended family. Her knitwear brought ooh's and aah's from her friends and people on the street. Even the professionals at the local knitting store admired her handiwork. At one point, another customer in the store asked my mother to knit a dress on commission. After accepting the assignment, my mother was in a state of constant stress and agitation—and she never finished the dress. Knitting, an act of joy and love when she was giving away her work to her family, had become a tiresome and stressful enterprise.

You can be a peacemaker without making it your day job. It may be the best decision you ever make. However, if you want to spend your days mediating, you have to be prepared to take your skills to the marketplace. This means you must adapt your peacemaking commitment to job requirements or a practice setting and without compromising your core values.

If you opt for a paycheck in either the public or private sector, you will immediately be faced with protocols and demands that may differ significantly from the models that you learn about in books and training courses. For example, one of the largest employers of mediators in Los Angeles is the Conciliation Court within the Los Angeles Superior Court, a mediation service for custody and visitation issues. As a staff mediator, you receive top-notch advanced training, long-term supervision from senior staff, and a salary plus fringe benefits from Los Angeles County. Perhaps most important, you have an opportunity to mediate every day with a diverse range of people. Your skills would rapidly develop as you face challenges and pressures from the participants, their lawyers, the court staff, and the demands of the daily issues.

However, as a court staff mediator, you might be required to modify your views of mediation and skills to fit the framework of the job. The parties seldom voluntarily enter mediation; they are required to do so by statute and are ordered to participate by the court. So much for consensual participation.

Due to the demand for services, it may take two to three months for an appointment that may be limited to two hours, agreement or no agreement. So much for gearing the process to the participants.

Even if the parenting issues are tied to concerns about child support, the family home, or other financial issues, the mediator is restricted from addressing any issues other than custody and visitation. So much for linking issues for an overall agreement.

In over half the conciliation courts in California, if the parties do not reach agreement, the mediator is authorized and required by court rules to make a recommendation to the judge, using communications and observations from the mandated mediation session. So much for confidentiality and privacy.

Certainly, pressures and limitations differ from position to position, but every job in mediation will require compromises. If you work in an ombudsman's office, you will be restricted on the issues and parties that you can work on. If you work for a mediation provider firm, you may be required to sell the mediators on the firm's panel when you might know of better mediators elsewhere. Every position will have its requirements and its limitations.

Private practice is also not free of cross-pressure. You will face people who have done abhorrent things and might ask you to be an accomplice in their schemes to defraud the government or the other party. Parties may be willing to pay for only an hour of your time when you believe that the matter calls for at least three hours to do the job competently. Referring lawyers or accountants may request you to steer the parties back to their offices when you have real questions about the competence or ethics of those professionals. You may turn away people who could benefit from your services because they can't pay your fees—and you have your own bills to pay.

Keep your seat belt buckled; get ready for a wild ride!

As you can see, your commitment to make your living as a mediator may face major challenges. It happens in every field when reality comes face to face with lofty ideals and initial expectations. Through it all, unless you either take a salaried position in mediation or stay in private mediation practice, you will not have mediation as your day job—and not just you but your community may be the worse for your inability or unwillingness to manage these inevitable bumps.

Strategic Planning and Implementation of Your Mediation Career

In training and talking with mediators throughout the world, I have been continually amazed by a disconnect between what mediators do for the parties whom they help around the mediation table and what they do in managing their own careers. The disconnect is that mediators are skilled strategists in planning how to resolve the conflict of others but are reluctant or unable to plan strategically how to make mediation their day job.

Most successful businesses have a mission statement and a written business plan. Few mediators take the time or undergo the hard thinking to articulate in writing their vision for their practice and their key goals, and think through how to achieve them. Mediators have the training and ability to offer many services that the public would buy, yet they often don't review their inventory of services or fail to develop a marketing plan to sell them.

Few mediators take the time or undergo the hard thinking to articulate in writing their vision for their practice and their key goals, and think through how to achieve them.

I have struggled for years to understand why so many mediators are effective with their clients' goals yet so passive and apparently uninterested in their own. Of course, most mediators will say that they want to be successful yet will not take the baby steps to go from the old way (financial struggle and pressure) to a new way (financial self-sufficiency).

The foundation of your strategic planning is the Mediator Self-Survey in Appendix One. Before I take on a mediator for individual supervision, the mediator is required to write out answers to every question. Although you might not now be in a position to answer all the questions on this planning instrument, you should read it over to get a handle on the types of issues you should start thinking about.

There is one strategic planning tool that you can implement now: establish a personal board of directors. Just as companies assemble diverse and trusted people on their boards, you can do the same thing to help you set your personal strategic career planning objectives and priorities. It can be lonely pursuing a career change in an uncertain field. You may be pleasantly surprised to find that for the price of a dinner two or three times a year, people who care about you will be pleased to help you test your ideas, monitor your progress, and give you emotional support.

In establishing your board, try to select people who will offer different perspectives and challenge your thinking. You must be willing to trust your board members with your doubts, your fears, and your private and otherwise confidential thinking. You should be prepared to share your true financial and emotional picture—the good, the bad, and the ugly.

Throughout my mediation career, I have made several wrong turns, false starts, and unproductive efforts. Since I started regular personal board of director meetings in 1982, I have found my peaks and valleys leveling out and have enjoyed more satisfaction as a result of my efforts.

To give you an idea of what types of decisions you can discuss with your personal board of directors, let me share some of the topics of my own recent meetings:

- It's time to write a book on mediation career building. Should I take the time away from practice now, get a coauthor, employ a research team, or do it myself, as I did the last time?

- My last book was with the American Bar Association (ABA). Should I publish this book with the ABA or branch out to Jossey-Bass, which has published books by a number of leading authors in the mediation field?
- I have several opportunities to establish links with other Web sites or advertise on their sites. Which ones should I explore? How do links and advertising fit in with my overall Web strategy?

My personal board has provided invaluable assistance in these and other matters. I reciprocally sit on the personal boards of other mediators. (Naturally, when I attend their board meetings, I focus on their issues, not mine.)

Reflection and Continual Reevaluation

Several years ago, I was introduced to Donald Schön's *Reflective Practitioner,* a book that raised both my skills and my career development.[5] I incorporated Schön's innovative thinking into my own training courses. With the monumental book by Michael Lang and Alison Taylor, *The Making of a Mediator,* I found reflective practice thinking vaulted to a new level.[6]

Piggybacking on Lang and Taylor's building on Schön's theory, following are the essential elements of a reflective practitioner that can be translated into building your career as mediator:

- Engage in a continual process of self-reflection while you are taking strategic action in building your career and after you have taken it.
- Rely on theory and overall concepts of practice building to guide and inform you.
- Test out and experiment with your strategies.
- Be a continual learner by being willing to see perspectives, strategies, and experiences other than your own.
- Regardless of your initial success, never see yourself as an expert. Always acknowledge how much more you have to learn.

These guidelines can provide structure to implementing the commitments that you make in regard to peacemaking and becoming self-sufficient in this new field.

You will need to try them out, one by one and as a whole, in constantly examining and measuring your progress: where you are now and where you see yourself in your mediation career in six months, one year, two years, five years, ten years, and twenty years from now.

Successful Models and Mentors

The last step in making mediation your day job is to avoid reinventing the wheel. Although you may be talented and motivated, others have blazed the trail of a mediation career before you—struggling and overcoming many of the same challenges that you may now find daunting.

Other fields recognize the value of promoting, even requiring, mentoring relationships. Some guilds or unions require a period of apprenticeship before granting a union card or license. In order to qualify for a license to practice in most states, mental health professionals must undergo thousands of hours of supervised practice. Although not required by licensure laws, lawyers, managers, and other professionals have supervisors to monitor their work during the early years. These supervisors often become mentors, teaching and modeling by example. Even more important, a mentor is a source of emotional support that can build the beginning professional's confidence. A mentor's contribution can be imprinted in your professional style and strategy throughout your career.

I have had the honor of being mentored by several lawyers and mediators throughout my career: Steve Meyers, who taught me how to operate a law practice to improve legal access; David Binder, who taught me the basics of client-centered lawyering, in particular the artistry of client counseling; and Frank Sander, Jay Folberg, and John Haynes, who modeled how I could make a bigger difference for society as a mediator than I ever could as a lawyer. The biggest impact on my career came from my twenty-five-year relationship with Louis M. Brown, the father of preventive law. Lou has imprinted my values and my thinking to the point that when faced with a decision point, I often think, "What would Lou say to me now?"

There are many more potential mentors in the field than when I started in 1979. Mediation organizations such as the Academy of Family Mediators (now the ACR) have institutionalized a consultation program, making it a requirement for mediators to have ten hours of consultation before qualifying for Practitioner Member status. The Southern California Mediation Association has a mentor program that is free to any member who wishes to participate; unfortunately many volunteer mentors do not get enough work.

Be proactive in finding and using mentors; it is very gratifying for the mentors too! Seek a mentor's help in developing your reading list, deciding what courses to take, which conferences to attend, and when and how to establish your practice. Be sure to include your mentor in your celebratory moments as well as your crises; giving back is reinforcement not only for your mentor but for the mentoring process as a whole.

CONCLUSION

I hope you now see that it is possible to make mediation your day job in spite of the hurdles. If you have a commitment to peacemaking and an appreciation of the benefits of mediation, you're off to a good start. Let's now see if you have what it takes to be a mediator.

Do You Have What It Takes to Be a Mediator?

At the start of every basic mediation training course, I sense a disquiet in the room along with a buzz of excitement and anticipation. Participants from various backgrounds are all asking themselves, "Will I be a good mediator?" "Do I have the talent and the skills to make it?"

I have never met the perfect mediator, the bionic mediator. Mediation is in many ways an art, but it also is a science that can be taught. Most people who are committed enough to take a forty-hour course and follow up afterward have many qualities that will be of service to people in conflict. Everyone who enters the field has some sharp edges and weak spots that need to be rounded and strengthened.

PERSONALITY TRAITS OF MEDIATORS

The discussion in this chapter highlights some personality traits that mediators need. A mediator needs to take in information without making premature judgments. As you review the following traits and think you come up short on a few of them, don't throw in the towel. In the same way, as you are going down the list, if the qualities seem to be calling your name, keep your hat on: talent and predisposition toward being a neutral facilitator are only the beginning steps in your journey.

Good Listening

I am always amazed when applicants for mediator positions spend most of an interview telling me how well they listen! Truly good listeners *listen*. Mediators need to listen to both sides of the argument, understanding the situation clearly in order to help the parties solve the dispute effectively.

Think about your listening skills:

- In discussing issues of interest and importance, do you spend your time trying to convince the other person (or group) how right you are or how wrong he or she is?

- Are you truly interested in what other people are saying?

- Are you a student and learner of human behavior, or do you use the words of others as a platform for your own contributions?

- In discussions, do you enjoy connecting dialogue in which you feel good about the other people and their perspectives, or do you favor debate where you didactically try to advocate your own position and have the others concede that you persuaded them to your way of thinking?

Effective Communication

Mediators are constantly observing how others are communicating and searching for an improvement in the communication process. Because mediators are also part of the process, you must be able to hear what you are saying and see how it is affecting the participants. Fight and flight are the most common communication modes; it's much more difficult to manage conflict and have a meaningful conversation with someone with whom you have negative feelings or a lack of trust. In your communication with people in your life, think about the following:

- When you talk to people, do you focus on saying what you need to say, or do you also check out whether they understand and appreciate what you are saying?
- When you don't get your way, do you throw tantrums or take your ball and go home?
- Can you stay involved in dialogue when the other person isn't playing fair or acting responsibly?
- Can you adjust your communication style and approach to meet the needs of different types of learners?
- Do you know whether you learn best by talking? Hearing? Seeing? Touching? Experiencing? Do you need a combination of approaches to learn effectively?
- Do you indicate to others what they need to do to be effective in communicating with you?
- Is it important to you to gear your communication in a way that others can understand? Do you think about drawing a picture or a graph in your conversations with people whom you know connect with the visual aspects of life?
- Are you willing to repeat yourself (perhaps several times) or find other creative ways to get across a point?

❧ Practice Tip ❧

Work on your listening skills. In the middle of a conversation that is going nowhere, suggest that you and the other person take a walk or make a sandwich to incorporate some shared experience into the situation.

Patience

Mediation participants generally do not present or act their best. Think about when you have been in conflict in your own life. How compromised was your own behavior and ability to function? Then magnify the challenge to include being asked to prepare and negotiate constructively in a structured setting with someone for whom you may have little or no regard.

Mediators also face challenges to their patience. Disputants may have demands for quick results when one or both of them don't know what to do—or don't want to do it. Others may have a desire to succeed in mediation, but due to lack of experience or emotional barriers, negotiations may be tortuously slow or break down into hassles or diverted into tangents. Think about your own patience.

- Are you patient with others who don't act up to your expectations?
- How good are you at adjusting your expectations to the reality of the situation?
- Can you keep going with people who appear to want to fail?

❧ Practice Tip ❧

Work on being more patient. Mediators are often faced with people with differing abilities or capacities to perform. When you're on a hike, can you slow your pace to that of the slowest hiker? Can you do so comfortably even when others in the group become irritated with the slowpoke?

Tolerance and Neutrality

One of the keynotes of the mediation process is the neutrality of the mediator. While appearing to be neutral is important, actually maintaining neutrality is essential. Both being neutral and appearing that way are easier said than done.

Being neutral doesn't mean liking every participant or being devoid of biases in favor of or against certain people. Don't worry; mediators aren't saints. Every professional mediator I know has biases and develops nonneutral feelings toward parties. The key is to be able to recognize those feelings, acknowledge them, and work to make sure they do not pollute the process by favoring one party over the other.

Tolerance means taking your biases and being able to work effectively with different types of personalities and behavior without judging the actions or the people—in other words, accepting differences in the attitudes and actions of the parties without choosing between them and not requiring parties to adopt or live up to your own values, philosophies of life, ethics, perceptions, or behavior. A mediator accepts people as they are and helps them.

If you choose to be a mediator, you likely will be required to sit down at the table with people very different from each other and very different from you. Although you cannot be expected to like every party, your ability to maintain a nonjudgmental tolerant approach will be essential in your peacemaking work. Reflect a moment about your own attitudes.

- How tolerant are you of people who are different from you? When family members or friends think or act in ways that you don't like, do you accept them, or do you try to change them? When they don't change, do you argue with them or reject them? Do you accept and like most people?

- When people treat each other badly, can you nevertheless work with them? When people act stupidly or self-destructively, do you bleed for them or wash your hands of them?

- Are there particular ethnic groups, lifestyles, cultures, genders, or other categories of people whom you just don't like or with whom you have trouble working?

- In your own life, do you find that most of your friends and contacts are diverse, or are they more homogeneous in their backgrounds and outlook?

Handling Conflict Well

Mediators take on conflict; they enter into the conflict of others voluntarily, and often the conflict of the parties gets misdirected at the mediator. Few of us enjoy fighting with others—or even observing others having conflict in which we are not involved. Mediation participants may be out of control in their own lives, but you must be able to withstand it. If you are conflict avoidant, you may wish to reconsider working in mediation; there is no place to hide! If you strike back or otherwise get aggressive around conflict, you might be adding fuel to the fire. How do you handle conflict?

- Do you get nervous, sweaty, nauseous, or have other physical symptoms when someone gets angry at you or if you are in the room where conflict is taking place?
- If someone cuts in line ahead of you, do you confront the cutter, getting into a screaming match or even a physical fight?
- Are you able to talk through problems with people in your life rather than rejecting them or otherwise ending the relationship?

Empathy

Mediators are required not just to refrain from judging disputants; they need to be able to see the problem from the eyes of the participants and understand it from their different perspectives. Being able to walk in the shoes of the participants while maintaining neutrality is a delicate balance mandated in the mediator's role.

Being able to empathize with all participants enhances the trust-building process that is so essential for participants to follow the guidance of the mediator in matters large and small. Mediators demonstrate their empathy through reframing statements that capture the emotions, beliefs, and concerns of the participants in a caring, supportive, yet impartial way. In addition to reframing, you must model empathy in a variety of other ways that let each participant know and feel that you care about them and want to help both of them meet their concerns to the greatest extent possible through mutual agreement. How much empathy do you have?

- When someone you care about comes to you in pain, can you identify with what is going on even if that person's life experiences are very different from yours?
- When you listen to someone who is crying, yelling, depressed, or otherwise emotional, can you show how much you care and understand without giving advice?
- In your family or at work, can you show support for both sides of an argument without taking sides or getting into the fray yourself?

Persistence

Most people enter mediation with a sense of doom. They can't imagine getting out of the mess that brought them into mediation. Often it is the mediator alone who provides the energy and belief in resolution that motivates the participants to keep going. What is your level of persistence?

- Are you persistent in the face of apathy, negativity, or even hostility?
- When you hit roadblocks, do you stop in your tracks or do you jump over them, walk around, move them out of the way, or consult others about how to overcome them?
- Are you a high-energy person?
- During long days filled with challenges and tension, can you summon up extra energy to get you through the task, then fall apart on your own time?
- Can you put your own needs on hold when you sign up to help others?

Trustworthiness

When disputants put their important conflicts into the hands of a mediator, they reposit a great deal of trust. Participants must believe the mediator when hearing guidance and information about the process, reality, and the dynamics of settlement. When a mediator promises to do something—from making a telephone call to conveying an offer—the parties must feel comfortable in trusting the mediator to do as promised. Where do you fit on the trust grid?

- Do people believe you when you make a promise? Should they?
- Are you restrained and accurate in conveying the truth, especially when you know people want to hear something better?
- Do you follow through on your commitments, especially the details?

- Can you comfortably tell people that you do not know something, need more information, cannot tell them confidential information, or otherwise cannot meet their expectations?

Flexibility and Creativity

Disputants enter into mediation because they have not otherwise been able to work things out. One of mediation's greatest attributes is that through the exploration of options, often very unorthodox and creative options, people find agreement when it did not otherwise seem possible.

The mediator must use a nimble and creative approach while providing the safety of structure. At the same time, while various steps are needed to reach yes, the mediator must be able and willing to rearrange the steps to meet the needs of the parties. Think about how you use your creativity.

- Do you create your own recipes or construction projects that differ greatly from cookbooks and building manuals?
- Can you dream and tolerate the aspirations and dreams of others, especially when they do not seem to lead somewhere logically?
- When you're stuck, do you use every tool and resource to come up with a new solution, or are you bound by those proven tracks tested by you or others before you?

⚜ Practice Tip ⚜

Learn to improvise. When you are driving, try to use your intuition and look for signs of correct navigation rather than religiously following a map. Sing along to songs on the radio, ad-libbing lyrics when you don't know the words.

Being Positive and Optimistic

Remember the Little Train That Could, who said, "I think I can, I think I can, I think I can"? Mediators are just like that little train, with a bit of cheerleader thrown in. It is not surprising that mediation participants are often negative in their opinion of the other side and often are hypercritical of themselves as well. They often feel stymied at getting what they want and what they believe they are entitled to. In addition to their frustration, the financial costs of fighting are high, and most fear that they will get even higher.

That's where the mediator's optimism comes in. The mediator tries to show participants that their frustrations are normal and the quagmire is solvable. The mediator reinforces the strengths and coping abilities of each participant and models a positive vision for the outcome. Sometimes this positive and optimistic model is the sole difference between impasse and agreement. What's your level of energy and optimism?

- Are you a can-do person whom others go to when times are tough?
- Do you believe that most problems can be solved?
- When others are stuck, do you encourage them to stick it out?
- During struggles, can you keep up a smile, make a joke, or proffer a pat of support rather than dissolve into a funk?

MEDIATION TREE OF VALUES

I, like many other mediators, had major doubts about my abilities to be a mediator and handle the basic tasks. However, what excited me most about mediation was the fit between mediation's core values and my own. I never felt that fit in the practice of law, despite certain talents that I had for the job.

Values are so crucial to mediation that the Academy of Family Mediators devoted its 2000 conference to this subject. Molding the conference participants into a community, the mediators present collaboratively built a tree of values (see Figure 2.1). The keynote speaker, John Paul Lederach, concluded his keynote address:

> When I approach the topic of mediation and values, I think the discussion can take us to the heart of the very purpose of the field, if we are able to envision values as social energies rather than rigid beliefs. If we can understand values as process-structures, we not only shift our understanding of mediation, intuitively we recognize that the mediation process proposes a paradigm shift for the ways in which we think about people and relationships that is relevant to every human endeavor. . . . Mediation represents the wave of the new millennium. It is to social process what quantum and chaos theory are to Newtonian Theory.[1]

In his book *Techniques of Mediation,* Walter Maggiola provides a list of personality characteristics that a mediator should possess.[2] Go down the list and see how you fit in with this checklist:

- The patience of Job
- The sincerity and bulldog characteristics of the English and the wit of the Irish
- The physical endurance of the marathon runner
- The broken field-dodging abilities of a halfback
- The guile of Machiavelli
- The personality-probing skills of a good psychiatrist
- The confidence-retaining characteristic of a mute
- The hide of a rhinoceros
- The wisdom of Solomon
- Demonstrated integrity and impartiality
- Fundamental belief in human values and potential, tempered by the ability to assess personal weaknesses as well as strengths
- Hard-nosed ability to analyze what is available in contrast to what might be desirable
- Sufficient personal drive and ego, qualified by willingness to be self-effacing.

Figure 2.1 Tree of Values

AFM Tree of Values

These mediation values were suggested and built upon throughout the conference to symbolize the values that AFM members share and cultivate, upon which we base our community.

Work for peace and justice...
Connecting to be...Transition...Self-Determination
...Connect with divine intelligence...She-is-compassion...
Peace...Better way for conflict...To hear others' ideas...
Compassion...Responsibility...Strive for excellence...Create
peaceful options...Neutrality...Moving beyond oneself...Share...
Questioning assumptions...Integrity...Taking a risk...Teaching...To contribute
to the repair of the world...She-is-Compassion...Restore trust...Harmlessness...
Support and connect with higher consciousness...Living the journey...Learn and connect
...To do...Harmony...Justice...To know myself better...He shares table...Vocation
...Promote harmony...To be me and let others be who they are... Growing, repairing,
changing, energizing...Make a positive difference...Wisdom...To make a positive impact...
To nurture and care for oneself...Create peace...Be all I can be–in relationships...Curiosity...Strive for
excellence...Service to community...He-Shares-Table...Movement...Commitment to work...
Giving back....Honesty...Creativity...Creating space...Compassion and respect...Kindness...Listening
transparency...Informed choices...Honoring...Connectedness...To reduce the destructive effects of
conflict...To connect and reconnect...Patience...Hope...Effective results...Compassion...
Self-determination...Humility...Respect...Positive perspective...Harmlessness...Non-malfeasance...Serve
others...She seeks truth...To get inspiration...Non-coercion of disputants...Humility...To help create just
peace...Motivate...To connect on value level...Rendir una mano al neccsitado...To grow... Sulha=
forgiveness...He-Cultivates-Hope...To give and to receive...To connect...Besserung der menschheit...
She preserves dignity...Seamless value system...Return and give back knowledge obtained
during life...Actualize potential...Equity...Freedom...Power...Competence...Balance in life...
Peace...Artistry...Total self expression...Empathy...Fairness...Hope...Speak only what
is true...Justice...Actively listening...Energy...Experimentation/research...Flexibility
...Gaining understanding...Respect...Recognition...She-Forges-Reconciliation...
Exploration...Trust...Give parties' control...Giving a voice...
Contribution...To believe...Choice...Faith...Patience...Child safety...
Difference...Fairness...Being self aware...Dignity...
Empowering...Behavior
harmonizing.

Reprinted with the permission of the Association for Conflict Resolution (a merged organization of AFM, CRENet and SPIDR). Originally printed in Mediation News, Spring/Summer 2001, *19*(2).

After looking at the tree of values from roots to branches, think about whether some of the key values of mediation mirror your own:

Empowerment—Do you believe that people should have control over their own destiny and reduce their dependence on forces, institutions, and professionals?

Collaboration—Do you believe people work more effectively when they are working together?

Fairness—Do you believe that people should get a fair shake out of life and that human action and institutions should be designed with fairness as an outcome?

Satisfaction—Do you believe that although the customer may not always be right, what customers say and feel about their satisfaction are important in evaluating a product or a service?

Options—Do you believe that people do better with choice?

Creativity—Do you believe that the process of creating new ideas and opportunities is a value in and of itself?

Hope—Do you believe that it is important to have a belief in the possible?

Reconciliation—Do you believe that people benefit by being in relationships with each other, especially after a rift?

Transformation—Do you believe that people can change for the better and that change can be facilitated by the way conflict is resolved?

Rational problem solving—Do you believe that people can find solutions through dialogue and thinking through the problem?

Peacemaking—Do you believe that peace and its pursuit are values in themselves?

These values are not a wish list. Every day mediators incorporate these values and others on the value tree into their work. It is little wonder that most mediators love their work; it is a living reflection of their lives as they want to live them.

Do these values align with those you already possess? Are you patient, flexible, optimistic, and willing to develop these skills and traits? Personality and values are important aspects of working as a mediator. We'll see why in the next chapter.

Can You Do the Work?

Mediation is generally understood to be a process to resolve a conflict with the facilitation of a neutral third person. Can you be neutral? Could you see yourself having a career as an individual who is selected and entrusted by people in conflict to help them resolve their differences?

Mediators have many personality types, come from different educational and professional backgrounds, and are motivated by various political and social personal agendas and priorities. I have seen young school children and ex-convicts do better jobs at mediating disputes than some attorneys or licensed therapists. In training mediators, I am regularly amazed at the variety of approaches and types of people who are effective at resolving conflict.

*In training mediators, I am regularly amazed
at the variety of approaches and types of people
who are effective at resolving conflict.*

So if you wonder if you can be a good mediator, there is no easy answer. This chapter addresses some common mediator roles and tasks and discusses some of the talents, skills, values, and perspectives that are required for competent mediators.

Following are common roles that a mediator performs:

- Host
- Teacher
- Emotional counselor
- Referee
- Facilitator
- Idea generator
- Reality tester
- Negotiation coach
- Conflict manager
- Recording secretary

HOST

A mediator provides a safe place for parties to discuss important and difficult issues of their lives. The mediator is responsible for ensuring the comfort and safety of the parties and anyone else attending the mediation.

You must be prompt and keep time commitments. As a role model, you must come early and prepare the mediation room for the participants. This means you must be able and willing to plan your schedule to be free of conflicting commitments and to plan your day so you do not breeze in at the last minute or even late while the participants become increasingly tense as they wait for you.

As part of your planning, you need to have a sense of what will encourage good communication. Chairs need to be arranged, confidential documents put away, and visual learning tools (flip charts or overheads) set up and workable. Tables and other furniture communicate a level playing field: no participants should sit higher than others or have the sun shining in their eyes, and you should also be on an equal setting with the participants. Food and drink need to be ordered and presented in an accessible fashion so that disputants can "break bread together."

You need to be inviting and sensitive to the needs and quirks of your guests. You need to be able to anticipate trouble and be able to plan strategically around it. Just as you wouldn't seat two long-time enemies next to each other at a wedding, you may need to arrange for separate waiting rooms for initially hostile parties. You need to take the initiative to walk out and greet participants rather than wait for them to be ushered in. In the same way, when your guests leave, you should not only walk with the parties to the door of your waiting room or the outside door, but all the way to the elevator, gate, or their car. These good manners demonstrate your respect for them and their participation in the mediation.

TEACHER

Do you enjoy imparting knowledge for a variety of learning styles? Is it important to you to be a role model for collaborative behavior and reflective decision making? Are you tolerant of people who need constant repetition, repeated positive reinforcement, or special tutorial help? Are you aware of and responsive to different types of learning styles?

Mediators are teachers. You will be required to design curricula and learning plans for classes of two parents in divorce mediation; groups of lawyers, parties, and insurance adjusters in civil disputes; boards of directors or company departments in workplace mediations; or even for a hundred or more citizens and their advocates in a community mediation.

Like any other teacher, you should enjoy making presentations, often using a range of pedagogical tools. You will need to scribe conversations and proposals on a flip chart or white board, prepare and distribute handouts for class use and homework, and involve your special class in interactive discussions that will maximize balanced involvement and reinforce lessons learned.

As a teacher within the mediation process, you will have the opportunity to teach substantive material such as legal information, negotiation theory, child development research, financial analysis, and court procedures. Even more important, you will be able to teach people how to listen respectfully, articulate demands and offers, generate options, and make lasting decisions.

EMOTIONAL COUNSELOR

Some people visibly weaken in the presence of conflict. If you are so conflict averse that you cringe when others display emotion and anger in front of you (not to mention *at* you), think very carefully before going into mediation.

In many ways, a mediator is the point person of conflictual interaction and behavior. *Triangulation* is a psychological term for two people in conflict involving a third person to make a triangle of communication to ease the problem between the first two disputants. They each either direct their anger at the third person (scapegoating) or each tries to ally with the third person to cut off the other. As mediator, you are a designated triangulatee! Mediation participants will either project their anger at you or try to bond with or manipulate you to get at the other participant. In either case, it gets very hot. Are you ready to stay in the kitchen?

The truth is that as a mediator, you volunteer for action in that hot kitchen. In Hebrew the word is *Rodef Shalom,* a pursuer of peace.[1] It is not enough for a *Rodef Shalom* to resolve conflict when people come to you for resolution. A *Rodef Shalom* seeks out those in conflict to offer resolution. You must be willing to bang on the door of that steamy kitchen, invite yourself to the table, and be ready for the heated conflict that may be directed your way.

In the midst of this setting, you must be ready to understand and support the feelings of people who may be behaving at their worst. As Judge Anne Kass of Albuquerque has said, "When people in conflict get hurt and scared, they often look and act stupid—and they say stupid hurtful things."[2]

As a mediator, you will be faced with a difficult challenge: to be tolerant, accepting, nonjudgmental, and supportive of each party without favoring any party or any party's position over another. You must be supportive and neutral at the same time, quite a balancing act. Your training will help prepare you for this challenge: to be supportive and neutral in the middle of hostile and often damaging emotional combat.

---

*As a mediator, you will be faced
with a difficult challenge: to be tolerant,
accepting, nonjudgmental, and supportive
of each party without favoring any party
or any party's position over another.*

REFEREE

Like a referee, a mediator is responsible for knowing the ground rules and ensuring their compliance. However, could you imagine a referee assembling both teams at the fifty-yard line and having the players develop their own ground rules? Or could you imagine the referee watching illegal blocks or several players go offside and waiting until a player comes to request a penalty flag—and then consulting with both teams to determine whether to assess a penalty and, if so, how much yardage to mark off?

Welcome to the role of the mediator. If you want the power to decide or to order people around (especially those who misbehave badly), mediation may not be for you. All mediator power starts and ends with the players. They invite you into their conflict to help them. The participants themselves are responsible to determine if there will be ground rules and have the ultimate power to negotiate the rules that will affect their own mediation process. It can be very heady to have people select you and entrust you with their important and often private business. Can you accept this responsibility without needing to control or have the last word? You must be willing to let go of the need to control while at the same time providing structure, balance, and a steady, trusted hand to facilitate the adoption and enforcement of ground rules.

You must be willing to let go of the need to control while at the same time providing structure, balance, and a steady, trusted hand to facilitate the adoption and enforcement of ground rules.

This means that unlike litigation, where a judge or an arbitrator makes the decisions, all decisions in mediation—even those about who will be present, when you meet, who speaks first—are made by the people who are in conflict with each other. Does this get messy? Absolutely. It is true that trains run more on time when there is a train dispatcher with absolute power over train schedules. But mediators are not train dispatchers. Since mediation provides the parties with self-determination and empowerment, you must be ready for initial chaos, delays, and even having the mediation train derail occasionally.

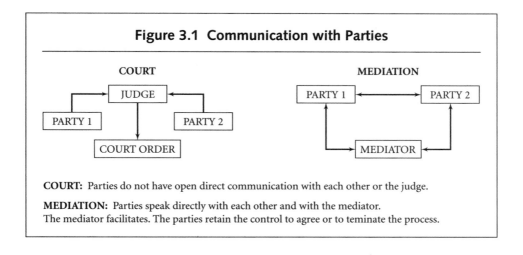

Figure 3.1 Communication with Parties

COURT

PARTY 1 → JUDGE ← PARTY 2
JUDGE → COURT ORDER

MEDIATION

PARTY 1 ↔ PARTY 2
PARTY 1 ↕ MEDIATOR ↕ PARTY 2

COURT: Parties do not have open direct communication with each other or the judge.

MEDIATION: Parties speak directly with each other and with the mediator. The mediator facilitates. The parties retain the control to agree or to teminate the process.

At the same time, just as a referee sometimes gets spit on or the police get attacked by angry citizens, you may find yourself in the middle of unleashed emotion and violence. Hostile residents of a housing project, disgruntled employees, betrayed divorcing spouses, or even angry business executives sometimes get out of control.

I have two basic ground rules that I ask participants to adopt: no hitting each other and no destruction of my office. Over the years, both rules have been violated. I have found myself in situations where I had to scream at parties to get back into their seats, order parties to take a time-out for an hour or the whole day, physically restrain parties from fighting, and literally push people out of the room or pin their arms when they were throwing *my* papers around the office! Even with ground rules, mediation can be dangerous, and outbursts can happen at any time. Many mediators have been lulled into a false sense of collaborative tranquillity only to find an eruption minutes later. Are you willing to take these risks?

I have two basic ground rules that I ask participants to adopt: no hitting each other and no destruction of my office. Over the years, both rules have been violated.

FACILITATOR

Most of the time you will be using your words, not your fists, to translate your experience and training into mediation progress. You will use your life lessons and specific training to help parties get to the table, stay there, and move in the direction of resolution rather than prolonging the conflict.

You will facilitate agreement by honoring the participants with respect and acknowledging that they have the answers within them and may need some help in reaching beyond their state of conflict and moving toward resolution. That movement—from the old patterns and behavior that clearly have not been working toward new perspectives and behavior—is the foundation of a mediator's work.

The twin goals of helping participants to attain empowerment and recognize the value and worth of the other side are at the heart of the facilitative approach.[3] To be a mediator, you must already have or must learn to incorporate a respect for the self-determination and capability of people to find and accept their own solutions—solutions that they can all live with and that will work effectively for them. These solutions may be very different from what you would do in your own life or even very different from what you would prescribe to solve their problems.

As a facilitator, you will provide guidance and structure for safe interaction. You will be trained to help parties hear each other and be heard themselves by using a myriad of communication skills. The bedrock of mediator facilitation is the ability to reframe the words and positions of the parties so that the party speaking might mollify hard stances and the party hearing might hear better and take in the information, possibly to reflect on and create movement on that end.

You will neither be wearing rose-colored glasses nor insist the parties do so either. Because conflict is pernicious and the parties were not able to reach resolution before starting mediation, you will work with the parties to help them realize that in order to get settlements that will be in their best interests, they may have to approach the other side (whom they probably do not trust and may even detest) in new and counterintuitive ways. You will encourage them to make these changes not to be nice or cooperative, but to get what each wants and needs but is not getting due to the conflict.

Some of these changes in approach may be:

- To concentrate on what the parties have in common rather than on what separates them.

- To realize that they are dependent on the other side to resolve the conflict.
- To understand that proving the other side wrong won't get them what they want; the truth of the past is irrelevant. What counts is how they will solve the problem so that all parties can move on with their lives.

Perhaps these approaches seem well meaning but naive or Pollyannish to you; certainly, you think, they don't work in the real world! In fact, mediators employ this counterintuitive worldview to settle conflict every day. To be a mediator, you need to be open to exploring this approach in your training and your work in the field.

IDEA GENERATOR

One of the marvels of mediation is that the parties are not constrained by statutes, cases, or court rules in creating their own agreements. For example, sometimes a heartfelt apology (or even mutual apologies) will resolve a conflict. You can scour the law books and will not be able to find a precedent that mandates or even sanctions apologies by litigants as relief available by a judge or a jury.

As a mediator, you will be impressed, inspired, and perhaps even awed by the creativity that people have in coming up with their own solutions. If you are a stickler for generally accepted rules and tried-and-true methods, you may be limited in your mediator role.

The best mediators I know not only think outside the box; they are willing to create wholly new boxes. It is not uncommon for parties to be stuck because one or both are hidebound by their own myopic thinking or reliance on legal authority or workable solutions from their own personal framework. Many people are afraid of or even strongly resistant to innovative and untried options.

As a mediator, options—traditional or off-the-wall—are your best friends. Do you like to brainstorm? Do you like to encourage others to do so? Many conflicts get resolved because the parties never knew that win-win options existed. For example, many divorcing couples argue over child support. If they go to a trained family mediator, they might learn that they both can end up with more money if they convert tax-free nondeductible child support into deductible family support. The supporting parent would pay more money each month but end up saving money with the tax relief. The supported parent would pay more taxes but end up with more money in pocket. They both do better simply because they learned about a new option through mediation.

Creativity and innovation can be learned; you don't have to be born with these traits. Many mediators enter and stay in the field due to the satisfaction and stimulation that comes from helping people maximize their potential by exploring new and creative options.

REALITY TESTER

The companion to unrestricted brainstorming is managing expectations and testing proposed agreements to maximize their potential for durability and down-the-road satisfaction. While getting every conceivable option on the board may be exhilarating, being doused with reality can be stark and depressing. If you hate giving people bad news, your mediation success will be hampered. Sometimes the messenger is directly blamed for a sobering message.

Reality comes in many forms. Often people have an inflated view of their legal position. Other times they have distorted views of the profitability or costs of a particular financial decision. Sometimes they make assumptions about how the other party will react to a proposal or be able to comply with an agreement. Or they expect that a complex problem can be resolved in an hour or two.

As a mediator, you will be challenged in maintaining your empathy and support for participants and still being willing to confront them with reality. This may be difficult for you if you have a strong need to be liked; few people enjoy their worldview to be challenged. Still, you have to learn to deliver the news so that the parties can hear it and still maintain their trust in your neutrality. This is a tough mission that you must be willing to accept.

NEGOTIATION COACH

Negotiation requires a combination of integrity and guile. As mediator, you will need both. The participants must trust you, yet you have to be able to see all the pieces on the board and help the parties move them so they can reach consensus.

Negotiation is part of life. We start as children negotiating with our parents for things we want, and we never stop. Yet few of us are trained in negotiation theory or savvy in negotiation techniques. Mediators are trained in negotiation, but it is still more art than science. You must like (or at least be tolerant of) the give and take of negotiation.

You will need to have a deep toolbox to assist parties who may have very limited tools or experience in negotiating important agreements. Mediators set the stage for parties to have enough data and understanding of the other parties' concerns before starting to bargain. You must have the patience and the strength to withstand the pressure to get to the bottom line and delay actual bargaining until the parties are ready to do so effectively. This is not easy. If you are prone to greasing the squeaky wheel, you might prematurely accelerate the negotiation process, and your effectiveness will be compromised. Being a mediator doesn't mean winning a popularity contest. You may even need to hold off the joint demand of both parties for immediate solutions to let the mediation process unfold.

It is not uncommon for disputants to want to get the mediation over with quickly. Yet knowing that early positioning may hurt negotiation, you may need to work with the parties to forestall this demand, trading it for an extended dialogue and encouraging a dialogue to explore commonality. It is a push-pull between the mediator and the parties: the parties driven by their anxieties and the mediator trying to modulate their adversarial negotiating positions that get in the way of reaching ultimate agreement. This means you must be willing to balance the commitment to client empowerment with a gentle touch for timing and approach.

CONFLICT MANAGER

How well do you plan, handle details, and follow through? These talents are essential in managing the pace and structure of the mediation. Many believe that mediation is confined to the interaction during official mediation sessions. But conflict management and mediation extend to your telephone conversations, e-mail, and other correspondence to and from the parties. You need to interact with experts, lawyers, family members, therapists, employers, and a host of other interested parties. The best mediators anticipate events outside the room that can affect the negotiations and work with the parties outside formal sessions to prepare them for the inevitable difficulties inside and outside the mediation room. You must be diligent in returning telephone calls and timely in sending out correspondence.

Your role as conflict manager also comes into play when parties do not reach agreement. More and more, mediators are called on to mediate the next step in the dispute resolution continuum. Rather than rushing off to court with its increased conflict and cost, mediators help the parties retain control and carefully design a precourt process. The most obvious example is arbitration. The mediator can help the parties design the rules, frame the issues, and select the decision maker. Yet arbitration is just one postmediation option. The mediator can help design an appraisal or evaluation process with mutually selected neutral experts to provide nonbinding data and analysis. Some examples include custody evaluations, business or real estate appraisals, or workups by accountants of financial and tax matters. Parties often return to the mediator after the data come back from these evaluations.

Finally, once agreement is reached, the mediator as conflict manager can work with the parties to negotiate a draft provision to handle future disputes. By helping parties prepare a future mediation or other ADR mechanism, the mediator can help the parties avoid unnecessary future conflict. To perform this function, you must become a student of other processes for resolving disputes and adroitly bring this knowledge into the mediations that you handle.

RECORDING SECRETARY

How developed are your writing skills? Mediators record the progress of the mediation in many ways. Almost every mediator is skilled in flip chart scribing so that concerns, demands, and agreements are recorded during mediation sessions. Yet accomplished mediators don't stop there. They write summary letters, interim memoranda of understanding, and instructions to parties (how to divide personal property, how to write an employee reference letter, how to process an agreement in court). In some states, mediators write the final agreements, drafting court documents, partnership and corporate documents, promissory notes, and letters to creditors and other third parties.

You may find mediation attractive because of the high level of personal interaction. You may be less interested in filling out forms or writing, but these are important functions of the job. Parties need these drafting services that support the mediation and are willing to pay for them.

CONCLUSION

You now have an overview of the tasks you will be expected to perform as a mediator and the aptitudes, skills, and values that will be helpful to you. You can rest assured that all mediators have strengths in some areas and weaknesses in others. If you feel confident that the job of mediator seems to be one that you are capable and willing to take on, let's now explore what training you will need.

Education and Training

There is no universal agreement as to what educational and life experiences are the best preparation for a career in mediation. It is a hot topic that can be broken down into two main areas: what best prepares mediators to be competent in the field and what mediators need in order to demonstrate their competence.

Although there is some turf wrangling and ox goring inherent in these questions, fortunately, your career preparation may be independent of the outcome of this debate. Mediator organizations have different standards and requirements regarding necessary preparation and training, and these views shift frequently. Different jurisdictions have widely varying approaches to ensuring mediator competence, ranging from total deference, to the free market and individual choice, to a highly structured scheme to certify mediators. No state has yet adopted a regulatory license requirement for mediators, although such movements are currently being hotly debated.

*Mediator organizations have different
standards and requirements regarding
necessary preparation and training,
and these views shift frequently.*

To help you with your strategic planning, this chapter examines six main topics:

• Premediation education and background

• Basic mediation training programs

• Academic programs in mediation

• Advanced mediation education and training

• Consultation and supervision

• Requirements for certification

PREMEDIATION EDUCATION AND BACKGROUND

You can go into mediation from almost any educational or vocational background.

Work and Life Experience—No College Degree

Mediation is one career in which a college degree is not required either to practice in most states or to be a member of the leading mediation organizations. Mediators with good people skills and life experience can be highly effective with a high school education. I have observed startling results from mediators who have solid reputations in building trades, as business owners, as lay educators and counselors, and from almost every other walk of life.

If you fit this category, your determination, enthusiasm, and self-study in conflict resolution and general college courses will improve your skills at the table and in practice building.

Undergraduate Education

Almost any academic major can prepare you for a career in conflict resolution, so you should obtain a broad education in areas that interest you. In addition, a number of colleges have undergraduate courses in conflict resolution (Manhattan College in Riverdale, New York, has a major in peace studies).

To explore your interest in the field, you might attend summer courses in conflict resolution or work as an intern at a community mediation center or in private practice (be prepared for the experience to be unpaid). Even better, you might take a year or two to work in a helping capacity, preferably in a new cultural or geographic setting, for example, in the Peace Corps. Your experience in providing service and being tolerant of differences will help you develop some of the key characteristics of successful mediators (see Chapter Two).

Advanced Academic Degrees

As in your choice of an undergraduate major, pursue an academic graduate course that interests and excites you; any background will be useful at the mediation table. In particular, you should develop your problem framing and resolution conceptual thinking. Taking conflict resolution or negotiation courses or writing your thesis or dissertation on mediation topics might strengthen your commitment, but you can also pursue such direction after completing your graduate studies.

Many esteemed mediators pursued a career in peacemaking after obtaining a graduate degree. John Haynes, a professor of education, was the first president of the Academy of Family Mediators. Joan Kelly, an internationally acclaimed researcher as well as mediator, is a psychologist. Bernard Mayer, noted author and international mediator, is a social worker. In these and many other examples, the mediators used their intellectual talents and combined them with developed people skills to rise in the profession.

DO I REALLY HAVE TO GO TO LAW SCHOOL?

The question that most people (who are not lawyers) considering a career in mediation ask is, "Do I really have to go to law school?" As with most of life's central questions, there is no right answer.

Currently, the debate rages inside and outside the mediation profession as to whether only lawyers can be competent mediators. Some states give lawyers preference in credentialing or membership on court panels. Many mediators with a law background see this as a positive trend; others do not. Many mediators with backgrounds other than law see the intrusion of the law profession into mediation as the beginning of the end of mediation as an independent profession; others believe that because the lawyer's office has been the gateway for conflict decision making, the involvement and support of lawyers can help mediation grow for those from law and nonlaw backgrounds alike.

If you are already a lawyer, you do not have to return to law school to take the dispute resolution and skills courses that you may have missed; you already have the credibility that a law license commands. However, as you will see throughout this chapter, your law school education has only partially prepared you for a mediation career: you have much to learn.

THE DECISION TO GO TO LAW SCHOOL

In planning your career, you should focus on your personal goals and make your own decision about whether to go to law school along the lines set out in the following discussion.

If You Are a Licensed Professional

If you have a license in a professional field, such as therapy, accounting, or contracting, you probably have much training that can be applied to mediation in your field. Your license provides you with initial credibility. You can learn much that law school could teach from taking basic and advanced mediation training, as well as law-based courses in your area of interest (family, employment, business, civil litigation).

If You Have an Advanced Degree or Significant Work Experience But No License

Although you do not have a license that carries with it credibility and accountability, think very carefully before spending the money and deferring income for the three years of law school. Will the increased knowledge and credibility that you will gain from law school be worth the investment? Your experience or graduate education (or both) counts for a great deal at the mediation table, and your other option is to start your mediation career right away and pick up legal knowledge or a juris doctor degree down the road.

If You Have a College Degree with Little or No Work Experience

This is the toughest position to be in. Unlike licensed professionals or those with substantial work experience, you have neither the experience nor a professional education or license to launch your career. Your choice is stark: Do you invest in a law school education plus mediation training and education, or do you go straight to mediation training and education and build your career, bypassing a formal legal education?

If You Have a Passion for Learning About the Law

You might benefit from the law school education itself regardless of the career path you ultimately choose. You would learn not just substantive legal theories and concepts, but you would sharpen your reasoning and problem-solving abilities.

If You Feel You Need a Law Degree for Career Security

Whether through your own search or through encouragement (or pressure) from your family, you may have an internal voice that says, "Whatever you do in life, complete a professional degree and license so that you will always have something to fall back on." If this voice speaks loudly and you are willing to devote the time, energy, and the resources to three tough years, regardless of your intrinsic interest in law school, it might be a good career insurance policy.

If You Are Not Sold on Mediation as a Career

Law school would give you time and information to weigh mediation as an alternative to other career choices available to law school graduates. You would come out better prepared and more credible as a mediator than you are now. And if you decide mediation is not right for you, many other opportunities would be available with a law degree.

If You Are Absolutely Sure You Want to Be a Mediator and That a Law Degree Will Accelerate and Enrich Your Career Path

There are few potential mediators who are so fortunate to have such clear career direction with the commitment and resources to prepare for a lifetime of peace-making. Following this path, you would go to law school for three years with the full understanding that after receiving your J.D., you would start building your mediation career. This direction is appropriate if you want to go into a particular field (entertainment, litigation, corporate, or real estate law) and realize that law school would prepare you to mediate in that field. Alternatively, you may desire to mediate intergovernmental disputes or other areas in which law school training could help you better understand the environment and dynamics of the field.

If You Know You Want to Be a Mediator with or Without Law School

If any of the following situations describe you, you may consider skipping law school, going back at a later time, and starting your mediation career now:

- You can't afford, or do not want, to be out of the workforce for at least three to five years.

- You are so hungry to start mediating that you do not want to defer that hunger for such a long time.

- You want to avoid the adversarial and competitive culture of many law schools.

- You know you want to be a mediator but are afraid that you will be diverted from your commitment by the many opportunities and choices offered during your law school experience.

- You do not have the necessary fire in the belly that you need to get through law school.

In Chapter One, you saw the financial and time commitment that is necessary to be a mediator. Law school requires even more. Unless you hunger for law school or know you need it, law school may not be right for you even if mediation is.

MEDIATION EDUCATION AND TRAINING

Professional Training

Mediation is a profession that you can enter laterally from your existing profession.

Law. The father of modern mediation, O. J. Coogler of Atlanta, was a lawyer, as are many leading mediators who have come from private law practice, the judiciary, and government service. Some mediation within courts and bar associations require a law license, but just as many do not. Lawyers who go straight into mediation do not command incomes comparable to those of their law school classmates who begin as associates with large firms. To date, most lawyer mediators have come into peacemaking as a second career due to their desire to be of service and have more control over their lives. With graduate programs in dispute resolution available to lawyers, increasing numbers of law graduates are choosing mediation as their first choice of career.

*With graduate programs in dispute
resolution available to lawyers, increasing
numbers of law graduates are choosing
mediation as their first choice of career.*

Therapy and Social Work. Licensed mental health professionals were early pioneers of mediation and influenced many of the professional values, training, and practice during the late 1970s and 1980s. Social workers such as Lynne Carp Jacob of Chicago and therapists such as Mary Lund of Los Angeles are examples of mediators who also continued practicing in their fields of origin. Because of the rigorous supervision required for licensing in most mental health and social work professions, it is understood that mediators with such licenses have both adequate training and the accountability of their licensing boards.

Business. If you have an M.B.A. or have worked in human resources for fifteen years or so, your qualifications for mediation may be superb. All of your experience in organizational politics, sales, or accounting adds to your suitability for the job.

Teaching. Mediation is teaching—sometimes in a class of two! As a teacher, you not only have many of the process skills; your knowledge of peer mediation, parent-child mediation, and negotiation within the school system (for example, over such matters as compliance with the Americans with Disabilities Act) may prepare you well. See www.CRInfo.com or contact www.ACR.com for information on conflict resolution in education (CRENet).

Clergy. The training and life of service of clergy are invaluable bridges to mediation. You are already a peacemaker. You find mediation work very familiar and consistent in your present life's work.

BASIC MEDIATION TRAINING PROGRAMS

With the exception of a few states, whatever education and background you already have would not preclude you from a mediation career. That should start with a carefully thought out mediation-specific education and training program.

The most popular entree into the mediation field is the completion of a basic mediation training course of twenty-five to forty hours. Shorter programs concentrate on more generic mediation skills and are generally required for participation on court and organizational mediation panels. Longer courses generally feature specialized training in substantive material in addition to the generic process. For example, the Academy of Family Mediators (now merged into ACR) requires a thirty- to forty-hour family mediation course as a partial requirement for its sixty hours necessary for Practitioner Status.

Although basic training courses differ as to emphasis and manner of presentation and student involvement, the core curriculum generally includes some or all of the following components:

- Introduction to the field of mediation with an opportunity to meet the other participants and recognize the value of collaboration within the training room

- Overview of Mediation: definitions, premises; values, functions; and skills and interpersonal skills that all mediators need

- Nature of Conflict: effect of conflict; methods to manage and resolve conflict; how to handle conflict in your own life

- Listening and Communication Skills: active listening; summarizing; reframing; use of different learning styles

- Facilitating Negotiation: theories of negotiation; planning negotiation; converting positions into interests; overcoming resistance and challenges to resolution

- Structuring the Mediation Process: roles of the mediator; roles of parties; who should be at the table; different formats; use of lawyers and other experts

- Starting the Mediation: telephone intake; orientation and education; scheduling; setting up a safe environment; opening statements of the mediator and the parties

- Framing a Discussion: setting an agenda; identifying interests; ground rules; balancing time between the parties; avoiding premature negotiation

- Use of Separate Meetings and Joint Sessions: caucusing; planning and inter-session meetings; contact with the mediator by parties and interested persons

- Maintaining Neutrality: understanding and recognizing bias; balancing power; managing nonneutral feelings and pressures from parties

- Dealing with Diversity: gender, economic, and cultural differences
- Bringing Closure and Avoiding Impasse: methods to break deadlock and weave movement of the parties into concrete, workable agreements
- Drafting and Implementation: writing up the agreement; mediator's role with the court and other documents; coordinating attorney review; monitoring adherence to the agreement
- Dealing with Ethical Issues: confidentiality, lack of capacity of the parties, conflicts of interest, dealing with crimes and abuse
- Trends and Policies in Mediation: understanding the issues important to the profession

If these subjects interest you, scan the listing of books and other resources in Appendix Four to get a jump on learning more about the exciting foundation of a mediator's craft. While you can learn much from advance reading and research, the true value of mediation training is the experience you will undergo by being part of the training process. Just as it is difficult to tell someone else what Ben and Jerry's ice cream tastes like, mediation training courses must be experienced rather than described.

Mediation training typically encompasses the following areas.

Role Modeling

Every competent trainer demonstrates the approach and method of mediation formally and informally in managing the class. The way the trainer greets the class, organizes the seating and name tags, arranges for food, stays on schedule, and answers questions all model for you and the other participants. High-level trainers show you how to handle various aspects of the mediation process. Rather than throw you into deep water and criticize you for your mistakes, competent trainers model an aspirational way of doing the job. At the same time, even trainers inevitably make mistakes from which you can learn and gain confidence that no one does a perfect job at the mediation table.

In many ways, the training is an inexact metaphor for the mediation process itself. The trainer plays the metaphorical role of mediator, and you and the other trainees play the metaphorical roles of mediation participants. Each aspect of the training can be a metaphoric model of the mediation process. For example, the way the trainer deals with too many things to do in too little time will show you how to handle the same problem in the mediation room. If students come in late or are interrupting each other, the way the mediator intervenes may be the best learning experience for how to handle the same problems with difficult mediation participants.

Observation

Usually a variety of trainers demonstrate mediation skills live or via videotape. This gives you the opportunity to see different approaches and techniques so you can stock your own mediator toolbox with tools that fit your own personality and preferences. You will also observe your fellow trainees, and this experience may hit home faster because of the shared level of experience.

Simulated Role-Play Experience, Games, and Exercises

Most training programs teach by doing. The trainer models the importance of preparation by having clear and concise fact and instruction sheets with an orienting discussion, plus time for questions so that you will understand the purpose of an exercise and what you are expected to do. Playing the roles of the parties, lawyers, experts, as well as the mediator, you will develop an understanding of and empathy for the complexity of the issues and the skills being taught.

Learning from the Class Participants

Your colleagues in the training room may be your best trainers. You will talk with each other about difficult concepts, share the experience of being critiqued, and even critique each other. If you decide to go into private mediation practice, you will probably earn back the price of your basic course tuition by referrals from other class members. The other participants will see you up close and personal. They will learn about your life experience and your talents and observe you resolve conflict in the safe practice setting of the training room. You will share meals, breaks, and often social activities with your classmates over the duration of the course.

At the end of the training, there is often a closing ceremony in which you will have a chance to share your impressions and feelings with your classmates. Following the course, many classes form e-mail chat groups or mediation study groups, or they just make themselves available to each other for consultation. The personal and professional changes that you and your classmates will undergo through your training together may last throughout your career.

ACADEMIC PROGRAMS IN MEDIATION

Instead of starting your mediation education with a basic training course, you might consider a growing variety of academic programs leading to a master's degree in mediation or a certificate in either general conflict resolution or in a specialized focus (such as family, employment, or government). These programs offer the opportunity for a broad range of courses with a structured format for intense reading and exposure to the field.

✿ Practice Tip ✿

Conflict resolution education can help you perform in the workplace.

College degrees and certificates can help you get jobs and improve your career trajectory. Maria A. Perez-Bisbal has a master's degree in conflict resolution from the University of Massachusetts, Boston, and is working as an international fundraiser for nonprofit organizations in New York City. She entered the program after practicing as a lawyer and says that her dispute resolution background has been quite helpful: "I have been exposed to the aspects of theories of conflict, cross-cultural conflict management, organizational conflict, and to workgroup dynamics. Not only am I a better consultant, but my company is now asking me to train all the employees in conflict resolution skills."

Programs are offered in connection with accredited law schools and in a variety of other academic and professional settings. The purpose of the advanced study programs is to provide you with the knowledge and credentials to enter the field of mediation. All programs have some residential component requiring you to be on site for periods as short as one to two weeks or as long as six months to two years. Programs differ in their reliance on visiting and adjunct faculty. Resident faculty can help you outside class. Although they are often well-recognized practitioners and excellent teachers, visiting faculty members rarely have time for office hours and often zip in and out without being available for consultation or to help with extern or job placement. The cost of these programs ranges from minimal state fees of $15,000 to $35,000 for private tuition alone, plus room and board, books, and supplies. Graduates of these programs apply their mediation education in a variety of fields beyond private practice, including management, teaching, and policy development

Is this high cost worth it? Currently, there is not sufficient follow-up to determine the impact of the dispute resolution program on the graduates' incomes, career options, career choices, and self-confidence in the field. There are no findings on the impact of the education on those that receive it. From such research, we could determine what dispute resolution graduates are doing and how much they are making. David Matz and Eben Weitzman, professors in the program at the University of Massachusetts, Boston, are designing such a study. After testing the research methodology on their own graduates, they will make the findings available to all other dispute resolution graduate programs in the United States for their use and adaptation. Matz and Weitzman are planning to gather information from all programs, analyze it, and disseminate it to the conflict resolution field.

When you are comparing programs, look particularly at their writing requirements and extern programs. If a program requires a dissertation or other publishable paper, you will increase your opportunity for close collaboration with at least one, and perhaps several, faculty members. You also will produce a tangible product to demonstrate your knowledge and creative thinking to be used on the employment circuit. Extern programs are invaluable in placing graduate students in practice settings. These experiences help you develop practice skills through observation and practice and provide direct and indirect employment opportunities.

Finally, in researching programs, take a careful look at the placement staff and services provided to the school's graduates. Most important, ask for the placement status of recent graduating classes to see what type of entry possibilities you will have after making the investment of time and money.

Choosing a Conflict Resolution Program

John Windmueller, a doctoral candidate at the Institute for Conflict Analysis and Resolution program at George Mason University in Arlington, Virginia, has provided the following advice on choosing a graduate program:[1]

Funding

- What sort of funding does the program offer students?
- Is funding guaranteed for a certain number of years, or must it be renewed every year?
- What percentage of master's and doctoral students receive funding?
- Is funding available for attending academic conferences?
- How is in-state tuition handled? Some schools allow students to start getting in-state tuition rates after only a year of course work. If your home state and the school's state are both members of the Academic Common Market, you may qualify for immediate in-state tuition rates.

Getting to Graduation

- What percentage of incoming master's or doctoral students complete their degrees?
- How long does it usually take for students to complete a master's or doctoral degree?
- How long does the institution specify for completing a master's or doctoral degree?
- How many credits of course work must a student take each semester to be a full-time student?
- What are the thesis or comprehensive exam requirements?
- What (if any) foreign language requirement is there?
- Can students apply any past credits? (This question is usually relevant for doctoral students who have already earned a master's degree.)

Classes

- What is the breakdown between core or required classes and electives?
- Are there specialty tracks to choose from?
- What is the average class size?

The Community and Culture

- What is the typical demographic profile of students and faculty (for example, age, race, gender, master's versus doctoral degree seekers, tenured versus non-tenured faculty)?

- How would you describe the relationship between students and faculty: formal with strong lines of authority or informal and collaborative?

- Do students have an organized group to represent their interests?

- Are most students full time or part time?

- Where do most students live, and what is the town or city like?

- What role do students play in such matters as decision making on curriculum, faculty hiring, faculty promotion, and admittance of new students?

- What regular nonacademic activities are there, such as celebrations and traditions?

- What is the history of the department? When was it created? Are there some core principles it was founded on? What changes is it in the midst of? Where will it be going in the next four years?

Professional Development

- What teaching opportunities are available for graduate students?

- What mentoring opportunities exist between students and faculty?

- Do students often collaborate with faculty on research or fieldwork?

After Graduation

- What do typical master's and doctoral degree alumni do both immediately after graduation and then later in their careers?

- What does the institution do to help graduates move ahead in their careers?

- Does the institution hire many of its own Ph.D.s back to teach? (This issue is a bit controversial. Some argue that hiring alumni or alumnae to teach is "academic incest." Others argue that not hiring any shows a lack of faith in the graduates the department is producing.)

Questions Specific to Conflict Resolution Programs

- What is the respective emphasis placed on theory building, research, and practice?

- How does that emphasis get played out in courses and graduation requirements?

- Does the program have a particular level of conflict it focuses on (for example, interpersonal, group, community, organizational, state or policy, or international)?

- If the program has an international focus, does it concentrate on a particular region?

- What professional associations do the faculty and students participate in?

- What is the academic background of the faculty: anthropology, international affairs, law, psychology, political science, religion, or sociology, for example? This is a new field, so very few will have a specific background in conflict resolution.

- What theories are at the core of the program? (For example, at ICAR it used to be basic human needs theory and the problem-solving workshop intervention process.)

- What core values drive the program (for example, what is the role of pacifism or social justice concerns)?

- What does the choice of the program's name indicate? Often a lot of information is packed into the choice of a name. Why is it "conflict transformation," for example, instead of "conflict resolution" or "conflict management" or "dispute resolution"? Or why is "analysis" included or not included in the title? You can often discern a lot about the theoretical and ideological background of a program in this way—or perhaps about the lack of a shared or thought-out theoretical grounding.

- Are the department and faculty actively involved in any conflict interventions? If so, what are they, and what role do students have in them?

- What skills does the program teach? Is a typical graduate ready to mediate, facilitate, lead a training, teach a course, or intervene in a large multiparty dispute?

To get this information, talk to faculty, current students, and graduates. And talk to as many people as possible. There are inevitably a lot of perspectives, and you'll need to hear several to make an educated decision. Don't rely on just the perspective you get from orientation sessions. Search for and read articles and books published by the faculty. If you're looking into the doctoral program, read the dissertations of recent graduates.

ADVANCED MEDIATION EDUCATION AND TRAINING

The slogan of my own training institute is, "Mediation Training Is Never Over." Completion of a forty-hour training course is only the start of training. Many successful mediators take several basic programs from different instructors. It is virtually impossible to cover all of the necessary basic material in forty hours; each trainer emphasizes different areas. Also, being exposed to a variety of trainers will help you round out the imprint of your first role-modeled experience. You will learn that there is no single right way: different trainers model vastly different approaches, and all of them have value. Too many mediators decide that their first trainer models the one true way and take a nonmediative pejorative view of other models. I have even heard the statement, "What you are doing is not true mediation" (implying there is only one right way, which is the way the speaker does it). By broadening your training experience, you will preempt the temptation to turn your first positive training experience into a judgmental and myopic approach that would prevent you from being a career learner.

Even if you choose to complete an advanced degree or certificate in mediation, you will still need extensive advanced work. Remember the study tour of Tom Altobelli (see Chapter One), who took off six months to take more than five advanced training courses after he had completed a law degree.

After completing your basic mediation training, which should cover (or at least initially dust over) the generic mediation curriculum, you will have a wide range of advanced offerings provided in stand-alone trainings, at conferences, or as part of meetings or dinner programs hosted by a variety of organizations. Advanced offerings can be broken down into the following categories:

- Process and skills courses
- Substantive courses
- Practice development courses
- Policy and trends

Process and Skills Courses

Many training programs have two- to five-day courses in advanced mediation training. These courses range in the areas they cover, but they often include the following subjects:

- Thorny barriers to negotiation
- Effective co-mediation
- Working with lawyers in the mediation session
- Mediating same-sex couples
- Preventive mediation of relationships
- Mediated case management

  Some advanced courses concentrate on one advanced area—for example:

- Handling out-of-control clients
- Involving children in the mediation process
- Advanced convening strategies
- Teaching parties about mediation values
- Facilitative versus evaluative mediation
- Strategies for questioning and reframing

Substantive Courses

Mediators who complete a basic mediation course realize how much they still need to learn if they wish to mediate in a particular field of conflict. Following are some examples of the topics of advanced courses by area of practice:

Employment and Workplace
- Developments in sexual harassment law
- Mediating equal employment opportunity claims
- Military civilian disciplinary actions
- Designing a corporate dispute resolution program

Family and Divorce
- New trends involving premarital agreements
- Operating computer child support guidelines

- Mediating parental geographical relocations
- Effect of parental alienation syndrome on adolescent children of divorce

Real Estate
- Facilitating a homeowner association meeting
- Drafting dispute resolution clauses in home sale contracts
- New laws regarding title vesting during probate

Practice Development

More and more mediators are interested in learning how to become financially self-sufficient in their mediation work. Courses in marketing, practice management, strategic planning, and financial oversight are well attended at conferences and in private training programs.

Policy and Trends

You need to know where this evolving profession is headed, both to guide your career and be effective at client intake. The issues discussed in the Epilogue are the major trends in the field today, and there are courses available in all of these subjects.

CONSULTATION AND SUPERVISION

In many states, psychotherapists and clinical social workers are required to work under the close guidance of an experienced professional in their field before qualifying for a license. California requires three thousand hours of such supervision. Borrowing from this model, you can increase your skills and professionalism by working with an experienced mediator after you have received your initial training.

The best-recognized model of consultation today is offered by the Academy of Family Mediators (now merged into ACR). In order to obtain and renew Practitioner Member Status, you must have ten hours of case consultation with another Practitioner Member or other experienced mediator approved by AFM. These hours can consist of both individual and group consultation (with a maximum size of six mediators per group). Consultation hours can be obtained free at the yearly conference, or you can choose among Practitioner Members in your community. You could have your consultation over the telephone or e-mail, or your chosen consultant could be in another city. Some consultants charge for this professional service; others do not.

In a group case consultation, you would share a recent case in which you served as a mediator. The other group members would offer their ideas to help you think reflectively about the important strategies, skills, and ethical and communication issues raised by the presentation. In an individual consultation, the teaching issues are the same, but you would get the full attention of your consultant, and the focus would be on your issues alone. Consultation can accelerate your entry into the field or help raise the level of your skills if you are already in practice.

Consultation can accelerate your entry into the field or help raise the level of your skills if you are already in practice.

Supervision is a more long-term mentoring experience that is generally provided by a senior staff member if you are mediating for an organization or interning with a more experienced mediator. You would have a variety of options within your supervision: role play, observing others, being observed, co-mediating with a more experienced mediator, and regular debriefing opportunities.

REQUIREMENTS FOR CERTIFICATION

Certification is a way of ensuring mediator competence. The California statutory requirements for a basic mediation training are considered minimal in the field. Virginia's criteria for evaluating a mediator's performance are considered state of the art but continue to evolve as they are upgraded. (The Epilogue has further discussion on this subject.)

Unless and until mediator licensing occurs, certification is one way that the public can gain confidence due to the seal of approval awarded to the certified mediator. Florida has the most advanced certification program. You do not have to be certified to call yourself a mediator, but consumers are becoming savvy about using certified mediators first, and most organizations in Florida use only mediators (even on a volunteer basis) who have completed the certification process.

CONCLUSION

There are many resources to choose from in obtaining education and training that meet your needs. Your own circumstances will determine whether law school is right for you. However, whether or not you have a law school education, mediation training and follow-up consultation and supervision are essential to your success as a mediator. Now let's look at job opportunities in mediation.

Job Opportunities in Mediation

Most mediators today do not have day jobs as mediators; they use their knowledge, training, and commitment to peacemaking in other day jobs or volunteer their time to mediate on evenings and weekends. This situation is changing. As more and more individuals and companies demand mediation services and legislation develops requiring mediation early in court and administrative proceedings, job opportunities will grow, and mediation will become the day job for many more who are trained and committed to the field.

SALARIED POSITIONS

If you want to be gainfully employed as a mediator, your first major question may be: Do I need and want a steady paycheck, or do I want to be in business for myself? There are two avenues to explore: the opportunities for staff positions in government, the courts, and the nonprofit sector and options available in private practice. Because a shortage of paid positions has historically herded most mediators into solo private practice, let's first explore the opportunities developing in paid positions and then look at the growing options for solo practice in the private sector.

Government

Propelled by budget restrictions and a desire to use public resources to benefit society as opposed to paying lawyers to fight with citizens in litigation, public jobs in dispute resolution are on the rise. Mediation is being mandated by legislation, regulations, and administrative acts in municipalities, counties, states, and the federal government.

The showcase legislation is the 1996 Administrative Dispute Resolution Act requiring every department of the federal government to set up ADR and mediation procedures internally and to use mediation as a primary means of resolving disputes with citizens, other federal agencies, and other state and local entities.[1] This legislation should encourage mediators to enter the field and ensure career development and security.

Agencies of state and local governments have similar mandated mediation programs. In fact, as certification and possible licensure of mediation are being explored nationwide, some states are creating agencies to study, monitor, and perhaps regulate mediation activities. These efforts will need staffing, and mediators with the background and training in the field discussed in Chapter Four will have an edge.

Two types of employment opportunities exist within court systems on every level of government: staff mediators and administrative and policy positions. Many court programs depend on volunteers to mediate court-mandated programs, but staff positions are on the rise. In California and many other states, courts have maintained staffs of professional mediators to act in every child custody and visitation case before the parties are entitled to a court hearing. These mediators are generally licensed therapists and social workers, but mediators with backgrounds as lawyers also qualify.

Not only are civil mediation programs that use a mixture of volunteers, private providers, and staff growing on the trial level, but many appellate courts have adopted mediation programs as well. Many of these court programs now require mediators to be licensed attorneys. It is impossible to predict which way the wind will blow on this controversial issue.

Not only are civil mediation programs that use a mixture of volunteers, private providers, and staff growing on the trial level, but many appellate courts have adopted mediation programs as well.

If you want an opportunity to teach, manage, and mentor other mediators, each of these burgeoning court programs needs people to manage these programs.

Court programs are growing to examine how mediation can be better used. For example, California has developed the Administrative Office of the Courts, an agency whose mission in part is to study and recommend policies for improving the resolution capability of the state's massive court system. Companion nonprofit agencies such as the National Institute of the Courts in Alexandria, Virginia, and the American Judicature Society in Chicago have vibrant programs that are studying the impact of mediation. The Superior Court of Maricopa County in Phoenix, Arizona, operates a national training program for other court administrators and judges in how to set up programs to serve litigants who represent themselves without lawyers, many of whom need and want court-based mediation programs.

Teaching

If you find your own life and career changed by your training and work in mediation, you may wish to teach and inspire others. Appendix Three contains a list of many educational programs offering courses, certificates, and degrees in mediation. Each of these programs needs teachers.

Many high schools, community colleges, and universities offer individual course offerings in mediation and related subjects, such as negotiation, group and meeting facilitation, the study of conflict, and communication. Peer mediation—that is, teaching students how to mediate their own conflicts and those of other students—is growing rapidly to address everything from squabbles over paint and paper in preschool to gang violence in high schools. There is even a national organization, Conflict Resolution in Education Network (CRENet), dedicated to promoting conflict resolution in schools and other educational settings. It has now become part of the national umbrella organization, the Association for Conflict Resolution, headquartered in Washington, D.C., but CRENet retains its mission and energy and is a source for teaching opportunities.

Stephen Marsh, author of the *ADR Newsletter,* (www.adrr.com) offers five paths for teaching conflict resolution:

- Teach in a law school setting.
- Develop a program yourself starting with the continuing-education program at a local college.
- Obtain a graduate degree that applies to dispute resolution.
- Obtain a Ph.D. in Business management services with a focus in conflict resolution.

- Branch out from your current undergraduate teaching, and add a class on the psychology of conflict, negotiation, or other course related to your area of expertise.[2]

Nonprofit Institutions and Agencies

The array of job possibilities for mediators in the nonprofit arena is truly staggering and is a subject deserving far more attention than I can devote here.

As you can see from Appendix Five, numerous organizations are dedicated to the promotion of conflict resolution, and each has open staff positions from time to time. Related professional bodies also have departments dedicated to mediation. For example, the American Bar Association Section on Dispute Resolution in Washington, D.C., has a staff to serve over eight thousand members of the section. Staff members develop conferences, monitor legislation, operate an e-mail listserv, publish a quarterly newsletter and books, and otherwise promote and support efforts in the field. The Better Business Bureau, National Association of Securities Dealers, and other businesses and professions also have ADR departments or task forces with paid positions, as do bar associations on the state and local levels.

One avenue into the mediation field is to work with a foundation that provides funds for dispute resolution work. The Hewlett Foundation, led by Steve Tobin, has been a major instrument for growth and change in the field, as has the Ford Foundation. You might investigate staff openings in such foundations that have current or potential programs in supporting mediation work.

If you have a long-standing commitment or interest in particular issues, you might look into developing related mediation programs that need professional staff. If you are concerned about the rights of people with physical or emotional disabilities, for example, the American Disability Act Mediation Association has an ongoing mission. Wayne Moore, legal director of the American Association for Retired Persons (AARP), promotes preventive and dispute resolution programs for AARP's members. If you have a concern about crime and developing new options for restorative justice, Judge Michael Towne of Hawaii, the Inglewood-Centinella Youth Diversion Program in Los Angeles County, and many other programs work closely with police departments and prosecutors to operate victim-offender mediation programs. In such programs, the criminal defendant and the person hurt by the crime sit down face to face to discuss a way that the victim can be compensated, receive a direct apology, or otherwise work out this problem outside the customary options of incarceration or fines.

Almost every community has nonprofit mediation centers to serve the conflict resolution needs of the underserved and train members of the community to serve as mediators. Each of these programs considers mediation training and experience to be prime qualifications for administrative, training, or staff-mediator positions.

The Private Sector

Many companies are creating dispute resolution programs to handle and train company employees to resolve internal complaints, provide mediation benefits in employee assistance programs, and prepare and represent management in mediations. Many in-house counsel offices are hiring mediation-trained lawyers to monitor their overall litigation program and encourage their outside counsel to use mediation strategically as the first step in dispute resolution. Business and accounting consulting firms such as Arthur Andersen and PricewaterhouseCoopers have entered the mediation field, offering expertise in the preparation for mediations and serving as neutral mediators themselves. Expanding their base with their business clients, these firms specialize in mediation involving accounting and business issues.

The number of mediation-related Web sites is on the rise, offering a variety of job opportunities (see Appendix Four). The field of on-line dispute resolution is growing quickly. Sites like www.squaretrade.com and www.onlineresolution.com use mediators to help clients solve disputes on-line. In addition, content-rich sites like www.mediate.com need people to write content on mediation issues, manage mediation programs, and bring mediation values and perspectives to their sites. If you have a technology or sales background, your opportunities in this area expand even more.

Straddling the divide between staff positions and private practice are the growing opportunities in working with mediation provider organizations. Nationwide companies such as Judicial Arbitration and Mediation Services, American Arbitration Association, and Mosten Mediation Centers are hiring people with mediation training to serve as mediators, case managers, and marketing and sales representatives and to provide general business management. Many statewide and local mediation firms offer entry-level and career positions. For example, the prestigious San Francisco mediation firm of DeGregorio and Haldeman uses beginning mediators as case managers to handle intake, convene parties, perform contracting and payment functions, and otherwise support the work of the professional mediators.

Straddling the divide between staff positions and private practice are the growing opportunities in working with mediation provider organizations.

PRIVATE PRACTICE

Even with the growth of paid positions, most people entering the field of conflict resolution opt for private practice. Before discussing the many forms of private practice, it is important to discuss whether private practice is right for you. Start by answering the following questions:

- Do your financial situation and obligations allow for the possibility of little or no income for the first three years and erratic income after that?

- Do your work habits and discipline enable you to be a self-starter, work alone, and manage your own time?

- Are you emotionally prepared for the uncertainty and risk that private practice entails?

If your answer is less than a clear yes for all three questions, you might defer your entry into private practice to a time in your life when answering yes is more likely. You may consider solely focusing on a paid position or starting slowly and doing mediation part time before you give up your nonmediation day job. Private practice is not right for everyone, or the timing may not be right. The challenges of succeeding in private practice are daunting enough without feeling major anxiety due to financial or emotional pressures. Assuming that you want to take the plunge, you have many options for solo practice, as well as the alternatives of forming partnerships, groups, networks, panels, or mediation provider organizations. Career paths are rarely linear. Many mediators start with a salaried position and stay there. Others use a salaried position to get started and head off for private practice at the first opportunity. Still others abandon their private practices for staff or management positions. You will have to find your own way.

Part 2 of this book explores the practicalities of building your own mediation practice.

Building Your Career
as a Mediator

Creating Your Mediation Signature

The twin foundations of a mediation practice are craft and clients. Without a developed set of skills at the mediation table, you will not be able to maximize your effectiveness to help people who entrust you to help them solve their problems. Yet without clients who are prepared to pay for your services, your mediation skills will get rusty and may never be used.

If craft and clients are the symbiotic components of your practice foundation, the mortar that binds them is your mediation signature—the way you are known among your peers, your referral sources, your clients, and the community at large. The growth of mediation has changed the process of selecting a mediator since I started in 1979. Consumers now have much more knowledge about the services offered and their options in the marketplace. Referral sources rarely give the name of just one mediator. It is becoming commonplace for parties to shop for a mediator by interviewing three, five, or even more candidates, comparing mediation style, background and experience, availability, and price. A clear mediation signature gives prospective clients more information about you and increases the chances that they will select you.

*Referral sources rarely give the name of
just one mediator. It is becoming commonplace
for parties to shop for a mediator by interviewing
three, five, or even more candidates, comparing
mediation style, background and experience,
availability, and price.*

I constantly ask mediators at all stages of practice development, "What is your mediation signature?" I'm surprised at how many cannot answer this question. There are many talented and committed mediators who have all the necessary training and preparation, but they either are not making mediation their day job or are not making enough money through their mediation work to keep the doors of their practice open. I have found that if you have a clear sense of your mediation signature, your chances of building a successful practice increase dramatically.

Let's look at some examples of mediation signatures. Bernie Mayer, a social worker by training, has a signature for handling public policy disputes, particularly in Eastern Europe. Susan Haldeman of San Francisco is known for resolving complex civil cases with her superb reframing skills. Robert Bush and Joseph Folger are recognized for specializing in a transformative approach, and Michael McWilliams, former ABA president from Baltimore, is valued for his personal credibility and case evaluation skills. Michael Lewis and Linda Singer have made a name for themselves in resolving intercultural disputes, and Mark Ingram works with small business owners in southern Idaho. These well-known mediators are known for their respective mediation signatures, and each signature differs from the next.

A mediation signature is how you describe your approach at the mediation table and how you attract clients. To create a detailed inventory of what should make up your signature, turn to the Mediator Self-Survey in Appendix One. Then write out your answers to every question on the survey. Your ability to answer these questions cogently in writing will be the basis for every move in building your practice, from writing your practice brochure to determining what to say to a potential referral source at a networking reception.

Let's look at the ways in which you can begin to develop your signature. Don't worry if you can't answer every question in the self-survey. Make a list of areas you wish to explore; you may find help in the rest of the book or in resources listed in Appendix Four.

USE AVAILABLE RESOURCES

In working to define your unique signature, there are many books and resources available. The key is that most of the resources are either generically written for service businesses or for professionals. Very few books address building a mediation practice. This means that you will need to adapt the concepts and strategies already available from their business focus to your mediation practice development.

For example, the American Bar Association's Section on Law Practice Management (www.ABA.LPM.org) has a broad and well-written portfolio of books, tapes, and computer disks that are very instructive to mediators. So does Nolo Press (www.nolo.com), the self-help publisher. In the same way, there is a multitude of mediation Web sites (see Appendix Four) that you can visit to pick up pointers of how other mediators have defined their signatures.

Although your mediation signature will be unique to your personal background, talents, and goals, talking with other mediators will widen your perspective. We will look at some ways that you can accelerate your signature definition building.

Your Personal Board of Directors

Your personal board of directors, which I described in Chapter One, can be of great help in major decisions affecting your practice. Defining your mediation signature goes to the top of the list. Once you have done some preliminary thinking, schedule a meeting with your board to discuss what your signature should be based on: your experience, interests, style, and target market. Once you have made a first cut on your definition, check in periodically with your board to see how you are following through to communicate your signature in the marketplace.

Study Group for Mediators

Study groups are a great way to interact with other mediators who share your commitment to defining a mediation signature and strategically building a practice. The Academy of Family Mediators has consultation groups at its annual conference, and many local organizations, such as the Southern California Mediation Association, have outreach groups for the general membership, but these groups do not have the frequency, informal and intimate atmosphere, or the shared goals of a self-made study group.

Try to identify one to five mediators in your community who are working on developing their signatures (or are similar to you in other ways). In addition to meeting informally on a regular basis, your group can invite special guests, assign presentations, collectively read books in the field, or jointly write articles. As a virtual alternative, perhaps you could form a study group by e-mail with mediators you met in training courses or at mediation conferences.

Here is an e-mail sent out by Diana Mercer, mediator and author of *Your Divorce Advisor,* to members of one of my advanced mediation training courses:

> Hi All: It was great to meet everyone last weekend. It's always so great to work with experienced mediators & learn from each other. Is anybody interested in doing a Virtual Consultation Group? We could post questions to the group and solicit answers, recommend good books & web sites, or just tell war stories. What do you think? If you're interested, you can cut & paste the addresses in this message into your e-mail address book, and then it's started . . . and you never get caught in traffic, but you get perspectives from people from all over the country!

Your Trainers and Mentors

Defining your mediation signature should evolve over time. After completing the Mediator Self-Survey and writing a mission statement to stimulate your thinking, another productive use of your time is exposure to different signatures by observing others in their work.

A good person to start with is the trainer of your basic mediation training course. Trainers are not only experienced mediators, but they know you, and most trainers are genuinely interested in helping you develop your craft after the formal course ends. Trainers are often able to suggest opportunities for you to observe them or other established mediators.

If you wish to accelerate your practice development, you may wish to pay for individual or group supervision from the trainer of your choice. It is customary practice for therapists to consult with supervisors throughout their career, but particularly in the beginning of their careers, and many successful mediators have launched their careers by using this method. (Chapter Four explored this area.)

Another option for learning about your signature is to identify a successful mediator in your community and ask that person for mentoring. Most mediators understand your struggles and may be willing to meet on a regular basis for lunch or invite you to mediation activities in your area. It might also be possible for you to be a fly on the wall of your mentor's office. As a fly, you would have an opportunity to observe your mentor in sessions, on the telephone, while drafting letters and agreements, while collaborating with staff, and otherwise practicing mediation. In return for this invaluable modeling, you could provide feedback either verbally or in writing about what you learned. And if your mentor is open, you might share some thoughts for improvement.

USE YOUR MEDIATIVE PERSPECTIVE

Certainly, you can learn much from strategic planning work in other fields and from successful models in practice, but as a trained mediator you should have internalized many aspects of mediation theory and thinking. This theoretical framework can be the most fruitful source for creating your signature because it will permit your signature to be congruent between your craft at the table and your marketing. Operating a mediation practice might have some elements that overlap with other businesses, but first and foremost you are a peacemaker. If you "walk the mediation walk" in your strategic planning and business operations, clients and referral sources will know it. This is particularly important because the skills that are required to resolve disputes (listening, patience, flexibility to client needs and concerns) may be initially seen as being incompatible with the entrepreneurial characteristics (risk taking, hard driving, results oriented) needed for operating a small business.

Although it may be counterintuitive, using the same concepts for resolving conflict and applying them to building your practice provide you with congruence between your craft and your marketing. Let's use just one conceptual model, Christopher Moore's Circle of Conflict.[1] Moore presents five sources—values, interests, structure, relationships, and data—as information crucial to resolving disputes. The same constructs can help you organize your thinking about your signature.

Values

Identify and use your personal values (such as helping others, empowerment, and creating options) as one set of criteria for practice success. Your practice signature must be integrated with your lifestyle, political philosophy, religious beliefs, and family priorities. Articulating your values is the foundation for creating the vision for your practice.

Interests

Just as positions of the parties during conflict may be clearer than the underlying needs and interests, the same is true in developing your signature. You need to dig deep to identify your actual and perceived interests that underlie your practice. You may wish to consider the following questions:

- Do you have substantive interests, such as an area of conflict (workplace, family, environment), that you wish to address?

- Is there an underlying philosophy or school of mediation with which you identify that will drive your practice?

- Do you have an emotional approach toward your work or toward your dealings with people? For example do you want to limit your workday to eight or so hours, or do you live, breathe, and eat your professional commitments?

- Are you able to integrate and make trade-offs among competing interests and find some objective criteria that will determine success in your practice (for example, amount earned, time off, or number of people helped)?

Structure

The structural components of your mediation practice can have an impact on your signature in a major way. Your ability to identify the patterns of behavior that work well can be translated into the essence of your practice. The way the organizational chart is set up can determine the distribution of power in your mediation practice, and that affects you, your staff, and your clients. The way you make decisions and handle time pressures are structural components of your signature. Finally, how you define your differing roles (mediator, boss, partner) is part of the structure for role expectations, which may take on a life of their own. For example, as a partner, you may have a shared expectation with your other partner to maximize income.

However, as a mediator, you may spend considerable unbilled time in order to get a job done right. You need to explain your peacemaking commitment to your partner so that your partner's expectation of profit making may be modified. On the other hand, your partner may not agree; then you have more talking to do until you can reach resolution. Your mediation skills are needed in your own life as well.

Relationships

The importance of communication with your clients and within your office staff could be a bedrock of your signature. A practice culture to avoid misconceptions or stereotypes of other people can create a tolerant climate. Just as ground rules are an intervention to prevent or react to poor communication, ground rules in the form of regular meetings, office policies, and a manual can serve the same function. And just like at the mediation table, a commitment to build positive feelings and encourage problem solving can be communication factors that help define your signature.

Data

Whereas a lack of meaningful information can contribute to conflict, in building a mediation practice your signature might include a commitment to increase information and decrease misinformation with which to make the best practice decisions possible. By paying attention to systems and technology, you can increase your ability to determine what information is relevant and how to get it, as well as develop common criteria with which to evaluate and make decisions from the data at hand. Finally, just as parties in a mediation may need a third-party expert to help assess data to resolve an impasse, you might need outside experts, such as accountants, computer consultants, and office management professionals, to help you make decisions that will improve your practice.

CREATE A VISION FOR YOUR PRACTICE

As business guru Tom Peters states about vision, "No topic is more important. There is no precise path to 'finding one.' The process of discovery is personal. Visions are aesthetic and moral—as well as aesthetically sound."[2] And in *The Fifth Discipline,* Peter Senge says, "If people don't have their own vision, all they can do is sign up for someone else's."[3]

Talk with any successful mediator whom you respect. Every one of them has a vision for his or her mediation work that has been lived out day to day and year by year in the mediation practice. Keynote speakers, national trainers, respected ACR officers, and well-paid private practitioners all had visions of their peacemaking work and have carried them out despite major challenges.

🌿 Practice Tip 🌿

Here are some questions to help define your practice's vision:

- What is the vision for your mediation practice in six months?
- What is the vision for your mediation practice in one year?
- What is the vision for your mediation practice in two years?
- What is the vision for your mediation practice in five years?

Developing a vision may be the most important step you take to build your practice and define your signature. Creating a vision may seem amorphous and overwhelming. The following eight traits of an effective vision, from Tom Peters' book *Thriving on Chaos,* can help you find yours:

- A vision is inspiring.
- A vision is clear and challenging—and about excellence.
- A vision makes sense in the marketplace and stands the test of time.
- A vision must be stable but constantly challenged.
- A vision is a beacon and controls your actions when all else is up for grabs.
- A vision is aimed at empowering you first, and your clients second.
- A vision prepares for the future, but honors the past.
- A vision is lived in details, not in broad strokes.[4]

Try answering again: What is your vision for your mediation practice in five years? Is it to empower people every day? To be so sought after by so many clients that you have a two-month waiting list? To have every client undergo growth, creating opportunity out of conflict? To have every client make just one step toward resolution? To create a system where people in conflict go first to a mediator's office? To make sure that people can resolve their disputes quickly so they don't have to live with burdens of conflict one day longer than necessary?

These are illustrative visions. You have to create your own. Again, Tom Peters has some tips for engaging in vision creation that I have adapted for mediators:

Look to your prior experiences. What have you done or strived for that was important? What did you not like about the way conflict was handled that you want to change?

Fiddle around, but make haste. Consult, think, and play with the possibilities. Then begin in fairly dramatic fashion (enroll in a mediation training course or register for a conference), and try out your vision on small events.

Take a baby step. Start living out your vision next Monday by implementing one small piece of it. (Make sure your candy bowl is filled. Get fresh erasable markers for your flip chart. Prepare one form to hand out to clients.)

Clarify over time. Start your journey, but be ready to take a new fork or even double back if necessary.[5]

DEVELOP A MISSION STATEMENT
BASED ON YOUR SIGNATURE

Once you have thought about the variables that compose your mediation signature—how your clients and referral sources think about your values, style, and services—you should reduce your thinking to a mission statement for your mediation practice. Your mission statement is primarily a guide for you and your staff. You can display it in your office, include it in your client marketing packet, set it out in full in your brochure, and use it as the basis for your strategic planning (these subjects are covered in Chapters Nine, Twelve, and Eleven, respectively).

Unlike a business plan, which should be comprehensive (and therefore lengthy), your mission statement should be approximately fifty to one hundred words. It should set out your basic principles and core beliefs about your mediation practice and include the types of services you aspire to provide, the purpose of your practice, and your vision. Look at mission statements of different businesses and professional service firms, and pick and choose the elements that you like best; then adapt your learning to your own practice. There is no correct mission statement. Yours must feel comfortable to you and reflect your own sense of your unique mediation practice.

---

*There is no correct mission statement.
Yours must feel comfortable to you and reflect your
own sense of your unique mediation practice.*

Here is the mission statement of Mosten Mediation Centers:

Mosten Mediation Centers is dedicated to helping parties heal conflict and move forward in their lives by providing caring, competent, thorough, and creative mediation services. We strive to treat our clients, our mediators, and each other with dignity and consideration through cooperation and respectful communication. Our vision is to create a work environment for each mediation center that is peaceful and supportive while providing balanced and secure lives for ourselves and empowering us to better serve our clients.

Take ten minutes to write your own mission statement. When you are finished, read it aloud. As you tinker with the wording, share it with mediation colleagues, family, and your personal board of directors in conceiving, drafting, and massaging their mission statements. You probably can develop your mission statement on your own, but if you are stymied, consulting with a mediator in the field or with a marketing professional can help you move forward.

TOOLS TO DEFINE YOUR PRACTICE STYLE

Most mediators learn their styles of practice from their training and early practice experience as modeled by their trainers, supervisors, and mentors. As described by Michael Lang and Allison Taylor in *The Making of a Mediator,* many equate "being a mediator" with doing those things that they learned during their novice and apprentice stages.[6]

But the key to defining your mediation signature at the table is taking a closer look at how you set up your process and what you do when parties walk through the door—and then translating those observations into an understandable picture of how you work. It is often not helpful to use broad labels such as *facilitative, transformative,* or *evaluative* to define your signature. These labels may mean different things to different people—and they may mean nothing at all. Let's explore some tools that may help you define the way you practice mediation.

Mediation Abacus

The simplest tool that I have found to define your signature at the table is the Mediation Abacus developed by John Wade from Queensland, Australia (see Figure 6.1). This inventory of formats and interventions can help you define your signature. The abacus sets out important signature variables on a continuum; rarely does any mediator operate solely on the margins.

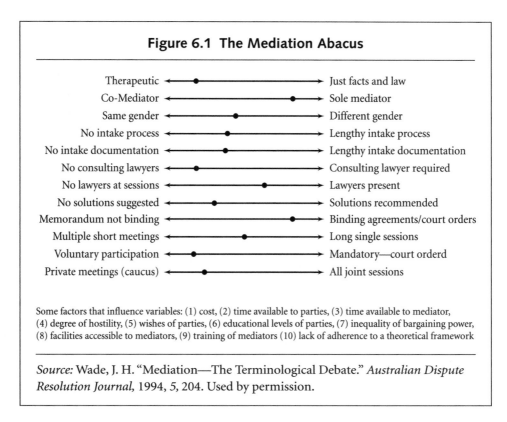

Figure 6.1 The Mediation Abacus

Therapeutic ⟵———●————————⟶ Just facts and law
Co-Mediator ⟵——————————●——⟶ Sole mediator
Same gender ⟵————————●———⟶ Different gender
No intake process ⟵————————●————⟶ Lengthy intake process
No intake documentation ⟵—————————●————⟶ Lengthy intake documentation
No consulting lawyers ⟵———●—————————⟶ Consulting lawyer required
No lawyers at sessions ⟵——————————●———⟶ Lawyers present
No solutions suggested ⟵—————●———————⟶ Solutions recommended
Memorandum not binding ⟵————————————●—⟶ Binding agreements/court orders
Multiple short meetings ⟵—————————●————⟶ Long single sessions
Voluntary participation ⟵————●———————⟶ Mandatory—court orderd
Private meetings (caucus) ⟵————●———————⟶ All joint sessions

Some factors that influence variables: (1) cost, (2) time available to parties, (3) time available to mediator, (4) degree of hostility, (5) wishes of parties, (6) educational levels of parties, (7) inequality of bargaining power, (8) facilities accessible to mediators, (9) training of mediators (10) lack of adherence to a theoretical framework

Source: Wade, J. H. "Mediation—The Terminological Debate." *Australian Dispute Resolution Journal,* 1994, 5, 204. Used by permission.

Therapeutic-Just Facts. Will the mediation be an opportunity for the parties to gain new insights and perspectives? Will healing the conflict and repairing the relationship be part of the agenda? Or will the parties shelve their emotions and concentrate solely on the facts of the controversy in order to settle the case?

Co-Mediator—Sole Mediator. Some mediators always work alone, and others work only in a co-mediation team. But the vast majority of mediators mediate both alone and with a variety of co-mediator partners. Your style of co-mediation may need its own abacus (see the Epilogue).

Same Gender—Different Gender. One or more parties may have strong views about the gender of the mediator. If all the parties are women, would it make a difference if you are a man? The abacus helps you focus on this variable.

No Intake Process—Lengthy Intake Process. Do you start mediating without meeting the parties or even talking with them before they walk in the room? Or do you have telephone or in-office orientation or screening procedures before you start a working session? (Chapter Twelve explores different models of intake.)

No Intake Documentation—Lengthy Intake Documentation. Do you require parties to fill out a questionnaire or forms before meeting with them? If so, how do you use this information?

No Consulting Lawyers—Consulting Lawyer Required. Some mediators will not work with parties if they are talking with lawyers outside the mediation room. Others require parties to hire lawyers for either full service or unbundled coaching. Where do you fit in?

No Lawyers at Sessions—Lawyers Present. Some mediators do not permit lawyers to attend sessions. Others mediate only if lawyers are present at every session. Still others start with parties only and bring in lawyers if trouble develops. Others start with lawyers present and have the parties work alone with the mediator once a comfort zone is developed. Do your clients and referral sources know how you handle this issue?

No Solutions Suggested—Solutions Recommended. Today, with the influx of more mediators with backgrounds as judges or lawyers, many consumers expect and want proactive solutions from mediators. Some mediators use both approaches depending on the situation. Traditional mediation training discouraged recommending a solution as such mediator conduct might threaten the parties' empowerment and the control. See the discussion on the facilitative-evaluative continuum.

Memorandum of Understanding/No Binding Agreement—Signed, Detailed Binding Agreements and Court Orders. Are you a one-stop shop where parties can both work out their disputes and have you or your staff draft final contracts and court documents? Or will your role be limited to helping parties resolve conflict and have other professionals (generally lawyers) handle all the paperwork? Do you differ in your approach depending on the clients or type of matter?

Multiple Short Meetings—Long Single Sessions. What do parties expect when they agree to mediate with you? Civil mediators generally use long sessions, and family mediators generally use several shorter sessions. See Chapter Twelve for discussion of format.

Voluntary Participation—Mandatory, Court-Ordered Participation. Will you accept mandatory mediation referrals from the court? How do you handle recalcitrant parties or lawyers?[7] Will you limit your practice to parties of participate based on their own reflective choice?

Private Meetings (Caucus)—All Joint Sessions. Do you favor one school or mix and match? Will you follow the desires of one of the parties, or do you operate on your own model unless there is joint consent otherwise? Will you stick to your model even with joint agreement of the parties to modify your model?

As you can see, the abacus highlights the extremes—for example, no intake process on one extreme and lengthy intake on the other. If you always start a working session with the parties based on a short telephone call from one party, you might put the dot all the way to the left of the abacus. On the other hand, if you have lengthy telephone calls with all parties and then have private office sessions with all parties plus an office orientation before any working session commences, your abacus dot would be on the far right. You might use one method of intake in family mediations and another in civil. Or you might use a hybrid system whether counsel are present or not.

Your ability to use the abacus will give more definition of how you work, and you can then communicate that definition to those using your services. A financial planner working with two business partners might want to refer to a mediator who can get to work right away and not demand a lengthy intake for two impatient businesspersons. A therapist organizational consultant dealing with the same parties might want you to have at least preliminary telephone calls with each of the parties before seeing them together and wants to refer to a mediator whose intake process permits this step.

It takes time to go through the abacus, but the process is worth the time investment. Once you are clear on the various components of your mediation style, you can translate that clarity into your marketing materials, your speaking, and your writing, and you can use it to orient your staff better.

What Mediators Do at the Table

The following list from Bernard Mayer's book *Dynamics of Conflict Resolution* provides another conceptual orientation for identifying your mediation signature:

- Help parties feel heard.
- Help parties hear others.
- Frame and reframe issues, suggestions, and concerns.
- Create a safe atmosphere.
- Manage emotions.
- Facilitate conversation.
- Explore needs.
- Balance power.
- Bridge differences of gender, culture, and class.
- Facilitate negotiation.
- Deal with impasse.
- Encourage creativity.
- Develop options.
- Weigh and compare options.
- Articulate and solidify potential agreements.
- Create dissonance.
- Apply appropriate pressure.
- Discuss implementation.
- Appropriate drafting.
- Help implementation.[8]

Just as with the abacus, you can go through each of these functions and think through how you handle this aspect of mediation work. For example, you might take the task of balancing power between parties and be able to discuss how you handle power imbalances and relate those to other mediator roles, such as reframing issues, creating a safe environment, and applying appropriate pressure.

The Style Index

If you are comfortable with the facilitative-evaluative paradigm, you might want to use Leonard Riskin's typology of facilitative-evaluative and broad-narrow mediator styles.[9] You can define your own signature based on this theory by filling out the Style Index for Mediators developed by Jeffrey Krivis and Barbara McAdoo.[10] In the Style Index, you can discover how you rate on the facilitative-evaluative and broad-narrow continuum in respect to defining the problem and your role as a mediator. Following are some sample questions, on which you rate yourself from 1 (Strongly Agree) to 10 (Strongly Disagree), contained in the Style Index:

> I prefer to look beyond the legal issues in defining the problem to be resolved.
>
> I urge the parties to compromise on narrow issues.
>
> The interests of the parties are more important to me than settling the case.
>
> I tend to decide how I will approach a case based on the legal documents, technical reports or legal briefs.
>
> To help parties negotiate successfully, I find it helpful to give an advisory opinion about the likely outcome of the case.
>
> I use private caucuses early to help the parties understand the weaknesses of their case.
>
> I do not have to understand the legal posture of the case to serve as the mediator.

After filling out the questionnaire and determining your own personal mediator classification, you then can reflect if you are satisfied with your current style and what changes you wish to make, if any.

Ten Roles of Peacemaking

In defining your signature, you may find that limiting yourself solely to the process of mediation is far too narrow. You may view yourself, and want others to see you, as a full-service peacemaker, with mediation only one of many roles that you play in your professional practice.

In his book *The Third Side,* William Ury discusses ten different roles of peacemaking, which provide a broader way in which to view your work:[11]

Provider	Equalizer
Teacher	Healer
Bridge Builder	Witness
Mediator	Referee
Arbiter	Protector

If you wish to use the Ury paradigm, look through your work and examine if your signature is accurately defined by calling yourself mediator or whether you need a more expansive definition. For example, in your neutral work, you may serve as an arbitrator on occasion. Do you wish to let others know about such availability?

In a less obvious illustration, following a successfully mediated agreement, do you offer the parties the explicit opportunity to have closure in a healing way? In his brilliant book *Resolving Personal and Organizational Conflict: Stories of Transformation and Forgiveness,* Ken Cloke offers mediators tools to help parties go beyond the four corners of their written agreement to attempt to heal their relationship that has been racked by conflict.[12] If you are trained in and wish to offer these healing transformative services, is that orientation part of your mediation signature? On the other hand, if you believe that such transformation is better achieved outside the mediation room, do you communicate that belief to your clients and referral sources?

CONCLUSION

These examples are meant to stimulate your own defining process that could range from the way you deal with impasse or difficult clients to how you organize lunch at an all-day session. In total, your definition will provide an orientation for clients and referral sources of what to expect if you are chosen as a mediator.

Now that you've explored the way you work and begun to develop your mediation signature, you're ready to set up your practice. The next chapter explores the ways in which you can provide more services to your clients.

Expanding Your Mediation Services

When I ask mediators, "What services do you offer?" the answer is often, "I offer mediation services." I generally respond, "If mediation services is your signature, what does that communicate to clients? How do those services differentiate you from other mediators in the marketplace so that potential clients will hire you?"

Calling yourself a mediator is like a store owner calling herself a businessperson. Is she a corporate executive or manager of a convenience store? The phrase *mediation services* tells the consumer very little about your individual services, style, or process.

Many mediators have a myopic view of the services that they sell: resolution of current disputes. That narrow view comes from the narrow traditional mediation training that they received, which results in the narrow practice in the field. But there are many more services you may not realize that you are capable of performing.

Even if you received training in only the resolution of current disputes and that product is the one being primarily practiced by mediators and currently requested by clients, it may be vital for you to explore other service products for which you already have the background, experience, and ability to provide—*and* that people want and are ready to pay for if they only know that such services are available.

One of the hottest trends in the legal profession is the unbundling of legal services to meet consumer demand.[1] Due to high lawyers' fees and a growing demand for consumer control over the process, lawyers are breaking up their traditional full-service package, where the lawyer does all the work and clients pay high fees and surrender control. Progressive lawyers are unbundling the full-service package and offering discrete services that clients can buy on an as-needed basis. This unbundling movement has led to legal hot lines, services over the Web, client-oriented seminars, and lawyer coaches who stand on the sidelines offering advice, ghostwriting, negotiation strategy, and other services while their clients represent themselves.

Mediators are adapting this unbundled approach to offer various discrete tasks of their services à la carte. Under this approach, you can break out many of your services and sell them on an individual basis, lowering the economic and emotional barriers that prevent an individual from entering mediation.

You can break out many of your services and sell them on an individual basis, lowering the economic and emotional barriers that prevent an individual from entering mediation.

SESSION-BY-SESSION MEDIATION

Many mediators use this approach but do not incorporate it into their mediation signatures. Essentially, you underscore client empowerment by offering your services session by session with no obligation to pay a large deposit or make an obligation beyond the initial one, two, or three hours. Because private mediation is wholly voluntary, every mediation participant has the right to end the process at any time. Many potential clients do not know that they have this control and that mediation is virtually risk free and affordable! This is the easiest service to offer; you may already do so. Your mission (should you choose to accept it) is to ensure that your services are affordable and available and subject to client needs and desires; then communicate that reality to your clients and referral sources.

MEDIATION CASE ASSESSMENT

Almost every competent mediator offers potential clients the opportunity to learn about the concept of mediation—how it works, its benefits and downsides, and how it compares with litigation, arbitration, and other binding (top-down) methods of resolving disputes. The essence of this service is that you probably offer it as a selling tool to convince the parties to retain you for the full package of mediation services.

You can unbundle the case assessment and offer it alone as a freestanding service. By offering case assessment along with your full-service mediation practice, you can help people in trouble learn about mediation, screen to see if mediation is appropriate in their situation, and assist them in finding the right mediator for them if they choose to mediate. This mediator could be you, but it very well may not be. For example, in Santa Barbara, California, an experienced mediator, Brian Burke, offers case assessment lasting two and a half hours for a flat fee. His primary service is case assessments; he rarely mediates the full case. In this way, parties can consult him without the built-in conflict of interest that full-service mediators face: people come to consult with those of us who are full-service mediators, and we sell both concept (mediation) and brand (ourselves as the mediator of choice). If you offer assessment as a stand-alone service, you not only can get paid for your time providing this important service, but you may find that clients feel more comfortable consulting you *and* might more readily hire you for full service based on their satisfaction with your neutral assessment performance.

This is exactly what mediation provider organizations such as the Judicial Arbitration and Mediation Service, the American Arbitration Association, and Mosten Mediation Centers do. The case managers or dispute resolution assistants who handle the intake calls are generally not the same people who serve as mediators. By erecting a Chinese wall between the intake and the mediators, the impartiality of the mediator ultimately selected is preserved, and the extraordinary time and stress of intake are borne by the administrators, not by the mediators. Actually, many mediators sign up with mediation providers or organizations to be freed from the intake work of handling telephone calls, sending out marketing packets, and handling the numerous administrative details involved in setting up a mediation. (Chapter Ten describes different types of mediator provider organizations.)

Within your own mediation practice, you may make a decision that your personal involvement with the potential clients is a bonding and effective sales link to being selected as the full-service mediator. If so, such personal involvement during intake would be part of your mediation signature (see Chapter Six). Or you might decide that you do not like doing assessments when other mediators will get the satisfaction (and fees) of handling the rest of the case. If so, *not* offering stand-alone assessment services can be part of your signature. The real point is for you to think hard about what services you are or are not willing to offer. You must also determine whether you wish to unbundle any of these premediation educational and counseling services and convert that thinking into defining your overall signature.

---

*Think hard about what services
you are or are not willing to offer.*

CONVENING AND CONTRACTING

Along the spectrum of full-service mediation, like intake and mediation education, convening the parties to get them to the table can be a stand-alone product that you can offer to the public. Virtually all ADR organizations tease out this service and charge for it in a variety of ways: by the hour, a flat fee, or a percentage of the claim involved.

At Mosten Mediation Centers, we have found that it takes approximately ten new client calls to translate into one case. About five of those calls are a demand for legal services; although we try to educate and counsel these clients about the benefits of mediation, most of these people hire attorneys or represent themselves in the traditional legal system. The other five calls are from people ready to mediate. Only one of those calls is from parties mutually ready to mediate. The other four calls represent one side of a dispute who wants to mediate but has not yet received agreement from the other side to mediate. Getting the other side to the table is called *convening,* and this service can be offered as a separate service.

Convening involves calling or writing to the other parties or their lawyers (or both) to persuade them to mediate. Convening can also include mediating the selection of the mediator, the venue, the dates of the session, the format, and allocation of payment. Once mediation is agreed to in principle, there may be negotiation over the contract terms of the written mediation agreement and some work to get all parties to sign the agreement and make their respective payments.

Convening and contracting take a great deal of time and skill. In fact, many talented mediators are choosing to perform intake, convening, and contracting as assistants for other mediators as preparation for careers as full-service mediators or as a career in and of itself. Others convene by day and mediate by night.

If you choose to offer convening separately, be sure to let your referral sources know. You may even want to prepare a separate brochure and set up an independent convening company to accentuate the discrete nature of this service.

MANAGING INFORMATION GATHERING

Because approximately 95 percent of lawsuits settle without a final decision by a judge or jury, how do all the lawyer fees and costs get spent in litigation? That's easy. Just think of all the depositions, subpoenas, interrogatories, document inspections, and other forms of discovery for which litigants spend their money. In fact, so much money is spent that many people run out of resources before a trial ever starts, resulting in a settlement that is more the product of frustration and a depletion of resources than of reflection and strategic decision making.

As a mediator, you have an opportunity to offer unbundled neutral services to stem this unproductive drain of energy and money. Many parties who are miles apart on ultimate settlement numbers might hire you to mediate the conflicts and complexities of information gathering. If you are successful, you can resolve many of the pretrial disputes without the parties' spending unproductive lawyer fees for multiple trips to court (so they can still have some money to beat each other's brains out in trial), where at least the parties will get a final result (assuming that any litigated result is final given appeals, collectibility, and posttrial modifications).

Here are just a few examples of information-gathering services that you can provide:

- Arrange for limited balanced initial document production, with a process to address later requests for missing documents.
- Mediate consequences for failing to produce discovery. Compensatory monies for extra work can replace fines or sanctions.
- Create manageable schedules and priority for discovery.
- Review submissions of documents and interrogatory and admissions answers, and mediate a resolution. Mediate conflicting claims over whether the information submitted is sufficient, whether discovery demands are too burdensome, or many other issues that needlessly cost money to resolve in court.
- Sit in on depositions or be on call to mediate objections or legal wrangles.

- Attend settlement conferences of lawyers and clients to increase the chances for resolution, making explicit agreements not to reach agreement but to frame the issues clearly.

- Help refine or consensually modify vague court orders that are not acceptable to either party.

In addition to cost savings, the real attraction of these information-gathering services to litigators is that as a mediator, you can gain the confidence of the parties to persuade but do not have the power to bully or impose your will. A bonus for the mediated approach is that in direct calendar courts, the judge who rules on numerous pretrial hearings also tries the case. When you serve as a mediator, the trial judge may never even know of the many squabbles that took place before the trial.

If the parties are impressed with your work as a mediated case manager, they may decide to give you a shot at mediating a settlement after you have cleared away the pretrial hurdles.

COORDINATING THE USE OF EXPERTS

Another cost drain in litigation is the battle of the expert witnesses. Despite eminent credentials, experts from different sides of a case rarely evaluate the same set of facts and reach similar conclusions. Unfortunately, experts themselves can become adversarial in defending their positions and jockeying for favor with the law firms that butter their bread. Runaway experts goaded by vigorous lawyers are a recipe for exorbitant fees and dissatisfied clients.

You may consider offering the unbundled mediated service of working with experts and the parties to mollify conflict and contain costs. These services are separate and distinct from your overall settlement work but may be the key bricks in the foundation for ultimate resolution. Experts can be the linchpins for settlement. More and more parties will be willing to use you to coordinate these necessary experts if they know you are qualified and available to do the work. You can provide these neutral services for cases involving experts:

- Mediate directly with the opposing experts. Even if you don't achieve agreement, you can help the experts propose a range of results that will provide more opportunity for compromise.

- Help the parties identify qualified, neutral, acceptable experts; mediate a mutually agreed scope of work; and help negotiate the expert's contract and fees with the parties.

- Work with the parties and acceptable experts to reduce their work and expedite the results.

- Help the parties digest and use expert information for settlement.

HANDLING EMERGENCY CONFLICTS

You may have witnessed (or been involved in) heated litigation in which letters are flying so fast between lawyers that the fax machines break down in both law offices. These poison letters often lead to emergency court hearings. There is no limit to the range of issues that can send overinvolved litigators through the roof and headed down to court. And the bills go up and up. Just like mediated case management for information sharing, case management for overactive lawyers, often playing out their own internal conflicts, is unbundled mediated service that both parties and their lawyers need and will pay for.

After one or two skirmishes, parties will learn how effective you can be in defusing disputes, and they will use you with more confidence in that case and other matters that each lawyer may have in the future. This is how you can build your mediation practice. Here are some unbundled emergency conflict services that you can offer:

- Mediate an agreement that will restrict the parties' right to seek court relief unless mutually agreed on. Before seeking court relief, the parties must first exchange letters discussing the problem and offering a proposed solution.

- Arrange for conference calls or emergency mediation sessions to diffuse conflict that rears up during the litigation or between the parties outside the court process.

- Establish timing, venue, and processes for emergency mediation sessions to precede any court filing and facilitate the discussion (and worse) at such sessions.

- Neutrally draft the results of emergency telephone or office sessions, and circulate the agreements for signature.

NEGOTIATING AND WRITING UP
THE TERMS OF THE AGREEMENT

This is the mother's milk of mediation work. Parties and lawyers will most often hire you to mediate their ultimate settlements. Again, your current clients are your best resource for future business. Remember to inform parties of your neutral drafting services when you are successful in bringing a case to a close.

You may have been trained to believe that mediators never draft ultimate agreements. Traditional mediation training taught that mediators help parties reach agreement in principle and write up a memorandum of understanding, leaving the final agreement or court judgments to be written by the parties themselves or to be drafted by the separate lawyers. This traditional approach is only one model of mediation. Experienced mediators often find that agreements that are wonderful in principle never get finalized due to excessive lawyer review, and the conflict rages on. Or the drafting process becomes so adversarial and costly that the savings of mediating the agreement become lost in the protracted wrangling over language.

If you are an experienced lawyer or are otherwise competent to draft contracts and mediator drafting is permissible in your state, you can be a mediator who can help the parties in the following ways:

- Neutrally drafting the final agreement for review by the parties and their lawyers.

- Supervising the requests for changes, identifying areas of agreement, and preparing open issues for resolution once the agreement has been circulated.

- Renegotiating the agreement. Too often, desire for renegotiation occurs when parties or their lawyers see the agreement written down in black and white in the drafts of the final agreement.

PREPARING COURT FORMS AND OTHER DOCUMENTS

Parties who reach agreement may need to sign more documents than just the final agreement or judgment (decree/order). Deeds, letters of resignation from partnerships and corporations, automobile title documents, credit card cancellations, employment reference letters, licensing changes, insurance beneficiary forms, checks to pay creditors, and other documents may be necessary. Just like closings in real estate or corporate formations or mergers, parties often want all these documents prepared for signing at one time in a mediation closing session.

As a neutral party, you can mediate what documents are necessary, who should prepare them, what form they should be in, the timing of preparation, and the manner of review. Often parties will want you to draft them. In some states, such work by nonlawyer mediators is forbidden as the unauthorized practice of law; some states even make it unethical for lawyer mediators to draft final documents, claiming such drafting is dual representation and outside the scope of the role of mediator.[2] In other states, with proper authorization by the parties, such restrictions can be waived in favor of your ability and neutral role to complete the job for the parties

If it is permissible for you to draft such documents and you are qualified to do so, not only will you contribute to the ultimate resolution; you will be able to generate additional fees that parties are willing to pay.

PREVENTING FUTURE CONFLICTS

A major role for the unbundling lawyer is that of a preventive legal health care provider. In many ways, as a mediator, you can provide needed preventive services—for example:

- Offer preventive mediation services to form relationships, not just end them. Examples include helping form business partnerships, marriages and cohabitation relationships, adoptions, joint ventures, and construction projects and helping families work on estate planning while parents are still alive. I recommend the videotape *Mediation, Arbitration, and Preventive Law.*[3]

- Mediate discussions prior to the settlement to include provisions for future dispute resolution.

- Mediate conflict and legal wellness checkups for parties to get together to monitor the workability of the agreement and provide a safe place to discuss modifying the agreement. (See Appendix Eight for a sample.)

CONCLUSION

It's more likely you can make a living as a mediator if you offer a variety of services—whether you're a staff mediator or in private practice. Knowing what services to provide is connected to knowing your target market, which we'll explore in the next chapter.

Defining Your Target Market

What is your target market? If you have trouble answering this question, you are a member of a very large club. Now that you have begun to define your mediation signature by clarifying and expanding your inventory of mediation service products, you are ready to answer the most often ignored question of mediator strategic planning: Who are or will be your clients?

Defining your target market is essential for two reasons. First, by understanding the needs of the population you serve, you can develop the skills and support materials to meet the needs of that market. Second, once your market is clarified, you can more effectively and economically communicate your mediation signature though advertising, brochures, public relations, and other marketing strategies.

DEFINING YOUR MARKET

Before thinking through the various criteria for market targeting, let's focus on the underlying premise of defining a market. You can differentiate yourself within an already established market through quality or difference, or you can expand existing markets or create new ones. The path you choose makes a major impact on the development of your practice.

Unlike going to a car mechanic when your car stalls or to the dentist when your tooth aches, most people do not think about mediation as their first option when conflict or legal trouble strikes. A 1997 study by the Rand Corporation found that only 7 percent of civil cases used private mediation.[1] The good news is that a major untapped market for mediation services awaits you. The bad news is that despite the virtues of the product, trying to sell mediation to people who are unfamiliar with it is very difficult. If selling mediation to people who already trust you is difficult, just imagine selling to people who do not know you! If it is challenging to persuade people with the angina of current disputes to try mediation, imagine the challenge of selling preventive conflict avoidance services (see Chapter Seven). If you have trouble getting your best friend to give mediation a try, think about the effort and expense of marketing mediation to people with all kinds of problems in other parts of your own state or across the country.

Experts in marketing link the definition of a target market and strategies of business development. In thinking through this connection for professional firms and consultants, David Karlson has developed the simple chart shown here to set out the options.

Marketing Strategies Chart

Low Risk	*Moderate Risk*
Mainstream mediation services to current clients	Mainstream mediation services to potential clients
Status quo	Moderate cost and growth
Low cost	
Low Risk	*High Risk*
New mediation services to current clients	New cutting-edge mediation services to potential clients
Significant growth	Slow growth
Moderate cost	High cost

Source: Karlson, D. *Marketing Your Consulting or Professional Service.* Menlo Park, Calif.: Crisp Publications, 1996.

Mainstream Mediation Services to Current Clients

If you want to get your feet wet with minimum cost, start with the clients you already have by offering the main fare of mediation: resolution of current disputes. Because you have achieved the trust and confidence of your current clients, you have already overcome the main challenge of marketing: get your customers to believe in your integrity and competence.

If you want to get your feet wet with minimum cost, start with the clients you already have by offering the main fare of mediation: resolution of current disputes.

If you have practiced as a mediator, your current clients (including those whose cases you have mediated in the past) already know that you do good work for a fair price. They may just need to be reminded that you are still in practice and available for work.

If your current clients are a result of your premediation profession or business, they still believe in you and will be ready to hire you as a mediator if you indicate you are trained and competent to be their neutral mediator. Building on that trust and confidence, targeting your current clients is the most economical means of marketing. Tom Peters reports that it costs five times as much to acquire a new client than it does to keep a current client.[2] Even if the client work is not ongoing and your role will be as a neutral mediator, Peters' point is still valid: market to your current clients.

If mediation is not your full-time job, your next strategic decision is whether you want to market your mediation services to nonmediation clients and risk losing them as clients. If you are an accountant and you do tax preparation for three hundred clients each year, there will be some clients who might worry that if you are a "born-again" mediator, your interest and focus will be on building your mediation practice rather than doing tax returns. You have to make this tough choice. If you concentrate on mediation, you could lose your accounting client base. But if you continue to do just tax returns, you may never live out your dream to be a peacemaker. This dilemma exists for lawyers, therapists, and in other fields whenever one tries to branch out or evolve into a second business or profession.

New Mediation Services to Your Current Clients

While taking advantage of the benefits of marketing to your current clients, if you roll out services such as mediated case management or mediation coaching services, you can do so at moderate cost with the expectation of significant growth over time. Although there is little current demand for those services, you can make them available to your clients through regular correspondence, e-mails, or on your Web site, so it won't cost you much to adopt a take-it-slow approach. This is definitely a low-risk strategy.

Mainstream Mediation Services to Potential Clients

This is a moderate-risk strategy that you can do with moderate cost with the hope for moderate growth. Essentially, by emphasizing your mediation signature of quality for resolving disputes, you will be attempting to increase your share of a market. It costs much more to reach out beyond your existing clients, because you need to sell both the concept of mediation and your brand. This double marketing challenge can yield new clients and more referrals as you are expanding your base.

Cutting-Edge Services to Potential Clients

If you are willing to invest substantial monies to finance your mediation practice, this double-barrel approach of offering new services to new clients has the best chance of accelerating your practice self-sufficiency.

To adopt this approach, you must be willing either to borrow money or use the cash flow from your current services to finance slow growth in the long term. You must devote the focus and follow-up to promote a market for new services and identify and sell to potential clients.

IDENTIFYING POTENTIAL CLIENT MARKETS

As a mediator, you have probably been trained to focus on the needs of the parties. The same approach works in building your practice: focus on the needs of potential clients.

Mediator-centered mediation focuses on the services mediators want to deliver rather than on the services that the public needs and wants to buy. These mediators concentrate on what they have to sell rather than on what fills the unmet needs of their potential clients.

This conflict between meeting your needs or those of your potential clients is tied to the consideration of whether to specialize or be a generalist. Let's examine four models and see how they will affect your market definition.

A common question among mediators is: Should I specialize or remain a generalist? Marketing expert David Karlson ties the answer of this question to marketing strategy. The wider your services and target market are, the harder it is to market effectively. You have to be all things to all people—and you have to market to everyone. Other mediators want to be open to resolving a large variety of disputes and work with clients and referral sources from different fields.

The Generalist: Wide Services to a Wide Market

This is the model that the majority of mediators adopt. These professionals mediate any type of matter in any subject area with any set of clients from any locale.

The advantage to being open to a wide range of services and potential clients is that referral sources can be confident that you will take all calls, assuming that you have the time and the parties are willing to pay your fees. Because you do not depend on a particular group of clients or limit yourself to one area of conflict, you will probably be seen as process oriented, and your impartiality and neutrality will be assumed. If lawyers are involved, you probably will defer to their substantive expertise and can use your broad knowledge as a tool in not becoming dependent on legal-based solutions. You will be free from dependence on any one segment of the population and can work with a variety of situations and clients.

Four Models for Mediation Practices

Generalist	*Specialist*
Wide services to a wide market	Narrow services to a narrow market
Narrow Market Specialist	*Wide Market Specialist*
Wide services to a narrow market	Narrow services to a wide market

Source: Karlson, D. *Marketing Your Consulting or Professional Service.* Menlo Park, Calif.: Crisp Publications, 1996.

As a generalist, you may be hampered by a lack of specific expertise so that referral sources may not put you on their short list. One reason for many generalists' having difficulty building profitable practices is that the marketing challenge can be overwhelming. Because it would take so much money to market to all potential clients, it seems that many generalists market very little or none at all. Some generalists such as Howard Bellman, Peter Adler, Bernie Mayer, and Jay Folberg do not have to market; they have plenty of business due to their experience and recognized talent. But most of the mediators with lean and hungry looks who can't seem to sustain a practice cling to their generalist philosophy. They love mediation and want to mediate anything for anyone. This infatuation with mediation as a philosophy and way of life often borders on proselytization and may either be off-putting to potential clients or prevent these generalists from developing consumer-oriented practices and marketing.

----

*Because it would take so much money to market
to all potential clients, it seems that many generalists
market very little or none at all.*

Narrow Market Specialist: Wide Services to a Narrow Market

This approach can permit you to offer a variety of services, both mainstream and cutting edge, to a market narrow enough to market effectively. It means that you are available to provide any mediation service to a narrow field, population, or geographical area—for example:

- Parents and children in a school
- Disabled persons
- Homeowner associations
- Divorced persons
- Financial planners
- Government agencies
- Trade associations
- Private practice therapists and family lawyers
- Readership of weekly neighborhood newspaper
- Corporate human resources personnel

Wide Market Specialist: Narrow Services to a Wide Market

This model is an opportunity for mediators with a distinctive process signature to market to a wide range of potential clients. Rather than focusing on the overall conflict resolution needs of any target market, you would emphasize your particular signature—for example:

- Mediated convening, selection, and contracting
- Coordination of multiparty litigation and class actions
- Neutral assessment and information for parties considering mediation
- Mediated relocation of residents in construction rehabilitation
- Intergovernmental contract disputes
- Coaching mediating parties in victim-offender mediations
- Neutral drafting of future dispute resolution clauses
- Neutral appraisals and evaluations for real estate and businesses

Specialist: Narrow Services to a Narrow Market

If you narrow your services and limit your marketing, you may be able to accelerate your practice by being identified as an expert mediator in a particular field who offers the highest-quality services. At the same time, because narrow-narrow specialists generally refer everything outside of their area, they receive reciprocal referrals from a variety of sources, including other mediators. One of the main advantages of this target marketing is that you can send out many repetitive messages to the same people to gain recognition and a higher share of the target market.

Here are some examples of narrow-narrow specialties:

- Child custody mediation within a small geographical area
- Neutral fact investigation for hostile-workplace claims nationwide
- Mediated case management for water intrusion cases in public housing projects
- Mediated strategic planning for family business with over $10 million in annual sales
- Case assessments for high-liability, low-damage personal injury claims

The downside of this approach is that unless you already have considerable recognition in a particular field, a distinctive process signature, or a name recognition in a geographical area, gaining a foothold will take some time. While you are ramping-up your practice, you may choose to handle mediations outside your narrow focus in order to make a living while you continue marketing to your narrow target.

CONCLUSION

As you start out your career in mediation, explore what target market works best for you. Without a defined target market, you will have difficulty developing a business plan (the subject of Chapter Eleven) or an effective marketing strategy (discussed in Chapter Thirteen). By thinking through your target market, you will have a head start in building your practice.

Creating a Mediation-Friendly Environment

Look around your office. Is it built to serve clients and their needs, or have you designed it primarily for the comfort of you and your staff? It is important to create an environment that makes your clients feel welcome and supports your mediation signature. This chapter explores ways to make your office mediation friendly—whether you work in a court program or a government agency or are in private practice.

꠵ **Practice Tip** ꠵

Give yourself a quiz to determine whether your office is mediation friendly.[1]

	Yes	No
Does my waiting room have educational materials for clients?	___	___
Do I have a dedicated space for a client library?	___	___
Have I prepared written instructions and checklists to help clients?	___	___
Do I have a staff training program geared to educate and assist clients in mediation?	___	___
Will my clients feel welcomed and that their comfort and empowerment is the top priority of my practice?	___	___

If your answers to the quiz in the Practice Tip are mostly yes, you already have the foundation for a mediation-friendly office. Many mediators talk about increasing their business by offering client-driven services, yet they do not set up a mediation-centered office. You have probably walked into those offices, where copies of the *Wall Street Journal* or *Golf Magazine* are on the coffee table. It's true that some clients are golfers, and others want to read about their investments. But let's be honest: In most cases, these mediators order the publications that serve their own personal needs, claim the subscriptions as a deductible business expense, and then toss them out in the waiting room for the clients as an afterthought.

Don't get me wrong. Taking care of our own needs is not an indictable offense. However, reaching out to a new client base requires commitment, clear strategic planning, and proactive steps to make your practice—and even the office environment—a management and marketing tool. If you want a successful model for a consumer approach, consider the following areas and aspects of your office.

Reaching out to a new client base requires commitment, clear strategic planning, and proactive steps to make your practice—and even the office environment—a management and marketing tool.

CREATING A WELCOMING ENTRY AND RECEPTION AREA

Your entry and reception area is more than a first impression for clients. It can be a mini–learning center to prepare clients for the challenges of participating in the mediation process. It will also give your clients a sense of how you approach mediation.

Stand outside the front door of your office. How imposing are the size and structure of your door? Does your office sign tell the consumer that you offer mediation services? Is the sign easy to read?

Open the door. What do you see? If you see a receptionist, is he or she smiling and oriented to serving clients? Does client service appear to be a priority, or will clients likely feel that they are interrupting telephone answering, filing, or accounting work?

What do the walls look like? Do the decorations indicate a client orientation, such as a sign displaying your mission statement, art showing helping people, or even photographs or stories about the office staff to welcome the clients? A little sign can reinforce your approach. Here is an example:

> Welcome to our Mediation Office. We try to honor our appointment times but appreciate your patience for any delay. While waiting, we encourage you to learn more about your situation by reading the brochures in this room or visiting our client library, where we have a large selection of client-oriented books and videotapes. Please ask any staff member for assistance. It is our pleasure to help.

What kind of furniture is there for clients to sit on? Is it comfortable and easy to get up from or is it imposing or of such a stainable color that clients worry about a coffee spill? What do the clients have to read once they are seated and waiting? Are there informational handouts in sufficient quantities about your area of practice? Are your client brochures or articles by or about your involvement in mediation easily and pleasantly displayed and welcomingly accessible?

BUILDING YOUR CLIENT LIBRARY

If informed client consent is the bedrock of mediation, clients must have access to sufficient information. Think about doing your own taxes. You have to learn the rules, gather up your receipts and other documents, make some judgment calls in applying the Internal Revenue Service rules and regulations to your facts, and then learn how to prepare and file a tax return by hand or choose and learn to operate a computer program that will do the job.

If that's not easy for you, imagine what it's like for individuals trying to handle their own negotiations in a mediation session. Try walking in their shoes. How does it feel for them to be in your office? What tools, resources, and space are available to your clients to help them solve their own problems?

The client library can be the client's home and learning center within your mediation office. Many offices of lawyers, therapists, and courthouse self-help centers are now installing client libraries as well.

A client library is a collection of consumer-friendly books, videotapes, audiotapes, brochures, and other resources. The materials should be easy to read and to access. Ideally, the client library should have chairs and tables (or even just a writing ledge) so that clients can comfortably do their own work there rather than using your office or the public waiting room.

You might provide computers so clients can draft their own documents or modify their drafts from home if they bring in a disk. Clients can use computer forms to fill out their paperwork. In child support matters, clients can run the numbers using statewide guideline child support software in order to educate themselves and realistically prepare for the mediation session. Cutting-edge client libraries provide Internet access.

When clients aren't visiting, the client library can serve as a breakout room for caucuses or an extra consultation room or inspirational working area for your mediation intern. Even if you do not have an extra office or fancy computer gadgets, you can still set up a client library in your waiting room. All you need to get started are a few books, a couple of videotapes, a video player (no recorder needed), and a monitor. Earphones are a nice added feature if the video player is in the waiting room.

The very existence of the client library symbolizes that clients rank high in your priorities and that you highly value client empowerment. The library demonstrates to clients that you are willing to devote expensive office space and purchase significant resources to provide for their education. In addition to providing needed help to clients, the client library is a cost-effective marketing tool. Think like a client. If you were shopping for a mediator, would you choose one who has a client library or one who has no place to sit and no resources to use?

The very existence of the client library symbolizes that clients rank high in your priorities and that you highly value client empowerment.

The client library also serves as another waiting room and learning classroom. New clients get a sense of the firm and necessary information to get a grasp of their problem. By leafing through books on your shelf, returning clients deepen their understanding and perspectives and may uncover unmet needs and concerns that you can address.

It costs so much in hard dollars to acquire new clients that being able to serve needs beyond the presenting problem helps amortize the high marketing and management costs to operate your practice. Your current client base should be your highest profit center; tools such as the client library that help you maximize your current client base cannot be overvalued.

Show videos to clients. Sometimes parties may watch a video together and are able to work out a full settlement on their own before the session ever starts.

Another use of the client library is to serve as a child care center. It is ideally better for your clients with dependent children to make arrangements for them outside the office. But we don't live in an ideal world, and sometimes the kids come along in tow. Provide age-appropriate videotapes, books, toys, and games in your client libraries so that children can be happily amused while their parents do their business with you.

The client library can also be a preventive classroom. Before every mediation, each client can be given a conflict-wellness checkup. The checkup is a thermometer for legal health, and the client library is a perfect place for your clients to self-administer the written checkup questionnaire or read material on preventing

⚜ Practice Tip ⚜

There are two basic ways that your clients can use the client library: self-selected or at your direction. Once they are seated in the client library, many clients browse and self-select material that they want to use. The library's collection can be listed in a notebook or accessible by computer. At our office, most clients use the library without much staff help at all. That's the point. You should have clear written or videotaped client instructions so that you do not need to spend staff time to explain the library to clients.

I do not lend books to clients; they must be read on premises. In eleven years of operating a client library, we have never had a book or videotape stolen. But mediators who do lend books from their client libraries (Academy of Family Mediators president Nina Meirding is one of them) report about a 100 percent return rate as well.

future disputes in their lives. Maryland Legal Services Corporation is developing a legal checkup for the Web, and I already have one on my Web site (www.Mosten-Mediation.com). As these technological developments increase, your clients will be able to improve their legal health from your client library or from home (see Sample Checkup in Appendix Eight).

PROVIDING INFORMATION TO EDUCATE CLIENTS

Firm brochures, client newsletters, and client checklists, whether developed commercially, by mediation associations, or in-house, are becoming commonplace.

Mediation-friendly offices take client education to the next level. The cornerstone of this educational effort is a well-designed, well-presented, and timely mailed information packet. Technology is changing these practices as well. Our own staff has gone from exclusively sending packets, to complementing packets with a referral to our Web site, and now frequently solely referring callers to the Web site. Despite this growing trend of Web use, many of our clients don't use the Web or also want the hard copy information packet even if the Web is accessible to them. Make sure you can meet your clients' needs in various ways.

The purpose of the preoffice client information packet is to help a prospective client make an informed decision to take a step on the path of using and paying for your services. The step you are seeking is for people interested in mediation to

---

✿ Practice Tip ✿

A client information packet should be the first step following a client inquiry by telephone, Web site, e-mail, letter, or a drop-by visit to your client library.

The first step following the telephone call is not to set up an appointment; rather, it is to prepare prospective clients for receiving a client packet. If clients are in a hurry, they can pick up the packet personally or have it sent for overnight delivery. Because mediation is so new for many people, if clients can have a few days to read and digest the packet before an orientation, they will get much more from that first office visit.

Client Information Packet Contents

- Brochures describing the practice and mediation process
- Mission statement
- Short biography
- Articles about you
- Articles by you
- Mediation agreement between parties and mediator
- Directions to office and parking information
- Business card

The material should be attractively arranged in a quality bond double-pocket folder with your practice name printed on front. Color copies should be used, if available. All duplicates should be made directly from originals.

---

schedule an appointment or at least telephone your office for further or clarifying information.

Many mediators do not send out any client material in advance because they do not have any material prepared. Others believe that because the client called the office (often by way of a solid referral source), a mailed package might talk the client out of coming in. This approach is not without some validity; the client was going to come in anyway and might see something in the mailer that could make him or her decide to keep looking for a mediator. Most mediators, however, find that information reinforces rather than harms sales and increases satisfaction down the road. It is much better to provide too much information about how you work and charge. If this information dissuades some potential clients from trying mediation or trying it with you, that is a price you should be willing to pay.

You should think carefully about what you want your prospective clients to know about mediation before they come to your office. Then customize your packet accordingly. You might want to have client information copied, sorted, and put into usable form to be provided to clients when needed. This requires an investment in copying costs, staff training, and operation time.

DISPLAYING POINT-OF-SALE INFORMATION

Once a prospective client arrives at your office, the education and marketing should not stop; they just take a different format. Using retail language, consumer information available in your office is distributed at the "point of sale."

Your clients are the same people who visit banks, video stores, and travel agents. They are consumers who are accustomed to receiving and assimilating information before making purchasing decisions and in deciding whether to switch brands or service providers. They expect nothing less from your mediation practice.

What information do you want your clients to have in their marketing packets and what information do you want displayed in your office?

- Structure and operation of your mediation practice: locations, hours of operation, type of payment accepted, methods of quality control
- Areas of mediation practice: employment, real estate, family, governmental, community
- Types of services: disputes, conflict avoidance, coaching and consultation in mediation
- Descriptions of processes: how mediation starts, the format used, the use of lawyers
- Your firm's mission statement and mediation pledge (see the Epilogue), professional values, and organizational affiliations
- Biographical information of mediators and staff: qualifications, personal and professional interests, individual or group pictures, firm scrapbook, quotations, or awards

- Books or articles that you have written or that are of specific interest to your clients, plus book reviews or summaries
- Published articles written about you or your mediation group

Once you have decided what you want featured in a point-of-sale display, you then have to determine how you want it displayed. You have many choices: on tables, in attractive files, in brochure stands, in wall or standing frames, in scrapbooks, or just signs informing clients of the types of information available.

✿ Practice Tip ✿

Keep your information up to date, in order, and refilled. It will not do clients any good if you intended to have point-of-sale information, but it ran out last week. Staff planning is needed to keep a supply on hand, with the originals tucked away and never used (have you ever tried to read tenth-generation copies?). Have an ongoing monitoring system to replace dated material with fresh copies.

How does this approach differ from your current practice regarding point-of-sale literature? If you currently have *National Geographic* magazines on the waiting room table and limit your client handouts to an intake sheet on a clipboard, you are forgoing opportunities to educate and to market.

DESIGNING, FURNISHING, AND EQUIPPING YOUR OFFICE

Your office should be physically set up to facilitate your work. In addition, providing materials that appeal to different kinds of learners will encourage productive mediation sessions.

The Table

Instead of sitting in your comfy executive chair with the parties sitting on the other side of the desk (often with the sun in their eyes since it flows over your shoulders to make *your* reading easier), a round table will break down barriers. Because it has no sides, the round table creates a collaborative working atmosphere for you and the parties; it also doubles as a mediation table à la King Arthur. If you don't have room in your office for both a desk and a round table, you might consider using a desk that has one rounded end that accommodates up to six people.

Aids for Adult Learning

We all learn in different ways. Some learn by hearing, some by seeing, some by touching, and others by experiencing. Because as a mediator you are also a teacher, you might want to provide materials that will enhance learning and client success in putting your tutorial into practice. During the first meting with the parties, try to assess their distinct learning styles.

Aural Learners. Aural learners need to listen again and again to the session in order to get a full grasp of the discussion and properly participate and complete homework. Have an audiotape recorder available so that these clients can take a cassette tape home to replay. They will often listen to the tapes in the car or at home and sometimes invite a friend to listen to the tape to get another viewpoint. Sometimes mediation parties will have the tapes transcribed so that they can review the information quickly and thoroughly. Be sure to mediate the parameters of the use of such audio tapes so that both parties feel comfortable that their privacy is protected.

Visual Learners. Summarizing your points visually and in different colors reinforces learning for most people, and especially for visual learners. You can prepare outlines or major points for consultation on a flip chart before the client arrives. You can also give homework assignments for parties and counsel to bring in photographs, videotapes, computer graphics, or other visual tools to educate.

Another choice is to use an erasable white board or draw on a piece of paper that can be duplicated to give to clients to take home and perhaps share with their out-of-session advisers. White boards are easy to see, but because they are erasable, the information needs to be copied before it is erased, which can be a big hassle.

Tactile Learners. Some clients learn best by literally getting their hands on the job. They need to experience writing, drawing, and touching the forms, so have these learning aids available. You may want to devise in-session assignments for these tactile learners so they might actually write out proposals and tape them on the wall for review. I have even devised a bundle of mediation services made out of Popsicle sticks and yarn that clients can hold and take apart to teach the concept of unbundling the mediation process into distinct parts.

Experiential Learners. These clients have to do it to get it. You can play different roles in order to practice and gain empathy for another's perspective just by being in someone else's shoes. In caucus, you can play the other side: your clients can play themselves and verbalize the conversation and deal with the hurdles you put up. Then your clients can play the other side to get an appreciation for their needs and concerns while you model their role. Very few clients do worse after this practice, and many find that it truly helps them overcome fears and stimulate their thinking to improve the important mediation session that could resolve a major crisis in their lives.

✦ Practice Tip ✦

When you work with experiential learners, videotape the role play so the parties can see how they appear to others.

HOSPITALITY SERVICES

You might increase your client bonding and prevent peckish behavior as a result of hunger by having a supply of grub in your office. I recommend installing a ten-foot-long shelf in your mediation room on which you set out red licorice, pretzels, hard candy, and other treats. If you have a small dispenser for bottled water, no one will have to take valuable time to get a drink outside the office. Clients greatly appreciate these intangibles; they recognize that you have planned and shopped for their comfort as well as yours.

TRAINING YOUR STAFF

As your practice grows and if you hire employees, how do you train them to complement your mediation-friendly approach? Where do client-centered priorities fit in with all the tasks and long-term priorities facing your staff? For example, where in your priority chain should your secretary place sending out client information packets? If clients are working on budgets or an opening statement and need help, how should your staff use their time when they are also under pressure to meet other deadlines?

These priority conflicts occur daily. If mediation is new for clients, it may be even newer for your staff whose needs are important both due to their function in the office and their place in your life.

Here are some ways to train staff in a mediation-friendly office:

- Commit to making client service your top priority. Put that commitment into a written pledge, or incorporate it into your mission statement.

- At each staff meeting and in other communications with your staff, clearly communicate that you have made the client the first priority, and you expect staff to have the same priority. Invite questions and hypothetical situations (some raised in this section) to help your staff make the transition to client-first service.

- Reflect your commitment to your personnel policy and compensation structure. Your staff should be rewarded monetarily for putting clients first and never criticized for letting other priorities slip for attending to clients' needs (unless you specifically make a different choice ahead of time and communicate it to the staff member).

- Be very specific about priorities. For example, what is more important: answering a new client call or completing the monthly accounting? You are responsible for giving advanced guidance and clarity to your staff when the choices come up.

- Don't do everything at once. Introduce changes slowly and one at a time, and be considerate of the varied learning styles and approaches of your staff.

- Set up a compliance and monitoring structure so that questions can be answered, help given, and progress implemented.

An example of the staff training process outlined in the Practice Tip is deciding which articles should go into a mediation packet. You must decide that sending a mediation packet is important and that staff time and financial resources will be invested in this project. Then the decision should be shared and staff ideas considered as to how best to implement this decision. It should be worked out what will go into the packet and who will be responsible for stocking, assembling, and sending out the packet. If they haven't done so already, staff should be oriented as to the key points of the material in the packet so they will have firsthand knowledge of the material and can share that knowledge with clients. Staff should be encouraged to take home and read copies of articles and other material. If there is to be a cover letter, will it be a form letter or customized? Who will prepare and sign the letter? Time parameters for getting the packet out after a telephone request from a client must be established. It should also be decided what circumstances, if any, would supersede mailing out a client packet as a priority. A staff person should be assigned to monitor compliance with this procedure and a date set to assess the implementation. This type of staff training is necessary for each innovation infused into your office as it evolves into a mediation-friendly environment.

❧ Practice Tip ❧

Educate your staff. Familiarity with the products of mediation increases staff commitment, loyalty, and acceptance of these changing job tasks.

CONCLUSION

If every aspect of the physical space, the procedures, and the people in the office is geared to marketing and providing client-oriented service products, clients will be able to participate in the decisions and work product necessary for them to solve their problems and maximize their opportunities. Your environment may be as important as your skills to contributing to the agreement readiness of your clients.

Your office environment can serve an important supplemental role to your own mediation strategies and skills. You probably could function in a traditional law office or even a courthouse hallway, but a mediation-friendly office serves your clients needs that much better.

⁊ℰ Practice Tip ℰ⁊

Make your office client-friendly in these ways:

- Make client service your top priority.
- Turn your waiting room into a mini–client learning center.
- Make your decor comfortable and inviting to clients.
- Use round tables and comfy chairs.
- Devote money, space, and staff time for a client library.
- Perform conflict wellness checkups during the first office visit.
- Send out client information packets with every client call.
- Set up and promote an information-packed Web site.
- Offer and display useful information to educate your clients.
- Use visual aids and other educational resources.
- Adjust your style to different methods of client learning.
- Supply snacks and beverages for clients.
- Train your staff to make client service their top priority, and reward them accordingly.
- Allow client waiting time to be client learning time.
- Prepare easy-to-read client instructions and forms.
- Display articles written by or about your legal staff.
- Develop a client library that symbolizes client empowerment and is an excellent marketing tool.
- Recommend a useful book or videotape to your client following every consultation.
- Display point-of-sale information, and make sure you have sufficient copies of the material.
- Use flip charts and other visual aids to educate clients.
- Videotape your clients during their simulated negotiation role-play scenarios.

The Nuts and Bolts
of Private Practice

Setting Up Your Office

You may have devoted quite a bit of thought and training to develop skills to resolve disputes. How much attention have you given to the physical setup of your mediation office? This chapter focuses on the environment of mediation practice and how it contributes to agreement making.

FINDING A PLACE TO PRACTICE

If you want to be your own boss and go it alone, your first decision will be whether you want to practice out of your home or rent an office. Let's explore the various options in detail.

Home Office

Many successful mediators work out of their homes by necessity, others by choice. This option certainly cuts overhead, permitting you to take the initial risk more easily and giving you more freedom to make choices of case selection and other use of your professional time with less financial pressure. Not only does working out of your home eliminate commuting time and the distractions of an office, but many mediators think that clients prefer the more comfortable and less businesslike home atmosphere. Also, if your reduced overhead lets you lower your fees, most clients appreciate the savings, which also gives you a competitive advantage.

If you choose the home option, the best layout is to have a separate entrance or even a separate structure in which you can set up a mediation-friendly environment.

If such separation is not possible, attempt to have at least a separate room dedicated to your mediation work so that clients are not invading (or being subjected to) your living room or kitchen (with or without dirty dishes). Crying babies or barking dogs generally will not contribute positively to your mediation efforts. However, there will be some parties who will warm to the homey touch. Jamie Johnson Palmer of Batavia, Illinois, near Chicago, uses her gardens, gazebo, and gourmet touch to her marketing advantage. She walks mediation parties through her landscaped grounds before a session and has home-made muffins and cappuccino ready when they sit down.

Another option is the hybrid home office plan: you work out of your home for client telephone contact and paperwork, but arrange for suitable conference room space in which to see clients and conduct mediation sessions. Such arrangements can vary from full-time rental of a conference room to renting it by the hour or session. You can also choose from upscale professional office suites or work out of a local library or community center.

⚜ Practice Tip ⚜

Make yourself mobile. Many mediators market their availability to travel flip chart in hand to the parties' office or home or to the office of their attorney or other consulting professional.

Renting an Office

If you believe that you need a professional office environment in which to practice, the rental expense may be a low price to pay to enter the field, particularly if you receive referrals from other office suite colleagues that can defray part or all of the rent. Or you may lack the discipline to stay away from the refrigerator or the television and need to have a structured environment in the company of others to run your practice efficiently. When renting office space, a number of lease options are usually available.

Month-to-Month Lease. The virtue of this approach is that you do not need to obligate yourself to a long period of time when you are uncertain about your future. You can market your practice at full throttle with the stopgap that if it doesn't work out, you can terminate a lease obligation in thirty or sixty days and save yourself a debt of potentially tens of thousands of dollars. The other side is that you lack long-term security and can be booted without cause. You also may be in a less-than-mediation-friendly environment, and you would be foolish to put in costly improvements when your lease could end at any time.

❧ Practice Tip ❧

Find a lease to give you some security. To give yourself at least a minimum of security, try to negotiate a short set lease (six months to a year) so that you can at least build up your practice before you have to move. Also, see if you can negotiate a right of first refusal to extend your month-to-month lease before the master tenant or landlord leases your office to another tenant. But realize that this will not help you if the master tenant takes over the space herself to expand.

Long Lease. If you make the decision to rent an office, you still have further decisions to make. You can sign a long-term lease that may guarantee you the space for a sufficiently lengthy time to amortize the cost of setting up a mediation-friendly office. This decision will also underscore your commitment to your practice.

Rent for Services

When you have extra time on your hands and cash flow is low, this may be a good option. In return for reduced rent or no rent, you might barter with the landlord or master tenant to provide services. At best, you could provide mediation services for an agreed-on number of hours at a retail rate for the landlord's clients. Of

> ### ❦ Practice Tip ❦
>
> Have a way out. Try to negotiate an escape clause in a long-term lease in case your dreams don't come true (at least on your initial timetable). As an illustration, if you sign up for a three-year lease, negotiate your right to terminate the lease after eighteen months provided you give six months' written notice and perhaps pay the last six months' rent in an accelerated fashion.

course, to make this arrangement work, the landlord must be offering neutral and impartial mediation services, and you could not mediate any case in which the landlord has a financial interest. In this way, your filling in would not compromise your neutrality due to your separate financial relationship with the landlord.

The odds are that unless you rent from another mediator, your bartered services would not be doing mediation. If you rent from a lawyer, accountant, or therapist, you could help prepare their clients for mediation (with another mediator), but your work could just as easily be answering telephones, collecting bills, performing Internet research, running for sandwiches, or doing anything else that needs doing. If you ever even slightly feel resentful about being exploited, you must remember that the other time in your office is all yours!

Shared Office Space

One way to cut down office costs is to share the space, and thus the rent, with another mediator or even with a service provider in another profession. You can work out a flexible but structured arrangement. For example, you take mornings and your office partner takes afternoons. Or you could assign particular days to each partner, and make adjustments when necessary.

You are each sole practitioners, responsible for all other expenses on your own and solely entitled to your own income. You may want to share office space with someone with whom you have a co-mediation relationship. In this way, it may be easier to decide on office design and decoration, as well as carve out time for each of you to mediate alone and at other times together.

Executive Suite

You might find space in a suite of offices with access to conference rooms, a receptionist and waiting room, copiers, fax machines, coffee and refrigerator privileges, and other customized amenities.

Your personal office can vary in size depending on your budget. You can start small and increase your space as your practice grows without having to move office locations. Although the waiting room is commonly shared and there may be restrictions on the materials that you can display, you may be able to negotiate setting up a tasteful mediation display with brochures. In any event, your office will be your own, and you can set it up any way you want.

One added benefit to starting in an executive suite is that because all other renters are on their own, you may have a starter referral base right in your suite. Don't be put off if there is another mediator in the suite. See it as an opportunity for sharing resources (maybe even starting a client library together) and doing some co-marketing so that your suite can be known as a home for mediators.

NAMING YOUR PRACTICE

Every mediator faces this dilemma. Should you use your own name (John Haynes, Mediator) or another name, such as Peoria Mediation Center? If you use your own name, you can have the comfort of knowing that every dollar spent on marketing your name will likely go to you. You are building name identification with your own mediation signature. The downside is that if you ever want to take on associate mediators to leverage your time, it may be difficult because most clients will want you and consider any other mediator to be second best. Or, if you retire or die, your successors will have less to sell because the firm's identity is tied to your personal practice.

Being realistic, even if you use another name, your reputation will be very personal. And because you are selecting, training, and standing behind your associate mediator, clients may be most willing to use your associate, especially if the price is more affordable.

You might want to use another name purely for marketing strategies with a different slant. Your name may be geographically descriptive (Southwest Louisiana Mediation Services) or generically descriptive (Family Mediation Center), or it could describe your mediation signature (Transformative Mediation) or evoke an emotional image (PeacePipe Mediation, Settlement Mediation, or We Agree Mediation).

FORMING STRATEGIC PARTNERSHIPS

Although you are in mediation practice for yourself, you still may want to take advantage of opportunities to allocate fees and share services to maximize the return for both strategic partners. Such opportunities include serving on a panel, participating in a network, or working out an exclusive arrangement with a mediation provider organization.

Mediation Panels

Instead of doing all your own marketing, an organization that operates a mediation panel markets for you. In return, you either pay a fee to the panel and keep any income from your panel work, or you split the money received in an agreed upon percentage.

Some panels encourage clients to contact you directly; others receive the call, help the clients select a mediator, arrange and receive payment, and serve as a conduit for any concerns or complaints. Some panels provide facilities, but most expect you to mediate in your office or travel to the office of one of the parties.

Some panels are closed: you must be accepted based on your training, experience, or some other requirement. For example, many court and bar association panels require mediators to be licensed attorneys. Other closed panels such as that of the Academy of Family Mediators (now merged into ACR) require not only membership in the organization but a high-level qualification process to become a Practitioner Member (250 hours experience, 60 hours training, and 10 hours consultation in individual or group setting are among the qualifications listed on the academy's list and Web site, www.mediator.org). The Center for Public Responsibility in New York requires peer review and substantial complex business litigation experience. Other panels require special training from the panel sponsors, with expenses either paid by the mediator or the panel sponsor. The Dalkon Shield mediation panel sponsored by Duke University required a full day's training to be included on the panel. The mediation programs of the National Association of Security Dealers and the U.S. Postal Service require much more. Some community mediation programs require 25 to 40 hours of their training to participate. Other panels are open to any mediator who wishes to sign up. For example, the panel of www.mediate.com is open to any mediator free of charge regardless of training or experience. Open panels tend to be larger, and you will probably get fewer referrals. Those referrals that you do get tend to lead to fewer actual open paying cases than referrals received from quality closed panels. Neither closed nor open panels generally require exclusivity. It is understood that you may belong to several panels and that you are free to develop clientele in any way you choose. Your only responsibility to the panel sponsors is to provide competent mediation services according to the fee schedule and other guidelines that you agree to and advertised to the public.

Networks

A mediator network is a nonexclusive arrangement that offers you more support services and expectation of business in return for increased payment to the organization for the work performed. You will also be required to conform to overall features, fee schedule, and approach designed to provide the public with a quality, uniform product.

Using Mosten Mediation Centers (www.MostenMediation.com) as an illustrative model, all network mediators must have professional training with substantial experience and must agree to set their fees within the network's fee guidelines. Rather than refer to individual mediators for service in their own offices, local mediators throughout the country provide offices in each geographical location for local network mediators to use. Each network office must have a client library, display network brochures and other client reference materials, and adhere to other network requirements, such as a guarantee to set up mediations within five days from the agreement of the parties to use the network. Also, network mediators may participate in the national telephone and on-line mediation services and are eligible to serve on panels for MMC's strategic partners, including mediation service contracts with federal governmental agencies, among them the armed forces.

As with other mediation panels, most networks are generally nonexclusive. However, unlike panels, all calls and payments go into the network offices rather than directly to the mediator. Also, the network stands behind the quality of its mediators and maintains malpractice insurance to back up the competence of its mediators. Like a franchise, a network is designed to give consumers an assurance of uniformity of service; unlike a franchise, local mediators work as subcontractors with the parent company rather than own the rights to particular geographical areas.

Exclusive Mediator Provider Organizations

National and local mediator provider organizations (MPOs) such as the Judicial Arbitration and Mediation Service (JAMS) and the American Arbitration Association (AAA) have operational offices in various cities across the country staffed by their employees. Many of their mediators agree to mediate solely for the MPO; in return, the MPO provides them with marketing and administrative support, including an office and staff. Like networks, client calls and payment go to the MPO, and the cases are then assigned to a selected mediator. MPOs differ from networks in that they have traditionally marketed to lawyers, corporations, and other high-end users, while networks more readily use the Internet and mass advertising to target the general public. Most MPO mediations currently involve lawyer representation in setting up the mediation as well as in the sessions themselves. It is not surprising that most of the JAMS panel comprises retired judges, and many of AAA's mediators on its expert panels are judges and established business litigators who emphasize a caucus style mediation process favored by lawyers.

CONCLUSION

The office environment and organization of your practice are among the areas that you will need to consider as you establish a business plan, which will be fully described in the next chapter.

Strategic Planning and Investing in Yourself

This chapter will probably be the most boring for you to read—
and may be the most important for your practice development.
Mediators like working with people and making their lives better; running numbers and writing up business plans are generally not first-choice activities. Yet just as we were taught to eat our vegetables before getting dessert, the purpose of this chapter is to give you the conceptual foundation and understanding to build your mediation practice and enjoy a lifetime of peacemaking.

PLANNING TOOL KIT

The elements of your planning process will rely on the work you put into your Mediator Self-Survey (see Appendix One) and your mediation signature (see Chapter Six). Your understanding of your own professional values, style, inventory of services, and target market are the foundation for your planning process. This chapter describes the tools you need to develop your business plan.

Mission Statement

After honing your mediation signature from your work on the Mediator Self-Survey, you should develop a mission statement for your practice of approximately fifty to one hundred words. The mission statement is the core of your practice and the foundation for your strategic planning.

As you use the financial planning tools in your tool kit, constantly conduct a mission statement impact test:

- Are my assumptions consistent with my mission statement?
- Are the goals for practice development consistent with my mission statement?
- Are the sources of income and services offered consistent with my mission statement?
- Are the ways that I am investing capital and spending money consistent with my mission statement?
- Is the way that I am spending my workdays and leisure time consistent with my mission statement?

If your answers are yes to all of these questions, you are on track. If there is dissonance between your mission statement and your practice building plan, you have three nonexclusive options:

- Modify your mission statement to be consistent with what you are planning and doing.

- Modify your plan to comport with the core values and underlying purpose of your practice.

- Modify both your mission statement and your plan as symbiotic living reflections of your evolving plans and actions based on new information and your experience.

⚜ Practice Tip ⚜

Just like decorating your reception area, from time to time your mission statement needs reexamination and reworking. Attend the annual conference of the Association for Conflict Resolution or other groups of mediators to stimulate this reflection. Take additional training or seminars on mediation or on the process of strategic planning. Use your regular meeting with your personal board of directors to keep you on track. Encourage your board to test your planning and projects against the content of your mission statement. Even better, schedule a day on a regular basis (at least once every year) to look at your mission statement and see if you are headed where you want to go.

Budget of Capital Investment

Every business needs start-up capital. Most require infusions of fresh capital when the initial money dries up or expansion requires funds in addition to ongoing revenues. Your mediation practice is no different. It is common knowledge that most small businesses die because of undercapitalization. You must plan for necessary money to be put into your mediation practice at the outset and down the road. In 1994, after practicing mediation for fifteen years, I conservatively calculated my yearly out-of-pocket expenses at approximately $15,000 *excluding* any rent, remodeling, staff, office expenses, or money needed for my personal living expenses.

*Most small businesses die because of
undercapitalization. You must plan for
necessary money to be put into your mediation
practice at the outset and down the road.*

Investing in and nurturing a mediation practice requires annual expenditures in a number of categories. The following estimates are based on actual costs expended in my own practice.

• Books, videotapes, and consumer software: $1,000. Every profession has its literature. Mediation is developing rapidly, and as a cutting-edge professional, you must keep up your current reading and have resources for yourself and your clients. Videotapes are an essential building block of your client library and often cost well over $100 per videotape. You may need software for clients to prepare their own budgets, letters, and presentations and to run child support calculations. See Appendix Four for an overview of books and resources.

• Attendance at conferences (four per year): $4,000. Practicing mediation can be lonely, and you might get stuck in a rut. Attending conferences is vital to learning new skills and concepts and meeting and observing the top mediators in the fields in workshops and informal discussions. See Appendix Five for mediation organizations.

• Advertising, Yellow Pages only: $2,400. This minimal expenditure is only the ante to the game that appeals to the target market most ready to purchase your services. (See Chapter Thirteen for other advertising ideas.)

• Meals and entertainment: $4,000. Taking referral sources and colleagues to lunch and hosting an occasional open house reception can add up fast. Remember that this annual amount is only $333 per month or about $85 per week over the course of a year.

• Postage and duplication of brochures, packets, and materials: $1,200. This expense is in addition to any postage or duplication necessary for client work. This line item is for a marketing investment to potential clients and referral resources.

• Organization dues, $1,500. This is a cost of business. You need to attend and participate in mediation organizations on both local and national levels. Remember that other mediators are prime referral sources (see Chapter Thirteen). Your being active in organizations in your profession of origin (law, therapy, chamber of commerce) in order to get an inside track on referrals might also benefit your practice. See Appendix Five for leading mediation organizations.

• Study groups: $650. These informal gatherings are invaluable for your skill development and networking (see Chapter Four), but you still need to budget for monthly dinners, materials, occasional retreats, and other expenses. If you belong to a mediator study group and a study group in your profession of origin, $70 per month item may be low.

• *Total out-of-pocket costs:* $14,750 per year, or $1,230 per month. This amount is *in addition* to general overhead expenses (rent, salaries, supplies, insurance, and so on). See Appendix Seven for sample office budget forms.

In developing your capital budget, look to your costs of investment (not operation) for the next three years. Then plan out the source of that expenditure outside of current operations. If everything goes better than planned, your fee revenue will cut down your investment. Add up your capital outlay. Assume it will come from fresh money; then amortize the total over the next ten years of practice as the price for establishing your peacemaking career.

For example, if your capital investment line items total $25,000 per year for the next three years, amortize the total of $75,000 over the next ten years so that you hope to repay as capital return a minimum of $7,500 per year for ten years out of profits of your practice. Your income tax returns will book the expenditures as current business expenses and the future profits as current income; the label of capital repayment is only a game you will play with yourself to help you with the planning and investment process. Yet it's a game that is real: You will be investing actual dollars into your business with the hope of significant payoff down the road.[1] Table 11.1 shows out-of-pocket costs in developing a practice.

Budget of Time Investment

Capital investment is by no means insignificant, but your real investment is sweat equity: the time that you devote to your practice. The amount of time invested can be staggering. In 1994, at the same time that I calculated my out-of-pocket expenses, I also added up the number of hours that I spent building my mediation practice during 1994—fifteen years after starting. I did not count the hours that I

Table 11.1 Out-of-Pocket Costs in Developing a Practice

	Year 1	Year 2	Year 3	Year 4	Year 5
	Out-of-Pocket Costs				
Training and education	$7,000	$5,000	$5,000	$5,000	$5,000
Library	1,000	1,000	1,000	1,000	1,000
Brochures and other materials	3,000	500	500	500	500
Marketing	3,000	2,500	2,500	2,500	2,500
Professional services	3,000	1,000	1,000	1,000	1,000
Total out-of-pocket costs	17,000	10,000	10,000	10,000	10,000

spent billing for my mediation services, nor did I count the time that I spent doing legal work or building my law practice. I counted the hours solely devoted to building my mediation practice.

Take a moment to guess how many hours I spent during the year. If you spend 5 hours a week building your current business or career, that would be 250 hours per year—or over six 40-hour work weeks per year. Here's my answer. In 1994, I spent over 1,000 hours building my mediation practice: over 25 work weeks in addition to the time I spent working on client work and otherwise operating my law practice. This time investment was not a one-time thing for 1994. In the early years, I invested even more time. In the past twenty-two years, I have invested 1,000 or more hours in building my practice every year—year in and year out—and I plan to continue.

✿ Practice Tip ✿

Don't think that I am the Lone Ranger. Ask successful mediators how much time they spend in building their practices. Don't stop there. Ask successful lawyers or other businesspersons with thriving practices how much nonbillable time they spend on building their practice. If you want to make peacemaking your day job, such a time investment is necessary.

Where does this time come from? If you took off two years to earn an M.B.A. or three years to earn a J.D., that time would come from earning money in the marketplace. Or the time investment would replace personal pursuits such as a world tour, working in the Peace Corps, or staying at home with your children.

How did I spend that 1,000 hours?

Annual Hours	Activity
64	Four conferences on mediation, counting each at 16 hours of time investment per conference for travel, attending workshops, and networking
75	Attending local bar association and other nonmediation professional committee meetings and programs
90	Serving on boards of mediation organizations
90	Preparing and teaching mediation courses and making guest teaching appearances
210	Writing four articles
34	Preparing and delivering speeches to mediation and bar associations
56	Volunteering as a mediator at courts, community organizations, and Child Find Telephone mediation service
150	Meals with referral sources and mediation colleagues
100	Reading mediation books and articles
55	Mediation study group
75	Moderating Internet chat group

1,014 Total hours

Spending time developing your practice does not need to equate with a prison sentence in Siberia. I enjoy every aspect of developing my practice, from attending conferences to reading the literature. I cannot think of a more stimulating way to spend my life than becoming a better peacemaker and interacting with the sincere and interesting people who are part of the mediation community. If put under truth serum, I would probably confess that I would do everything on the above list even if I did not have a goal of building a profitable practice.

As you can see from the practice development time horizon chart, it is important for you to consider how your time planning will affect your practice building. The more quickly you wish to make mediation your day job, the more money and time you need to invest on the front end. However, the cold reality is that these activities take time—time in addition to your workday. You will constantly be faced with choices: Do I watch the afternoon football game or prepare materials for a workshop presentation? Do I eat lunch with my friends from the office or church, or do I have lunch (and pay) with a potential referral resource? Do I bring mediation books on the beach trip and read them before my sci-fi thriller? Wanting to be a full-time peacemaker means you are never free from these choices.

Practice Development Time Horizon Chart

- Start now or in the future?
- Full time or part time?
- How long can you keep investing time and money?
- Projected break-even date?
- Amount of cash reserves for unexpected expenses or delayed income?
- Ultimate income objectives?
- Projected retirement date?

The time devoted to building your mediation practice that replaces time for earning income or enjoying leisure is called *lost opportunity cost.* Every hour you invest in your mediation practice could have been used to put current money in your pocket or to enjoy yourself. Your available time is finite. You only have so many hours in the day, so many days in the week. If you spend them building your practice, you are either losing money or draining energy and focus from other pursuits. It is a trade-off. Is becoming a professional mediator important enough to you to make that trade?

This trade-off can be quantified in the amount of lost opportunity cost plus the investment of soft time beyond your 40-hour week. Soft time would otherwise be spent in personal pursuits, such as family, hobbies, sports, and relaxation. If you are currently earning $75,000, your lost salary income for the first year if you do not earn $1 dollar of income is $75,000. If you spend 500 hours in nights and weekends in addition and you value your soft time at $30 per hour, the annual soft time cost for the year would be $15,000. As you can see from Table 11.2, your total opportunity cost for the year would be $90,000. However, maybe you could expect $10,000 in mediation fee revenues for the first year if you project 100 hours of paid mediations at $100 per hour. This anticipates 8.33 paid hours per month or about 2.0 paid hours per week. If you met these projections, it would leave you with a net opportunity cost investment of $80,000 for your first year in practice. Remember, if you are investing $15,000 in out-of-pocket costs, your first-year investment would be $95,000 plus any monies you need for rent, staff, supplies, and other costs to operate your practice.

Table 11.2 Opportunity Cost Chart

	Year 1	Year 2	Year 3	Year 4	Year 5
Lost salary income	$75,000	$75,000	$75,000	$75,000	$75,000
Soft time: 500 hours @ $30/hour	15,000	15,000	15,000	15,000	15,000
Total opportunity cost	90,000	90,000	90,000	90,000	90,000
Income projection	10,000	25,000	40,000	60,000	100,000
Net income (loss)	(80,000)	(65,000)	(50,000)	30,000	10,000
Cumulative income (loss)	80,000	145,000	195,000	225,000	215,000

Because it takes at least three years to break even, you must project on a longer time line in planning your practice investment. As you can see from Table 11.2, you must be prepared to invest your lost income and soft time over several years. This long-term investment results in a cumulative investment that continues to grow until your marketing efforts start to pay off and revenue begins to build. Table 11.2

shows that with a 250 percent increase in fee income projected for the second year, your net opportunity investment decreases a bit—to $65,000 per year—but your overall cumulative investment would grow to $145,000 after the second year plus marketing costs and office expenses. You also need to be prepared to face the fact that even if your fees increased 250 percent, that revenue is still only one-third of what you were making before you quit your premediation day job.

As your income continues to grow, you should approach break-even on a yearly basis and start whittling down your cumulative investment. In these projections, you would hit break-even in year five, and your revenues would start replacing your current job income (remember, you still have marketing expenses and office costs). You should be over the hurdle and continue building your practice since you are still operating well under capacity. Using an hourly rate of $100, under these projections of $100,000 per year, you would be paid for 1000 hours of mediation for the year—about 83 paid hours per month and about 21 hours per week. You certainly have more time and energy to build—and you will.

The projections here are very modest. It is better to be ready for a long siege of capital and time investment and be surprised when your performance outstrips your projections. If you actually get paid for 16 hours of mediation weekly (two full working days), you can double your first-year income, reduce your net opportunity costs, and accelerate your journey to profitability. In the same way, if you work at your practice at half-time or less, you are taking a much safer road that requires less overall investment. The obvious corollary is that the half-time approach will extend the time in which you can be a full-time mediator. If you know that you have a low threshold for risk or have existing financial or family commitments—or if just thinking about the full-time plunge makes your palms sweat—a lower-risk path may fit better with the rest of your life.

If you know that you have a low threshold for risk or have existing financial or family commitments—or if just thinking about the full-time plunge makes your palms sweat—a lower-risk path may fit better with the rest of your life.

Full-time practice may not fit your needs. As you can see from the chart, there is a trade-off: less risk and cost on the front end with a longer time horizon and lower income potential down the road.

Opportunity Costs of Part-Time Mediation Practice

- Lower opportunity costs (less time invested)
- Lower income with increased time horizon
- Higher soft cost of time (you are overworked)

There are few shortcuts or easy tips to analyzing the time investment necessary to launch and build your mediation practice. Two keys are to budget your time commitment and to keep track of your time and analyze the results.

Developing a time budget is easier if you have a computerized calendar system that you can easily access. Looking at your life in week, month, and year blocks, you can set aside time to develop your practice as a high-priority appointment in your life. Every member of our staff at Mosten Mediation Centers is required to budget an agreed portion of their work week to market the practice. Each person has the responsibility to devote that time to practice building and to track the results of those efforts in fee revenue.

This brings up the second prong of the budgeting process: tracking your time. Use a billing program to record, and at the end of each day, add up your time spent on various activities. These software systems provide reports that will permit you to see your total time you spent on each practice activity: telephone intakes, initial orientations, mediation sessions, drafting, entertainment, reading literature, preparing press releases, and so forth.

Budget of Operating Expenses

This facet of your financial planning is straightforward. You need to make some predictions about your hourly rate and the number of hours that you will be paid for.

Hourly Rate. If you are a lawyer, therapist, accountant, or other professional, you might assume that your current hourly rate should be your hourly rate as a mediator. It is true that to lower your hourly rate as a mediator will mean either less income or more hours you will need to work to make the same income. However, it is also true that you have invested considerable time and money in your current profession that should justify your current billing rate. The same is not yet warranted for your career as a mediator.

Many mediators make a huge mistake by being unwilling to reduce their hourly rates. They will not work for less, and they don't, which generally results in plenty of free time. You should set your hourly rate as low as possible, fill up your time, and then slowly raise your rates as your expertise and the demand for your mediation services build.

Hours for Which You Are Paid. When you compute your time investment, put down every hour spent; in making income projections, you should predict the number of hours for which you will receive the hourly fee you set. Unless you are unique in your ability to collect fees, some people will not pay you or will not pay you in full, regardless of your careful practice management (see Chapter Twelve).

In making your assumptions of hours, estimate the number of hours per week, month, and year for which you expect to have client contact. Then discount the number of hours that you work but do not bill and the percentage of the fees that you do bill but do not collect.

You might estimate that you will have 4.0 hours of client contact per week. If you assume 4.3 weeks per month, you are estimating 17.0 hours of client contact per month (actually 17.2, but let's round down). If your hourly rate is $100 per hour, you can expect $1,700 per month gross income revenue before discounting. (See Figure 11.1 for these calculations.)

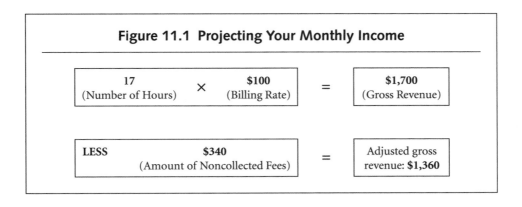

Figure 11.1 Projecting Your Monthly Income

| 17
(Number of Hours) | × | $100
(Billing Rate) | = | $1,700
(Gross Revenue) |

| LESS | $340
(Amount of Noncollected Fees) | = | Adjusted gross
revenue: $1,360 |

If 80 percent of your fees are paid in full, this means that you do not collect 20 percent. This translates into noncollectibility of $20 per hour, or $340 per month (17 hours at $20 per hour). Therefore, in making your income projections, you must subtract $340 from your total of $1,700, leaving you with $1,360 per month. Or, to make up for the $340 that you lost, you will need to work an addition 3.4 hours (the new total is 20.4 hours per month) and be paid in full for this time in order to keep up with your initial projections.

Professional Advice

In conducting your financial planning, you should consult the following professionals often and follow their advice:

Certified public accountant. In addition to preparing your tax returns and advising you about other required licenses and local taxes, CPAs are adroit at helping you plan budgets, project income, set up your bookkeeping system, and, most important, help you plan based on the reports generated by you and your bookkeeper.

Bookkeeper. Even if you input your data into a computerized accounting program, you should have a bookkeeper reconcile your bank statements and help you prepare monthly and yearly cash reports (income and expenses), as well as summarize your assets and debts in a balance sheet.

Business lawyer. The best money you will ever spend is to plan your practice's legal and financial affairs preventively. Even if you are a lawyer yourself, don't have a fool for a client. Consult a lawyer before you sign a lease or make a major equipment purchase or otherwise make large commitments. The money lost on a bad decision that could have been prevented will greatly affect your planning because you will have to come up with extra money to pay for your mistakes.

Involvement of Personal Board of Directors

If you go to the expense and time to prepare reports and budgets as part of your financial tool kit, make sure you share them with your board on a regular basis. A member of your board may see a pattern in your financial situation or even pick up an error that you may have missed. It's like looking at a financial X-ray: your board can look at the financial reports and try to detect some asymptomatic cause of financial trouble that can be cured if treated in time.

BUSINESS PLAN

Just as it was important for you to write out every answer of the Mediator Self-Survey, you must also write out your business plan. The writing process stimulates and concretizes your thinking process so that you can translate loose, flabby musings into clear goals and action. Don't try to do it in one sitting or be wedded to a particular order. Just as you start with easy agreements to build momentum at the mediation table, start writing your business plan by tackling the topics that seem the most familiar and comfortable for you to address. Write each topic on a separate sheet, and compile them in a loose-leaf notebook. You will be pleased (and amazed) at your progress as you finish topic after topic and your entire plan nears completion of the drafting stage.

Before starting to develop and write your plan, go to a local bookstore and scout the business section for books on business plans; every business should have one. The following key topics are adapted from one of the best books on the subject, *The Successful Business Plan: Secrets and Strategies,* by Rhonda Abrams.[2]

Executive Summary

In five or fewer pages, the executive summary should incorporate the essence of your entire business plan into a compact, readable unit.

Mission Statement

Insert the mission statement that you developed in your work in Chapter Six.

Description of Mediation Practice

Providing a detailed description of your practice will help your business plan. In a brief paragraph, describe the services you offer. Use your mediation signature to help you write this description (see Chapter Six).

Legal Name of Practice. Insert the name you have selected for your practice. (See Chapter Ten.)

⊱ Practice Tip ⊰

Write the executive summary before you start the plan to give yourself a blueprint. Then revise it after your entire plan is completed and your thinking has evolved.

Legal Form of Doing Business. If you are a corporation or partnership, include the compliance documents filed with the appropriate governmental agency. If you are a sole proprietor and need a fictitious business name or want to limit your legal liability, this is a good time to take care of these details. See the books offered by the American Bar Association Law Practice Management Section and Fred Steingold's *Legal Guide for Starting and Running a Small Business.*[3]

Location of Practice. Provide the address and location of your practice. Also describe the parking situation, and provide a general description of the building and neighborhood.

Demographics and Target Market. Describe your clientele by income and educational levels, types of problems, geographical location, and direct versus indirect users (professionals who refer as opposed to members of the public). Describe the needs, demands, and specific concerns of both your end users and your referral sources. (See Chapter Eight for information on defining your target market.)

History of the Practice. Describe the chronological and developmental growth of your practice. Start with the year you opened (or will open) your doors, and share the stages of change in type of practice, personnel, reputation, and awards and other accomplishments. Insert your long résumé and a one-page biography.

Mediation Services Offered. Delineate the different and discrete mediation services for which you are qualified and competent to offer. If you are not currently offering an expansion of services beyond resolving current disputes, explain why an expansion or unbundling of services is not in the best interest of your practice. (See Chapter Seven.)

Competition and Collaboration in the Marketplace.
Spell out how your mediation practice differentiates you from other professionals offering services to your potential client base. Address how the following professionals offer services that may compete with your practice or offer opportunities for cross-referral and collaboration such as co-mediation: other mediators, lawyers, other licensed professionals (such as therapists and accountants), related businesses

(document preparers, notaries, financial planners, real estate brokers), and court and governmental programs.

Marketing Strategies. After reviewing Chapter Thirteen, take the time to think through the following areas carefully:

- Marketing in your office with displays, materials, and office setup
- Advertising
- Public relations
- Networking with referral sources
- Writing and teaching
- Volunteering in the community
- Using your staff in your marketing efforts

Operating Your Mediation Practice. Be prepared to perform a full audit of the management and operations of your practice, and address each of the following elements:

- Staff. Describe each person with strengths and weakness in relation to an articulated job description.
- Office facilities. Give an office tour, room by room, pointing out the functional reality and potential for your space.
- Technology. Inventory and assess how your equipment and software meet your needs. At a minimum, address the following areas: computer capacity and software, internal e-mail and document networking, Internet access, telephone equipment and networking, duplication and collating, filing and retrieval, and postage and shipping capability.

Use of Contract Services. Inventory and assess the people you hire outside your practice to perform necessary services for you and your clients:

- Building management
- Cleaning crew
- Computer and telephone technicians

- Messenger and delivery personnel
- Insurance brokers
- Interior designers
- Bookkeepers and accountants
- Banks
- Attorneys
- Marketing and management consultants

Client Service and Quality Control. Perform a client service impact study on the following areas:

- Speed and competence of responses to client questions and concerns
- Supervision and review of written documents
- Method of client evaluation of services and analysis of result
- Acknowledgment and communication with referral sources
- Ways to ensure *kaisan*—that is, ongoing improvement (see Chapter One)
- Financial planning, monitoring, and execution

CONCLUSION

The tools provided in this chapter are effective only if you use them. If you find crunching numbers or extensive drafting to be difficult, ask for help from a colleague or pay someone to help you. Remember: *Prior preparation precludes poor performance.* Yet be easy on yourself. You may want to take the plunge into mediation practice before all of your planning is complete, and update your planning as you go along. The next chapter will help you improve your practice management once you get the doors open.

Managing Your Practice

Planning your practice is crucial, but operating it competently and profitably will ultimately determine whether your clients are satisfied and you make enough money to support your family. This chapter examines the key elements to help you run an efficient and profitable practice.

BE COMMITTED TO QUALITY

Your reputation and goodwill in the marketplace are ultimately determined by the quality of the mediation services that you deliver. In Chapter Six, you explored defining your mediation signature. Yet there is a vast difference between creating a signature and actually providing effective mediation services. Mediation skill building and strategic development are beyond the scope of this book, but they should never be overlooked. Review Chapter Four for the strategies to obtain mediation training and to improve your mediation craft constantly; your mediation training is never over. See Appendix Three for training opportunities.

Your commitment to quality does not end with how you resolve conflict. Your commitment extends to every aspect of your practice: the appearance and functionality of your office, the training and supervision of staff, the production of paperwork, and your appearance in the marketplace.

In his book *Thriving on Chaos,* management expert Tom Peters argues that to succeed in your mediation practice, you must be obsessed with quality.[1] He feels that if you knowingly ignore even one act of lousy service or sloppy paperwork, you destroy your moral authority within your office to demand quality at all times. You can demonstrate your quality obsession in the following ways:

- Never let a typo or misspelled word out the door—even if it means staying late or throwing out hundreds of printed brochures.
- If you ever hear a staff member be rude or nonresponsive to a client, make sure an immediate apology is made and a lesson learned.
- Check with clients, referral sources, court clerks, and other people in your practice orbit to make sure your quality meets their expectations.
- Discuss at office meetings how the quality of the mediation services is being maintained and can be improved.
- If quality lags, make sure that clients not only get redone quality work in a hurry but that you credit the bill or offer a refund to compensate your clients for having to endure your quality lapse.

Peters advises that any cost in refunds or time to repair shoddy work will inure to the benefit of your practice in the long run. He contends that it costs five times more to go out and replace a dissatisfied client than it does to maintain satisfied clients. Peters uses a mediation metaphor to make his point: "A well handled problem breeds more client loyalty than you had before the problem."[2] Just remember that conflict can be an opportunity whether it applies to your clients' problems or your own.

NEVER SETTLE FOR LESS THAN YOUR FULL POTENTIAL

You may have heard about the Levitt Total Product Concept that has been used in business and industry for the past twenty years. Developed by Theodore Levitt and endorsed by Peters, this four-level approach might help you think through the evolution of quality in your mediation practice:[3]

Generic Level: You are a trained professional who resolves conflicts.

Expected Level: Your mediation skills are competent, and your fees are fair.

Augmented Level: You know the current trends in the field, you provide comprehensive congruent client-oriented materials, and your staff is trained to initiate follow-up.

Potential Level: You have built and maintain a current client library, you have equipped breakout rooms as well as a mediation room with food and forms, and your entire staff is trained and committed to peacemaking and quality mediation services.

Think about your practice. What level do you expect and work toward? In referring to other mediators, I recommend that clients settle for no less than a mediator whose practice is on an Augmented Level. Let's examine some of the ways you can reach the Augmented and Potential Levels of mediation practice.

TRAIN YOUR STAFF IN MEDIATION SKILLS

Think about the best-run service business that you deal with as a consumer: airlines, retail stores, dentist offices, or restaurants, for example. A benchmark of quality is the way that support staff treat the customer with their understanding and knowledge of the ultimate product. An airline service representative may not know how to fly the airplane but is probably trained to know the features of the aircraft, factors in scheduling and delay, and what movies and food are being served. If you inquired about meal service, I doubt that you would stand for the answer: "I'm only a counter representative. That's the flight attendant's job, not mine."

Apply this point to your own mediation practice:

• Are your assistant and telephone receptionist knowledgeable about the benefits of mediation?

• Does your staff know the strategies and skills that you use to resolve conflict?

• Does your staff know how the forms and other materials that you have developed are used in your mediation work?

You are not operating at either an Augmented or Potential Level if your staff members are not well versed in these and other aspects of your work. It is your responsibility to either provide training in-house or pay for the tuition and time off for your staff to complete professional mediation training. We strive to have every member of Mosten Mediation Centers management and administrative staff (including interns) complete a forty-hour basic mediation course, and many take advanced and specialized courses as well. We require and pay for this staff training because we believe our clients deserve no less. Our professional mediators can deliver competent services only if they are supported by mediation-knowledgeable support staff. It is no different in your practice.

It is your responsibility to either provide training in-house or pay for the tuition and time off for your staff to complete professional mediation training.

OFFER INTANGIBLE ENHANCEMENTS TO YOUR CLIENTS

One method of reaching Augmented and Potential Levels is to find intangible ways of meeting client needs that are value-added to their mediation experience. These enhancements, some large and some small, can increase client satisfaction without increasing their bill. Following are some examples of intangible benefits that you can offer:

- Provide free parking.
- Send out for lunch during noontime appointments.
- Provide up-to-date mediation literature in the waiting room and client library.
- Keep candy bowls filled (and remove discarded wrappers).
- Call each party within twenty-four hours of a settlement to see how they are doing and to prevent day-after remorse.
- Fax and e-mail agreements to clients in addition to snail mail.
- Always have fresh markers and plenty of flip chart paper.
- Provide folders and notebooks for parties to organize documents.
- Arrange for a round table and comfortable chairs.
- Have dispensers of drinking water and glasses in the mediation room.
- Place writing pads and pens at every place at the table.
- Keep client files neat and make sure that confidential documents are put away when others are in your office.
- Provide consultation rooms for parties to meet their lawyers.
- Offer parties the opportunity to use your telephone and receive fax messages.
- After sessions, walk with the parties to the elevator or the front door of the building.

Try to think of other ways you can make visiting your office and participating in a mediation to be a satisfying experience for your clients.

DEVELOP CLIENT-FRIENDLY WRITTEN MATERIALS

When clients walk through your door, do you have prepared materials to assist them step by step through their mediation experience? Are those materials readily accessible to you and your staff to make sure your clients get them when they need them?

The key is to prepare; don't scramble. When parties come in for the first time, have a preprinted client intake form ready to be filled out, as well as a pen or pencil readily available and a clipboard or writing table to make filling out the form comfortable. This type of planning should take place at every stage of the mediation process. If parties are going to meet in caucus (separate meetings) as well as joint session, have a prepared written guide for clients to understand the caucus process and how to succeed in these private meetings. If you use opening statements, have an outline of common points that you can hand out to clients that they can use to prepare their own opening statement. If you use a written deal memo or memorandum of understanding, have preprinted samples so that your clients can review the boilerplate in anticipation of writing up their own settlement.

These are just illustrative examples of the forms you may consider preparing. You can develop your own forms, trade with colleagues, or buy them off the shelf from mediation practice books. Always respect the work product and copyright, and provide attribution and credit to the forms of others. Always obtain prior permission.

⟫ Practice Tip ⟪

Keep client materials at your fingertips. Regardless of the source of your written materials, make sure that they are ready when you need them:

- Keep a file drawer of commonly used forms in the mediation room. You won't have to leave the room and interrupt the dialogue flow.

- Never use the last form in a file without duplicating five more. Routinely inventory your forms so that you have sufficient copies.

- Keep the original forms in plastic sleeves in a notebook. Copy from originals rather than from other copies to make sure the quality is good. Be sure you have hard copy originals; you never know when your computer might crash!

ESTABLISH AN INTAKE MODEL

When the telephone rings, you are offered a highly targeted marketing lead that may turn into a revenue-producing case or just another telephone chat depending on how you handle it. Unlike every other form of marketing that casts out a line to potential clients hoping for a bite, the caller is approaching you! Getting the telephone to ring is the ultimate goal of all your marketing (see the next chapter). Now it is up to you to convert that call to an opened case.

✿ Practice Tip ✿

Review your intake procedures:

- What model do you use for case intake?
- Who handles the initial telephone call or Web inquiry?
- What steps do you and your staff take following that inquiry?
- How are phone inquiries converted to opened case files in your office? What are the sources of those inquiries? How are referral sources recognized?

Can you articulate your intake model? There are four general mediation intake models described below (see Figures 12.1 and 12.2). Review them to identify the workable model that you now have in place or to find a better method.

Short Intake: Mediator Talks Directly with Potential Client

Short means ten minutes maximum. The purpose of the call is to answer the caller's basic questions personally with the goal of following up with a mediation marketing packet or referring the caller to your Web site (see the next chapter). Your challenge will be to stay on the process of mediation rather than delve into the facts or personal concerns of the caller (this discipline takes training and practice). You will provide information about you, your signature (see Chapter Six), your fees, and your availability.

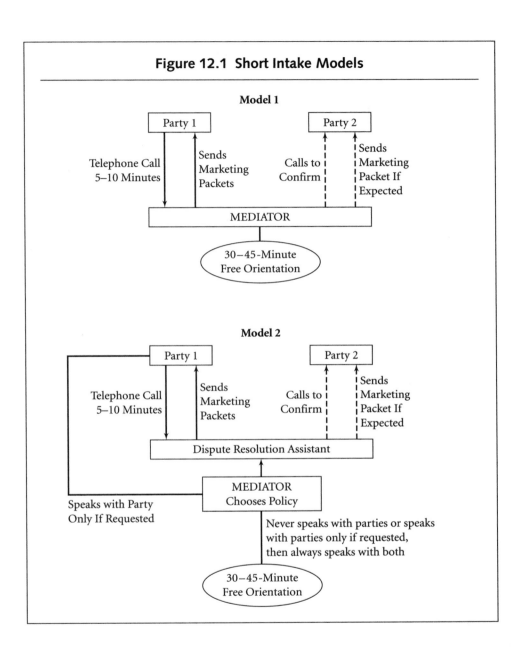

Figure 12.1 Short Intake Models

Model 1

Party 1

Telephone Call
5–10 Minutes

Sends
Marketing
Packets

Party 2

Calls to
Confirm

Sends
Marketing
Packet If
Expected

MEDIATOR

30–45-Minute
Free Orientation

Model 2

Party 1

Telephone Call
5–10 Minutes

Sends
Marketing
Packets

Party 2

Calls to
Confirm

Sends
Marketing
Packet If
Expected

Dispute Resolution Assistant

MEDIATOR
Chooses Policy

Speaks with Party
Only If Requested

Never speaks with parties or speaks
with parties only if requested,
then always speaks with both

30–45-Minute
Free Orientation

Figure 12.2 Long Intake Models

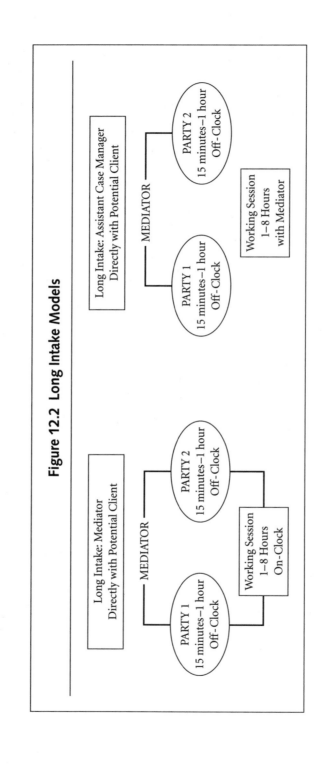

You want to stay brief for two reasons. First, your follow-up marketing packet and Web site will answer most questions. Second, you are off-clock (that is, not billing for this time) and want to keep your time investment to a minimum. Most mediators who use this model also offer a free office consultation for thirty to forty-five minutes. The free consultation then leads to private individual sessions or a working joint session, both of them on the clock (that is, this time is billed).

At the end of this short intake, the caller should have confidence in your tone and information and provide contact information for sending the marketing packet. Be careful to send a packet to the other party only if you are sure that the party is expecting it. You also might ask if the parties are represented by attorneys and if they want the lawyers to receive their own marketing packets. Remember that your credibility and neutrality as a mediator start with the way you handle these delicate issues.

Be careful to send a packet to the other party only if you are sure that the party is expecting it.

In this model, you might not have any contact with the noncalling party until the first mediation or orientation session. It's often a good idea for you to call the noncalling party before this session so you can get the other side of the story. This way, both parties will feel you are neutral going into the mediation.

Short Intake: Mediation Assistant Talks Directly with Potential Client

Everything about this model is the same as the short intake that you handle yourself except that another staff member takes the call. You should instruct your assistant to alert you if the caller insists on speaking with you. Most callers are willing to speak with your assistant since that is the procedure you have set up, just like we accept the nurse who takes our blood pressure or temperature at a doctor's office. If the caller does insist on speaking with you or another mediator, you need to have an established office policy about whether you will get on the telephone or have your assistant explain that in order to preserve your neutrality, you do not talk to either party until both parties come to your office for the free orientation session. Both of these policies are common in the field.

Long Intake: Mediator Talks Directly with Potential Client

Under this model, you would speak with each party for fifteen minutes to an hour without charge. The next stage would be a working session with both parties on the clock. Most mediators who use this model do not necessarily follow up the telephone calls with marketing materials due to the time spent on intake, but this is changing as more mediators are developing marketing materials to supplement their direct contact with potential clients.

Unlike the short intake model in which the caller does not reveal facts, relationship dynamics, or other concerns, such revelations are precisely the purpose of the long intake model. This approach gives you the opportunity to showcase your craft as well as to develop a bond with each party on the telephone. By taking a factual history and learning more about the conflict, you can also prepare for the joint working session and give parties information and guidance.

The major downside to this model is that after spending one to two hours on the telephone, the parties may never come in. Also, you may be concerned about perceptions about your neutrality since you will not have met or necessarily have spoken with both parties prior to conducting these long intake sessions.

Long Intake: Conducted by Mediation Assistant or Case Manager

This model works best when the dispute resolution assistant or case manager is highly experienced in intake and convening. The telephone calls must be followed by a detailed memorandum from the intake professional so that the mediator can be fully briefed before the working session. Obviously the bonding and personal relationship between you and the parties is sacrificed with this model, and you must decide if that loss is outweighed by your time savings.

Short or Long Intake with Counsel

Whether long or short or handled by you or your assistant, designing intake when lawyers are involved requires special preparation (see Figure 12.3). Lawyers are becoming more sophisticated consumers, so they often do not require an extensive orientation about the process of mediation in general. Rather, you need to educate them about particular aspects of your process—for example:

- Use of private sessions or conference calls prior to the date of mediation
- Whether you encourage or require premediation briefs, what the briefs should include, and whether the briefs are confidential with the mediator or shared with the other parties and counsel
- Hours of the session and how meals and snacks will be handled
- How offers will be presented: by you or by the lawyers themselves
- Presession sharing of boilerplate release language

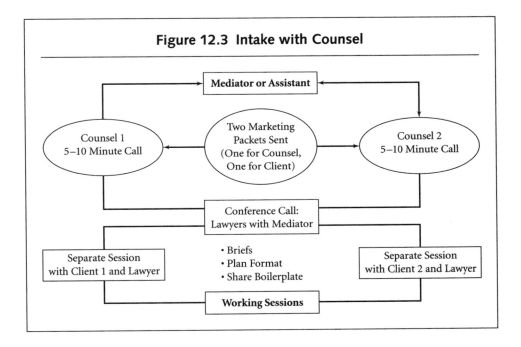

Figure 12.3 Intake with Counsel

You may need to be particularly adaptable in deciding your method of intake with counsel. Some lawyers are accustomed to dealing with dispute resolution assistants or case managers with both private mediators and mediation provider organizations. Other lawyers are concerned about the delicacy of their case and insist on speaking directly with you, either together or individually.

Single and Sequential Session Formats

Traditionally, most civil mediations have been set up so that the parties expect to meet and work out a settlement in a single session. Sometimes these sessions can last days and nights; exhaustion often contributes to settlement as much as skill. (See Figure 12.4.)

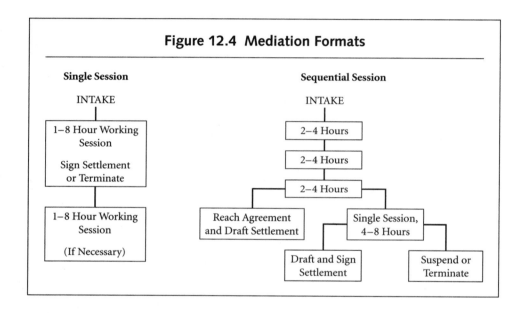

Figure 12.4 Mediation Formats

Single Session

INTAKE

1–8 Hour Working Session

Sign Settlement or Terminate

1–8 Hour Working Session

(If Necessary)

Sequential Session

INTAKE

2–4 Hours

2–4 Hours

2–4 Hours

Reach Agreement and Draft Settlement

Single Session, 4–8 Hours

Draft and Sign Settlement

Suspend or Terminate

A second model is to have a series of shorter sessions (two to four hours each) that are set by agreement of the parties. These sessions are often followed by a mediator's summary letter that serves as minutes of the session and outlines agreements made and issues still open for resolution. The parties continue to meet until an agreement is reached or the mediation is terminated by one or both of the parties.

In planning your sessions, you can offer either model or a hybrid. In the hybrid model, parties usually start with sequential sessions until an agreement is reached or impasse develops. The parties can then try a marathon single session to try to bring closure.

CUSTOMIZE YOUR WRITTEN MEDIATION CONTRACT

The prevailing law in most states requires a written mediation contract to be signed by parties to a mediation (see Appendix Eight for a model contract). This written agreement provides informed consent for consumers as to the mediation process and your fees. It also handles rules for confidentiality and inadmissibility of communications and documents prepared for the mediation in future court proceedings. You should prepare different mediation agreements for different types of mediations. For example, family mediations require different considerations than an employment mediation. A one-size-fits-all agreement may not meet the needs of your clients. See Appendix Two for mediation standards.

You may also want to have a standard agreement, but make it clear in your intake that the parties may modify it if they wish. Your agreement may call for a seven-day notice for cancellation and the parties may want to be able to cancel within twenty-four hours. But such requested modifications force you into having conflicting needs with one or more of the parties. It's a tough balance. Like working out fee and payment arrangements, you must delicately protect your own interests while remaining neutrally client centered. My mentor Louis M. Brown always said that a client should really talk with a second lawyer before making a fee arrangement with a lawyer! It is not so different when potential clients who need to trust you are negotiating with you at the same time. You must do your best to acknowledge your own needs and still remain neutral and client centered.

CLEARLY STATE YOUR FEES

Because saving money is a prime motivation for many consumers to try mediation, you have a professional duty to be crystal clear about how much you charge and what services you charge for.

Hourly Fees

Charging by the hour is still the prevalent method since you can never predict how long a matter will take. Because more mediators are providing services between sessions such as writing session summary letters, arranging for neutral experts, or handling emergency telephone calls, charging by the hour accommodates billing for these services.

Daily or Session Rates

You may decide to charge a flat daily rate or set rate for a multihour session. Many mediators add out-of-session charges to these flat fees; others set a flat rate and do not charge for out-of-session time. You also must set a policy for what you will do if the parties settle before the end of the arranged time. In the same way, if the session goes overtime, do you have additional set time periods, or do you charge by the hour—and at what rate?

Flat Fees

You may wish to offer a flat rate to mediate an entire matter, no matter how many or few hours it takes. This method is certain and clear, but it sets up a conflict of interest between you and your clients. You have an economic motivation to rush a settlement to maximize your hourly return, and the parties do not have a motivation to accelerate their settlement. One way to reduce this problem is to arrange for a flat fee incorporating a reduced hourly fee for a set time period and charge hourly thereafter. For example, if your customary hourly rate is $150 per hour, you might offer a flat rate of $1,000 for the first ten hours of mediation and $150 per hour thereafter.

Percentage Fees and Bonuses

Some mediators tie their fees to the amount of the controversy or negotiate fee components for settlements reached quickly or based on other criteria negotiated between the parties and the mediator. Except for very sophisticated and very wealthy parties, these types of fee agreements should be avoided. Your talent, skills, and experience can be reflected in your hourly or daily rate rather than vesting yourself with an interest in the outcome that can directly affect your neutrality.

PROVIDE EASY PAYMENT OPTIONS

In managing your practice, think through how consumers can pay for your services. Your hourly or daily rate might be competitive, but if you do not demonstrate flexibility in your methods of payment, you might find that potential clients will go elsewhere.

Payment by the Session

One way you can maintain a competitive advantage in the marketplace is to unbundle payment for your mediation services. Instead of having parties pay for the whole bill at the end or pay a retainer at the start, they can pay as they go. This generally means you will get paid every time they meet with you, and you can eliminate billing altogether.

If you don't charge for time you spend on the case outside the sessions, calculating your bill will be a snap. You either bill for the flat session amount or tote up the number of hours that you work with the parties. If you do charge for out-of-session work, add up the time in between sessions, and have an invoice ready at the beginning of the session.

⸙ Practice Tip ⸙

Although many mediators collect fees at the end of a session (partly because it may be unclear how long a session might last), try to collect at the beginning of the session to alleviate any last-minute hassle if (when!) parties bring up issues in the last five minutes or there is a stormy ending to the session. You don't want to be in the position of chasing parties into the parking lot in order to get a check. Also, in order to set boundaries and structure, think about setting an ending time to the sessions even if you have time open afterward. This will also allow you to collect a calculated fee at the beginning of a session.

Retainers

This method of payment came into mediation practice because many mediators come from law practice backgrounds. A retainer is a deposit paid at the outset of the services to ensure payment for part or all of the expected services. There is no recipe for setting the right amount. If you set it too high, you could scare away potential clients. If you set it too low, your time billed could vastly exceed the amount deposited so that clients will owe you money and you may have a risk of collection. If you have to err, do so on the low side. Research has shown that mediation participants have high levels of satisfaction, and satisfied customers pay their bills.

There is a way you can keep your retainer low and still ensure full payment. It's called a *replenishable retainer*. Unlike a traditional retainer, in which the fees you render are deducted from the retainer until the retainer is exhausted and the clients owe you money, with a replenishable retainer the deposit remains intact until the end of your services. Clients pay you regularly for the services that you render, and those payments are not deducted from the retainer; rather, the payments replenish the original amount of the retainer.

Let's say your retainer is $500, your hourly rate is $150 per hour, and you render three hours of service during a billing period, for a total of $450. Under the traditional retainer, the $450 earned would be deducted from your retainer of $500, leaving the client with a credit of $50. If you bill two hours in the next billing cycle (total fees $300), the parties would owe you $250.

Under the replenishable retainer method, the $450 earned during the billing period would be due and payable so the parties still had $500 on deposit (total fee paid: $950). If your next billing cycle is the last, the $300 fees earned during that period would be deducted from the deposit and the parties would receive a refund of $200; that is, you have $500 and they owe you $300, which means you owe them $200.

In both instances, the total bill was $750. However, with the replenishable retainer, the parties never owed you money. In fact, they received a check at the end, which generally boosts customer satisfaction.

❧ Practice Tip ❧

Tell your clients it is in their interests not to owe you money. They need you to be highly motivated and neutral to help settle their conflict. If you have to remind or pressure them to pay, this situation adversely affects your ability to help them, and it could turn out lose-lose instead of win-win.

Credit Card Payments

A consumer-friendly way to help parties finance mediation services is to offer them the option of paying by credit card. In fact, instead of having to ask for any retainer or payment at the end of a session or billing cycle, parties can agree to authorize charging services as they are incurred, reserving the right to question any charge after receiving a bill itemizing your services. Clients like this option because they can start without paying a deposit and can pay off the mediation as another credit card obligation.

OFFER SEVERAL METHODS TO ALLOCATE YOUR FEES

It is part of mediation lore that the parties must equally split the fee in order for the mediation to start. Equal payment does often encourage a level playing field and equal commitment to the process. However, there are many options to equal payment, so you should be adaptable.

In many employment mediations or those involving large corporations and consumers, the company will often pay 100 percent of the fees. In construction defect and other cases involving multiple parties of different sizes and potential liability, allocation usually puts a larger share of the mediator's fee on the lead plaintiff and defendant (usually the developer or general contractor), with smaller percentages for other parties (usually subcontractors). And in divorce mediations, due to differences in ability to pay, the parties may share the mediator's fee unequally.

You should always assure the parties that your neutrality will not be affected by who writes your check. More important, by modifying the equal payment rule, you will be making mediation services affordable and accessible while building your practice at the same time.

OFFER CONFLICT PREVENTION

If you provide competent mediation services and office support for raging conflict, your practice is destined to grow. Yet there is an even more important service that you can offer: helping your clients prevent conflict in the first instance. You can offer a number of services to help your clients avoid disputes in the future.

Conflict Wellness Checkups

When parties first come to your office, offer a conflict wellness and legal checkup along with your intake sheet (see Appendix Eight). This conflict prevention tool takes only a few minutes to fill out, and it can stimulate thinking that can spur client preventive action. Although you probably do not sell life insurance or offer family counseling, you can still help your clients reflect and consider steps that can make their lives better. Just like doctors who suggest that their patients lose a few pounds and most patients do not give up dessert, do not be discouraged if your preventive interventions do not appear to have immediate results. Prevention is often nondetectable and is a long-range process.

Mediation Reminder Postcards

How does it feel when you get a postcard from your dentist every six months to come in for a cleaning? Sitting in the dentist's chair may not be your favorite activity, but you probably appreciate the dentist for setting up a system that will keep your mouth healthy. You can do the same type of preventive planning for your mediation clients. If parties have arranged for settlement terms to become effective in the future, you can remind them of the terms and offer your availability to help. Here are some examples of reminder cards:

- Deferred payment dates in a settlement. Perhaps the parties need to negotiate an extension or other terms.

- Regular scheduled meetings. As part of a mediated agreement, parties might agree to meet regularly to work out problems. Your reminder letter can help make sure these meetings take place.

- Property being sold. The settlement might provide that real estate, company assets, or other property be sold in the future. You can be of help in reminding parties of this agreement and facilitating details.

Do not worry that clients might find your reminder letters to be intrusive or might impute a motive on your part to hustle business. Remember the dentist's cards. You know that it costs money for cleaning and you call for an appointment because dental health is important to you. Give your clients the same opportunity to prevent and resolve conflict.

Preventive Mediation Services

Many mediators are providing preventive mediation services in the formation and monitoring of relationships and ongoing projects and co-ventures. When parties are finishing up settling a dispute that has ripened into the need for mediation, they may be open to exploring preventive mediation the next time problems are at an early stage or they are entering new personal and business relationships. Make sure that parties and lawyers who are satisfied with your services know that you are available to prevent trouble in the future.

INITIATE A PROGRAM OF ONGOING EVALUATION

Most companies have some method of evaluating their services so that they can learn and improve. You get customer surveys at your auto dealer, when you stay at a hotel, or when you buy an insurance policy.

Start an evaluation program immediately. You can use the sample evaluation form in Appendix Eight and adapt it to your practice. Give the form to all parties, lawyers, and referral sources at the conclusion of every mediation. The most important task is for you actually to read the evaluations, share them with your staff, learn from the results, and initiate steps to improve.

CONCLUSION

Now that you have some tools to manage the clients whom you are serving better, get ready to improve your marketing efforts. The next chapter will show you how to increase your client base.

Marketing Your Practice Effectively

Once you have created your mediation signature, identified your inventory of mediation services, defined your target market, and set up your office, you are ready to get the word out about your practice. You will never have enough money to carry out your marketing goals fully. You will have many choices to determine a marketing budget. As you can see in the sample marketing budget in Appendix Seven, every marketing item has direct capital costs, staff costs, and the cost of your time. It is important for you to decide which marketing directions deserve most attention. You may choose to put all your available funds in your top two or three strategic choices. On the other hand, you may want to spread out your marketing dollars in as many directions as possible.

In regard to the source of marketing funding, the safest course is for you to use a comfortable percentage of your gross revenue from fees paid by clients. This assumes that your fee income exceeds your other expenses. Of all the expenses of starting a mediation practice, your willingness to invest in marketing may determine both the timing and possibility of profitability. Your choices regarding these expenditures are tied in with your overall approach to investing in your practice (as discussed in Chapter Eleven).

LAUNCHING YOUR PRACTICE

When you decide to open up your practice, you have many special opportunities for reaching your potential base of clients and referral sources. As with all other marketing, you will need to decide how much of the work you will do yourself and how much will be professionally handled.

Mailed Announcements

This is your chance to make a statement about your mediation signature and services to a targeted market. You can have the announcements graphically designed and professionally printed, or reduce costs by doing them in-house with a computer software program. These announcements are attractive, and you can increase the elegance by selecting high-quality paper stock. Use the money you save on graphics to add expansively to your mailing list. Don't pinch pennies; spend money on the extra postage to send announcements to everyone you know who might refer to your practice now and in the future.

Press Releases and News Stories

You can have your announcement printed in your local newspapers either of general circulation or directed to professional or business readers, or you can save money here and prepare a press release instead. Not only does a news story have more credibility than an ad, it's also free. Newspapers are always looking for local stories, and a new peacemaker in town may be considered newsworthy. Of course, there is no guarantee that the newspaper will run your story, but give it a try.

Follow-Up Letters

Using the same mailing list that you used to mail your announcements, write targeted letters on your letterhead discussing your mediation signature and how you can meet the conflict resolution needs of the recipient. These letters can be sent at a fraction of the cost of your announcements because there are no printing costs and can be produced as needed. Remember that multiple repetitions to the same potential customer is the key to effective marketing.

Office Open House Reception

If you are proud of your new mediation-friendly office (and you should be!), you may want to invite your family, colleagues, existing clients, and referral sources to an open house to help you launch your practice. You do not have to spend the money for a fancy catered spread; chips, salsa, and soft drinks will do the job. Remember that people aren't coming for the food; they are coming to support you or perhaps get business for themselves. In that regard, invite your guests to bring their own marketing materials to set out on a table. Consider putting those materials up on a community bulletin board in your client library on an ongoing basis.

Business Cards

Business cards also can be produced in-house with a computer program. However, local business centers can produce a very classy card at reasonable cost. Even the costs of professional printers are not excessive in their charges for business cards. You might also check out on-line printing options through www.iprint.com and other companies with very reasonable prices.

Stationery

Stationery can also be produced by your own software program. Many marketing experts urge that you develop a logo to give all of your written materials a uniform look. Logos are nice, but unless a graphic designer owes you a favor, you may wish to hold off on a professional logo. Very few clients will select your firm just because of your logo. Wait until you can afford some discretionary spending. Logos are frosting, not the cake or even the bread necessary for you to survive in practice.

Brochures

Brochures are the bread to keep your practice alive. Your hard work in defining your mediation signature will be translated onto this foundation of your marketing program. You can display the brochures in your waiting room, include them in client marketing packets, and carry them with you when you mediate or market off-site. You can produce brochures in-house, and they can be photocopied rather than professionally printed. Rather than pay for color printing, you can use colored paper stock with black ink. If you can live without your picture in the brochure, the cost per brochure drops even further. Based on your definition of your target market, you may wish to produce different brochures for different targeted areas of practice. For example, if you practice both family and employment mediations, you can produce two separate brochures with virtually no added cost.

Client Marketing Packets

Information is the key to informed consumer decision making. Client information packets should be sent out immediately after the first telephone call. These packets are expensive but are vital to your overall plan. The expense includes duplication of materials (color copies are even more expensive), the folder, the envelope, postage, and staff time. See Chapter Nine for sample contents of these marketing packets.

In addition to the initial marketing packets, you may wish to consider other client handouts—for example:

- The contract between mediator and the parties
- Client instructions for various aspects of the mediation process (such as ground rules and how to participate in caucuses)
- Legal and financial information
- Necessary court forms
- Relevant statutes
- Standards of Mediation Practice
- Templates of settlement agreements
- Community resources and experts

NETWORKING WITH REFERRAL SOURCES

While current clients offer the most inexpensive and best marketing targets, marketing to referral sources can be your second most effective strategy. Instead of spending your time and money on marketing to people who do not know your work or may use your services only once, referral sources offer the opportunity of quality repeat business from satisfied users of your services (see Chapter Eight).

The care and feeding of referral sources cannot be overemphasized. However, rather than relegating your efforts to an expensive present during the holiday season (which is better than nothing), you can develop a strategy to sell and reinforce the support of your referral sources throughout the year.

You will receive calls from potential referral sources indicating that your name has been offered as a potential mediator for one (or several) of their clients. Because mediators are barred from paying referral fees for ethical reasons (it compromises neutrality), the single motivation for a referral source is to make sure that you can facilitate the resolution of the client's dispute competently and economically. When a lawyer, accountant, human relations officer, or other professional refers a mediation case to you, the referral sources are risking some measure of their goodwill on your ability to get the job done. Therefore, anything that you can do to instill confidence in your abilities will increase the opportunities for that referral source to recommend you again and again as the mediator of choice.

When a lawyer, accountant, human relations officer, or other professional refers a mediation case to you, the referral sources are risking some measure of their goodwill on your ability to get the job done.

Provide Referral Source Information Packets

Just as you have a client marketing packet, you should also develop a packet for referral sources. You should use biographies and résumés that emphasize your educational background, professional experience, and the professional writing and teaching that you have done. You might also include a list of satisfied clients and referral sources (always get prior permission before you list names) with accessible contact information and encourage contacting the people on the list for a personal reference.

These referral source strategies are stressing your brand of mediation rather than the generic concept of mediation. Most referral sources have much more familiarity with mediation than will the ultimate parties, but not always. Include some of the information that you send to clients both to show the referral source what materials the clients are receiving and to provide some additional education about mediation. Like chicken soup, this added material on mediation can't hurt; it might even help. Potential referral sources will be appreciative of how you are educating their clients about mediation, as well as pick up an insight or two themselves.

You might go another step by providing articles or even your own guidelines on how the referral sources can best help their clients in the mediation setting.[1] Many lawyers, for example, fear a loss of revenue from litigation averted by a speedy settlement and therefore may be reluctant to refer clients to mediation. You might offer information to these lawyers on how they can unbundle their services by serving as coaches from the sidelines or even representing clients in the mediation itself. Other referring professionals such as therapists, business managers, and organizational executives can also serve as mediation coaches, offering helpful information, reality checks, and emotional support through the mediation process.

Practice Tip

Craft different résumés and bios for different work that you do. If you mediate business and employment matters, you may want one bio that emphasizes employment and another that highlights your business experience. If you teach as well as mediate, produce separate bios.

Strengthen Relationships

In addition to reasonable fees and competent service, you can reassure and assist referral services by stressing your accessibility and accountability to them and their clients throughout the mediation process. Referral sources do not want negative comebacks from mediation participants who complain that the mediator cannot be reached by telephone or does not deliver promised services in a timely manner. These referral sources are even unhappier if they cannot reach you on the telephone or you are unwilling to work with them to clarify and solve a problem raised by their clients. In *Thriving on Chaos,* Tom Peters points out that referral sources' and direct customers' satisfaction increases when you work out a problem successfully.[2] Sometimes they have more confidence in you than before the complaint or problem arose.

You can strengthen your referral relationship by mixing good manners and accountability throughout the mediation process. In addition to sending thank-you and instruction letters within days after receiving the referral and being accessible to the referral source during the process, you might consider writing a letter at the conclusion of the process. Without divulging confidential information, you can let your referral sources know that the mediation ended with a settlement (or not) and again thank them for their confidence and trust in mediation and their support of your efforts.

Encourage Feedback

Finally, just as you should seek direct feedback from your clients on their satisfaction level of your mediation services, you should do the same with referral sources. You can send out customized referral source questionnaires to seek their thoughts on their level of satisfaction and input for improvement. Going further, you can attempt to meet annually (or more often) with your major referral sources to discuss how you might better meet their needs. For example, if you have successfully mediated two or three employment matters for a company, it might come up during such an evaluation meeting that the company itself is having internal conflict and your referral source might learn that you also offer organizational facilitation or dispute resolution system design and consultation. Or it might be that some employees are missing a great deal of work due to divorce litigation; your referral source might learn that you also provide divorce mediation and that the company's employee assistance program might refer to you in conjunction with or even before offering referrals to divorce lawyers. Focusing on the needs of your referral sources is not only walking the mediation walk, but it is effective low-key selling of your services.

STRATEGIC MARKETING

There is no recipe to successful marketing. Just as you need a full array of skills and techniques to approach conflict resolution, you need a wide array of strategies to market your practice successfully.

Direct Mail

The most targeted advertising strategy is sending direct mail promotional pieces to your potential referral sources or the ultimate user of your services if that market is discrete and specialized. Direct mail campaigns can range from elaborate multicolored brochures with customized and personal letters to a simple postcard. The virtue of direct mail is that you directly target people you want to get your message and whom you believe have the need and awareness to contact you now or in the future. Unlike display advertising in a general daily newspaper or television and radio, you are not paying to reach potential users who do not have conflicts needing mediation or who might live too far away to use your services anyway.

You will be faced with the dilemma of increasing the quality of the mailing piece versus increasing the number of repetitions of your presence and message to the same targets of your mail ads. Opt for several direct mail pieces to the same recipient several months apart rather than put too much of your advertising budget into a glossy mailer that will be sent only once. Of course, it would be wonderful if you can afford to send out quality pieces on each of your follow-up mailings. If you have to choose, go for repetitions over a longer period of time.

Also, keep your expectations low. Most direct mail experts predict a 2 to 3 percent response rate. If you find that it takes fifteen new calls to convert to a mediation case, you can expect only twenty to thirty calls from a thousand pieces of direct mail sent out, which may yield one or two new cases. However, you will also benefit from residual delayed response and affirmed name recognition. The recipient may not call you when reading your mail piece, but your name may stick and be retrieved when that recipient or someone they know needs a mediator in the future.

Marketing Database

If you elect direct mail as an advertising strategy, invest early in a database that you can maintain yourself. A database is a computerized address book of names. Once you type in the name (input data), you can retrieve and reuse that name forever. Many inexpensive database programs also have mailing label functions that permit you to print the recipient's name directly on the label; then you or your staff can peel off the label and stick it on rather than individually typing or writing each address for each and every mailing.

If you do not feel that you are ready to start a database yourself, you can buy mailing lists from organizations, often with labels already printed. Usually, these are limited to a single use, which means you would be contractually barred from duplicating the list or using it in subsequent mailings without paying a new fee. Other organizations will not give out their lists but will send out your letters, brochures, or postcards to the people on their list for a fee.

Yellow Page Ads

People who call your office directly upon looking at your Yellow Page listing (whether in the phonebook or on the Internet) are the most targeted leads possible. People involved in disputes who do not have a source of referral will probably turn first to the Yellow Pages to find a mediator. This contrasts very favorably with a display ad in a newspaper or magazine where most of the people reading the ad are not ready to hire a mediator. The timing of your practice opening should coincide with your Yellow Page listing so that you can get a running start. The American Bar Association's study on Yellow Page advertising found a return of three to seven dollars in fees for every dollar spent on advertising. Lawyers who use advertising were very satisfied with the results.[3] If it works for lawyers, it may work very well for you.

At the first stages of your practice, you may want to invest in larger display ads since you probably do not have many sources of business. As your practice grows, you can cut down to a box ad or even just a listing. You also may want a broader reach by listing in multiple specialty areas as well as under mediation. For example, some Yellow Pages have subspecialty listings for mediation under lawyers (that you may use only if you are a licensed attorney) as well as specific practice areas such as real estate, family, and employment matters.

Display Ads

Unlike Yellow Page listings that reel in clients with immediate need, display ads in newspapers, magazines, and professional journals build long-term recognition and establish your identity in your target market. Do not expect any immediate results.

Also, since repetition is the key, if you choose to use display ads, be prepared for a long-term campaign—an absolute minimum of three months weekly or six months monthly, with a recommended run of at least twice this time period. Most publications will design the ad for you, but you might do better designing it yourself on your computer. Whichever route you take, make sure that you don't try to cram too much information into the space allotted. Leave plenty of white space. Certainly, the message of your mediation signature is important, but the name of your practice is even more so.

Web Presence

As you can see from the vast number of Web sites in Appendix Four, the Internet has become a major source for mediation marketing activity. Web strategies may yield you new clients; an equally compelling reason to have Web presence is to affirm your mediation signature to people who inquire about your services. Like a brochure or sending a résumé, referring people to your Web listing or Web site can establish your credentials further. It is very affordable to have a listing or even a profile with a mediation supersite, such as www.mediate.com, as an initial strategy, with future plans for your own site or even a separate domain down the road. Regardless of your strategy, find yourself a competent and reliable computer consultant, but write your own initial copy. After all, you know your signature best.

COMMUNITY OUTREACH

Another good way to get your name out there (and work on your skills) is to get involved in your community. If you do business mediation, join the local Chamber of Commerce and serve actively on a committee that interests you. Don't feel that your volunteer activity has to be directly linked to your practice. Actually, the relationships that you form from working on a charity pancake breakfast or serving on the program committee may get you referrals because you do not seem like a hustler. Think about your community and pick your involvement: with your church or synagogue, a home for troubled children, the local school or parks committee, or the political and social issues that are important to you.

Action Steps for Marketing

- Pick one marketing idea to implement.
- On one piece of paper, write down your steps to get there.
- Schedule your first task ASAP.
- Experiment with new techniques.
- Hook up with a colleague or small group to help you focus.
- Tell others about your marketing goals.
- Develop a separate computer file or drawer for the initiative.
- Act soon and often.

Source: Crandall, R. *Ten Secrets of Marketing Success.*

PRESENTATIONS AND TEACHING

One of your best (and cheapest) marketing strategies is to present workshops at conferences or offer classes on mediation. Being included in a mediation conference or college faculty will increase your credibility in the field, which can only lead to an expanded referral base. Even more important, by spending the countless hours preparing your overheads and teaching materials, you will increase your own expertise, which makes you more effective at the mediation table.

Once in the classroom or conference hotel, you will have an opportunity to showcase your mediation skills through your presentation. Your ability to adapt your teaching to the needs of the group, listen patiently, respond comprehensively yet tightly, and motivate participants will help build your reputation. You also will have a chance to connect personally with participants following your presentation or throughout a conference; such personal relationships are the foundation for later referrals.

If you enjoy teaching, the opportunities range from graduate dispute resolution programs to mediation modules in high school classes. You can even open your own school in your waiting room by teaching classes to current and prospective clients. You can advertise your classes by fliers, free announcements, and display ads. If only one or two students show up, give your full presentation. Not only are they entitled to the class as advertised, but you never know what will come from the one or two class members. Even if no one shows up, you still get some goodwill through your advertising.

ARTICLES AND MEDIATION PRACTICE MATERIALS

You might not enjoy speaking in front of groups or even networking at cocktail parties, yet you may be a superb mediator with lots to say and much to contribute to the field or directly to the public. Consider writing short articles for your local mediation organization, bar association newsletter, other professional journal, or local newspaper.

By thinking through, researching, and writing the article, you will improve your knowledge and effectiveness at the table just as you would in teaching or presenting. And there is an added feature: you can use the reprints of the articles (with permission of course) to include in your marketing packets, decorate your office, and include in your bio and Web site. Your articles could also lead to speaking invitations both within the profession and to professional and public groups.

Many mediators moan that they feel that they do not have much novel to say and that they cannot imagine being a published author. Remember that mediation is a booming new field with many hot issues of importance. Unlike Chaucerian scholars who have dissected every line of *The Canterbury Tales* many times over, there is much that you can contribute on mediation that is fresh and of interest to editors of all types of publications.

ℒ Practice Tip ℒ

If you don't know what to write about, go back to your basic mediation training manual and develop just one point that is of interest to you. Or if you are moved by your experience in mediation training or at the table, write an autobiographical piece about your own journey and experiences in mediation. I suggested this to Elana Weiss, a mediator from San Francisco, and she published a superb article in Fall 2000 *SPIDR News* about her experiences at her first Society for Professionals in Dispute Resolution Conference.

ORGANIZATIONAL WORK

Other mediators can make prime referral sources. Even if you are fresh out of mediation training and do not feel ready to write or speak, you certainly can volunteer your time with your local mediation organization. You will contribute to the field regardless of whether you are handing out materials as a conference helper, reviewing new legislation, or working to increase membership by serving on a committee. Mediation organizations can always use the extra help. In addition to increasing your own knowledge of key policy issues and trends in the field, you will develop relationships that will support and sustain you throughout your peacemaking career.

🌿 Practice Tip 🌿

If you choose to volunteer, carefully and strategically plan your involvement so that you demonstrate your proficiency and follow-through. It won't be much fun for you or of help to an organization if you volunteer in an area that doesn't interest you or for which you have little aptitude. The local mediation organization may need a treasurer, but if reconciling your own checkbook baffles you, turn down this opportunity. You can end up hurting your career and the organization if you're not committed to your work there.

KNOWLEDGE OF MEDIATION ISSUES AND TRENDS

Being able to discuss major issues in mediation cogently on the telephone with clients or referral sources and with colleagues at a conference will increase the effectiveness of your marketing efforts.

As the field of mediation becomes increasingly competitive, the knowledge and confidence that you demonstrate (without showing off) may give you a needed edge. Staying current in the field is crucial. Look at the hot mediation topics set out in the Epilogue that represent some of the most important issues and trends in the field. Could you now write a five-minute talk on each topic? On most topics? If not, are you prepared to study and correct the situation?

☙ Practice Tip ☙

When discussing topics in mediation, don't try to inject yourself or your brand. Stick to the substance of the issue rather than use it for self-promotion. You will have the opportunity to sell yourself in following up later. In discussing these issues, you improve your credibility—your best sales tool!

CONCLUSION

You can use a mix of the techniques explored in this chapter to meet your needs, and you'll be developing a solid business and making mediation your day job— but be patient. The seeds you sow today may not bloom for two or three years, but if you stay in the field, you will be able to harvest the results.

What Do You Do Next Monday?

You now have the information and tools to make mediation your career. The next step is developing your personal plan and taking action.

In my work with mediators on all levels, I have found that it is more productive to take action, almost any action, than to wait to develop the perfect plan. You may be enthralled with the vision of peacemaking, but the journey can seem so overwhelming that you may never make mediation your day job. The best way to start and to keep momentum is to take comfortable baby steps at your own pace toward a destination of a career in mediation. Such progress is virtually risk free. As you take one step after another, you will increase your knowledge and skill set and move closer to your goal. If you get satisfaction out of each step, even if you stop at any point on your career path, you will have gained insight, communication tools, and enjoyment from your journey. Whether you make mediation your day job or use your perspective and skill to help others in your current job, in your community, and at home, you and those close to you will have benefited from your hard work.

WHAT YOU CAN DO AT HOME

If buying and reading this book have been your first steps, you now have a modest investment of money and time in your early exploration of a peacemaking career. There are many other steps you can take by yourself at relatively low cost to move you along your path.

Home Reading Plan

Carve out a starter budget for building a peacemaking library and a reading schedule that will ensure you the time and likelihood that you will make steady progress. Each book purchase is a step in building a future client library (see Chapter Nine). Start a library catalogue of your books, and take notes as you read. These notes can be the basis for your personal description of the books that you can offer other future mediators or clients, or use to refresh your knowledge. Concentrate. Read these books as focused preparation rather than leisure reading at the beach. As you come to points within the text that seem important, write them down. For each point, follow up and write down answers to these questions:

- Why is this important?
- What can I do to develop this point in my career preparation [or building my practice]?
- When will I put this into action, and what baby step will I implement?

This follow-up is even more important than your initial reading. It may be the difference between your being a peacemaking dilettante or making it your day job.

Read your selections one at a time, and complete your notes before starting the next one. This focus and structure will reinforce the purpose of your home study plan rather than having several books open and not completed scattered throughout your house.

Go to the resources in Appendix Four. Pick one book to give you an overview of the field. There is no magic in your selection—just pick something that appeals to you. Make your own selections. (My personal top choices are reviewed at www.MostenMediation.com.)

Most of the books can be purchased at mediation conferences, directly from the publisher, on Web sites, or at selected bookstores. Articles require a bit more library research.

Surf the Web

Appendix Four contains a list of leading ADR and mediation Web sites. Many of these sites have interesting information that you can download to read and put into action. Other useful features are forums and chatrooms that offer you the opportunity to see the comments of other mediators and offer your own. Not only

Find authors through www.mediate.com., www.crinfo.com, or another source, and contact them directly to ask for a copy of your article of choice. Most authors have many copies on hand and are thrilled to provide their articles to interested readers. After finishing reading the article and making your notes, you might want to e-mail the author to offer a comment, ask a question, or otherwise begin a dialogue. Mediation authors are rarely paid to write articles, so part of our psychic income is to engage in dialogue with and mentor mediators who are interested in what we have to say.

have I initiated many vibrant collegial relationships over the Web but have received some welcome client referrals as well.

Complete the Mediator Self-Survey

Whether you are thinking about starting a mediation training program or building a private practice, be sure to put aside plenty of time to write out your answers to the Mediator Self-Survey in Appendix One. If you do not know how to answer a question, that's okay; you clearly have more reading and training ahead. Answer each question on a separate page so that you can use your responses in planning your business strategy and marketing.

LEARN WITH YOUR COLLEAGUES

Once you feel more comfortable with your knowledge of the field from your self-study, consider widening your circle to discuss and share your thoughts.

Join a Mediation Study Group

Many mediators in practice meet regularly to hone skills and network. If you are just entering the field, you can join a group to discuss mediation concepts and share readings. A logical way to form a group is out of your mediation training class, but you can also contact a local mediation organization to identify others who may be in your exploratory stage, or you could set up a virtual group.

Attend Mediation Seminars and Conferences

Before you invest the money and time to commit to a five-day mediation training course, look around for an hour or half-day program in your community. Local mediation organizations (see Appendix Five) and other professional bodies and business groups have programs that you might attend as a nonmember. Plan on attending at least one such program in the next few months.

Mediation conferences take place throughout the year in various parts of the country. Check out the Web site of your organization of choice, and find out when the next conference takes place. These conferences are treasure troves of excellent presentations and workshops at affordable prices. The real value-added is the professional connections you will make.

Enroll in a Training Course

Whatever your level, there is a training course that will hone skills and offer renewed energy to pursue your peacemaking journey. If you have taken most of the basic courses, take a training course with a very different orientation or in a different discipline. If you are comfortable with settlement conference evaluative caucusing, take a transformative facilitative training. If you specialize in families, enroll in a commercial training. When I starting training other mediation trainers, I enrolled in a corporate train-the-trainer seminar designed for personnel supervisors. I learned new skills and tips that I adapted to my mediation training. You can always pick up new tools and broaden your skills.

Select a Mentor

Building your career can be an uncertain and lonely process. One way to chart your own course is to walk in the tracks of those who have successfully navigated the journey before you. Whether that model is your trainer, an author, a conference speaker, the leader of local ADR organization, or a well-regarded practitioner, identify someone who shares many of your personal and professional values and skill sets. You can pay for formal supervision and consultation or just have casual on-the-run conversations. Your main goal should be to find out what your model does well, how it is done, and how you can replicate that success.

BE STRATEGIC ABOUT BUILDING YOUR PRACTICE

Think about how you care about and prepare for resolving the conflicts of others. Put that same thinking and preparation into building your practice. If you are serious about going into practice, start immediately to do the following:

- Develop your mediation signature (see Chapter Six).
- Inventory your current mediation services, and expand your services to meet needs in your community (see Chapter 7).
- Define your target market to differentiate your services from other mediators and to make your marketing more efficient (see Chapter 8).

Keep Track of Your Time

If you're already a lawyer, you know all about time sheets. If you're not, any lawyer will tell you about time sheets. Lawyers will tell you that unless they write down everything they do and when, large chunks of a day or week are forgotten. Clients rarely pay for services that never get on the bill. The same is true for building your practice. If you seem to be spinning your wheels, examine how you are spending your time. If you want to see the current amount of your investment in opportunity costs, keep your time and add it up (see Chapter Eleven). You can start this drill next Monday. By next year, you will have an entire database of your activity to analyze and plan from.

Think and Act Like a Mediator

Starting Monday, you can walk the peacemaker walk. In Chapter Two, you learned about the traits of successful mediators. Whether you choose to be a full-time professional or just use your mediation insights in your everyday life, you can start modeling peacemaking in everything you do:

- Listen to others at every opportunity.
- Make sure you are truly interested in what others have to say rather than use their pauses as a chance for you to break into the conversation.
- Be a learner. Identify one thing that you learn from every human interaction.
- Check in during conversations to make sure your conversation partner understood and is truly interested in what you have to say.
- Check in to find out if you truly understood what was being discussed.

- When you feel disappointed or betrayed, stay in the relationship rather than run away or get even.
- Adjust your communication style to different types of learners. If someone says, "I feel . . .," try directing conversation to emotions. If someone keeps saying, "I think . . .," focus on a logical presentation.
- Think about what you will say before you get on the telephone or enter a meeting of importance. Plan. Don't react.
- Work on your patience. When you feel as if you are losing it, try to get back on track.
- Keep your expectations down and your hopes high. Disappointment can be a conflict provoker of situations capable of a calm solution.
- While you can't be neutral in living your life, try to recognize and correct any biases or intolerance.
- Try working effectively with people who may be just a bit different from your usual circle of friends and colleagues.
- Try to find one thing to like in every person in your life.
- Take time in your day to listen to others who may be in pain or conflict.
- Look around at those in your family or at work who seem to be having trouble. Try to understand what it is like to walk in their shoes. Be willing to help.
- Do what is necessary to make sure your energy stays high throughout the day. Exercise, eat properly, sleep, and keep your own stress down.
- Make your word your bond. Take care to meet commitments, and cut down on exaggeration or distortion.
- Increase your use of the phrase, "I don't know."
- Find ways to express your creativity during the day.
- Go out of your way to give encouragement to someone who is struggling.

CONCLUSION

Mediation is about process, and the process you use in becoming a mediator is extremely important. If you start next Monday, your commitment, supported by concrete action, increases your chances that you will live out your dream and make mediation your career.

The Evolving Field of Mediation

Y ou are now seriously considering making mediation your career. The reality is that the field you are entering is changing and evolving rapidly. In China, mediation has been the primary method of resolving conflict for thousands of years, but historically in the United States, we have used the court system as the way to settle disputes. As a society, we are coming to recognize that this system is not working to our advantage, and we are turning to mediation as a far superior method of resolving conflict. Within the past two decades, mediation has grown exponentially and continues to become entrenched in our schools, courts, businesses, and governmental agencies—in every area of our lives.

In fact, you might not have even considered mediation as a career ten years ago. As mediation evolves as a profession, there are key issues and trends that you must be aware of and factor into your career planning in order to maximize your mediation practice.

This chapter focuses on a few of the hot issues swirling in the field. Some of the issues are being debated and decided within the mediation community itself. However, most trends are affected by forces outside the mediation field such as legislatures, the courts, the legal profession, consumer groups, and the media.

Your understanding and ability to discuss the issues in this chapter will affect your career and development in several ways:

- You can better plan for appropriate education and training.
- You can maximize your investment into private practice by being ahead of the curve.
- You can increase your referrals.
- You can improve your client intake success rate.

Although your practice is symbiotically linked to the growth of the mediation profession, I've divided the issues into two categories: trends that affect the profession are set out first, and those that more directly affect your own mediation practice follow.

ISSUES FOR THE PROFESSION

If you check regularly on a mediation listserv (see adr@aba.net) or a mediation Web site (see Appendix Four), you will be struck by the changes that are occurring and the debates beginning in our profession on nearly a daily basis. Here are just a few.

Certification and Regulation of Mediators

Permitting "a thousand flowers to bloom" has been mediation's history. Growing out of society's need for options to the legal system, you could hang a shingle to mediate without a state license—actually without any training at all. The proliferation of different styles and backgrounds has been a blessing and a curse for consumers. There is an abundance of choice and virtually no accountability. With the increasing interest and entry of lawyers into the profession, many wonder if mediation might become a subspecialty of law rather than an independent peace-making profession.

Uniform Mediation Act

One signal that mediation is here to stay is the movement to establish a model act on mediation that states can use as a template in drafting their own legislation. The drafting of this law has been a joint effort between the National Conference

Check out your state's approach to monitoring the competency of mediators and entry into the profession:

- What are the requirements to mediate in court or community programs?
- Is there a certification program that specifies necessary training or experience to permit you to be labeled a Certified Mediator?
- If so, what are the benefits of being certified and how does it affect the marketplace for mediation services?
- What are the estimated out-of-pocket costs and time commitments to become certified?
- If there is no licensure, determine the attitude toward licensing mediators in the future. What agency or profession would be in charge?
- Determine whether it benefits you to belong to a mediation organization in your state to qualify for certification or competency.
- What do you need to do to qualify for certification of competency by a voluntary mediation organization? For example, the Association for Conflict Resolution has standards for Practitioner Membership and Advanced Practitioner Membership. Do you qualify? What benefits would you get if you did qualify?

of Commissioners on Uniform State Law and the American Bar Association, and there has been a national effort to include diverse interests and points of view.

As this book goes to press, the Uniform Mediation Act outlined in Appendix Two is still a draft awaiting adoption as early as August 2001. It is important for you to track the final draft and take an active interest in any effort to introduce the model act into your state. A model acts as a further signal of the acceptance and institutionalization of mediation in our society.

Professional Standards

In an effort to have the mediation profession regulate itself, many of the leading organizations have adopted their own standards of conduct. Aspirational in nature, these standards are published and often are used by courts and legislatures and administrative bodies in setting guidelines. Two examples are set out in Appendix Two: The Model Standards of Conduct for Mediators (1994), jointly approved by the ABA, SPIDR, and the AAA, and the draft Standards of Practice for Family and Divorce Mediators that are state of the art and can be applied to areas outside of family mediation.

Emerging Duty to Advise About Mediation

Despite the obvious benefits of mediation, its relatively low usage stems from the fact that most people don't know what mediation is or how it could be used to solve their conflicts. Since the lawyer's office remains the gateway to most conflict decision making, proponents of mediation have long believed that if lawyers and their clients had a conversation about mediation and how it compares to other alternatives, clients would use mediation more often.

State legislatures, bar associations, and courts are now encouraging or requiring lawyers to tell clients about mediation before even filing a court action. This early client education is consistent with the benefits of use of mediation early in the life of a conflict. In Texas, for example, all divorce litigants in their first court appearance must file an affidavit indicating that they have been informed of mediation and have made an informed choice to proceed with litigation nevertheless. Colorado has a bar association rule requiring such advice by lawyers. Other bar associations such as the Beverly Hills Bar Association have voluntary ADR pledges that encourage lawyers to use mediation whenever it is appropriate, and many trade associations (for example, the Better Business Bureau) and individual corporations have also developed mediation pledges. These pledges are commitments to discuss mediation with clients, use it in one's own organization or in disputes with others, and work at avoiding conflict in the first place. The pledge can be a wonderful public relations tool for professionals and organizations, resulting in favorable press and encouragement for members to display their framed pledge in their offices and for the public to look for a mediation pledge in choosing with whom they wish to do business.

As more professionals such as therapists, accountants, and insurance adjusters become aware of and successfully use mediation for themselves and their clients, the increased use of voluntary and required incentives to use mediation may develop.

The Multidoor Courthouse

In a 1979 article arising out of the historic Pound Conference on Perspective on Justice in the Future, mediation pioneer Frank Sander of Harvard Law School dreamed of a multidoor courthouse. Sander argued that courts should serve society by offering a number of choices at intake: negotiation, conciliation, mediation, and arbitration, as well as traditional courtroom litigation.[1]

ADR Pledge of the Beverly Hills Bar Association

I recognize that there are various techniques available to help parties resolve disputes outside or in conjunction with litigation.

I understand that in many cases, Alternative Dispute Resolution (ADR) may be more appropriate for dispute resolution than traditional litigation. ADR includes, but is not limited to, mediation, voluntary settlement conferences, arbitration, and mini-trials.

I believe that attorneys should be knowledgeable about various methods of dispute resolution, and be prepared to fully explain ADR options to clients in order to ensure their informed consent regarding the resolution of disputes.

I believe that clients are entitled to be informed about (a) comparison of the costs of litigation with the costs of ADR; (b) creative remedies not available in the court system; (c) time and privacy considerations; (d) comparison of potential results of litigation versus ADR; (e) preventive methods to avoid future disputes and maximize the client's overall quality of life.

I have read the Beverly Hills Bar Association (BHBA) brochure *Alternatives in Dispute Resolution*. I shall have this brochure or similar ADR handouts available and shall give such handouts to clients early in the attorney-client relationship where appropriate.

I pledge that I will discuss ADR with my clients and opposing counsel and recommend its use in appropriate situations.

Date _____   Attorney's Signature _____

Name of Law Firm _____

In the near quarter-century since the Pound Conference, courts are beginning to understand Sander's wisdom. Many states now require neutral courthouse facilitators to serve as counselors and ombudspersons to citizens, helping them select alternatives to litigation to resolve their disputes. The Maricopa Superior Court in Phoenix, Arizona, has devoted an entire floor of its courthouse to a self-service center. In this consumer-friendly environment, litigants are referred to as customers and are provided information in both English and Spanish in easy-to-read pamphlets, videotapes, and accessible computer programs. They are offered community resources of mediators, lawyer coaches, and social agencies. In other courthouses throughout the country, client libraries and dispute resolution offices are housed in the courthouse as both symbols and resources for citizens to make informed choices about how to resolve their disputes. As judges and court personnel become more mediation friendly, this attitude symbiotically supports the growth in the private sector as well.

Take a field trip down to your local courthouse:

- Conduct a consumer-friendly impact study as to how a litigant would feel walking down the courthouse halls. Is there a neutral court facilitator? Are there settlement rooms with round tables, flip charts, and readily available computers and copiers? Are there easy-to-access and readable consumer-friendly materials in a client library format?

- Meet with other local mediators to share impressions of the conflict resolution features of your courthouse. Come up with consensus recommendations for making the courthouse more mediation friendly. Arrange for a group of mediators to meet with the presiding judge of the court to present and discuss the recommendations.

- Write an article about how mediation can be injected into your local court system. Make reference to your group recommendations, and freely credit others.

- Volunteer as a mediator in your local courthouse program. When you are on duty, model a mediation environment. Arrange for a flip chart, or bring your own. Provide coffee and some cookies or pretzels. Bring a small array of mediation books and literature for litigants and their lawyers to browse while waiting. Offer a conflict wellness checkup (see Appendix Eight and the discussion that follows) to parties whom you are helping.

Private Versus Public Justice

Many critics of mediation believe that mediation offers a two-tiered brand of justice: private justice for wealthy and upper-income disputants and public justice in the court systems for the poor and working people. Others feel that the privacy of mediation allows issues of public policy to be dealt with behind closed doors rather than in the openness and setting of precedent that the court system requires.

As awareness of domestic violence, environmental protection, and other public issues emerges, you will be faced with this legitimate concern. What cases should you turn down due to their policy importance? How far should you go in mediating issues of tax evasion, health dangers, or other issues affecting society when both parties want to keep the discussion private rather than have reporters or others in their industry learn about their trouble? In addition to being a mediator trying to make a living, you are also a citizen in this society. When do the two roles conflict?

⚜ Practice Tip ⚜

- Learn about your state's laws for prohibiting or permitting the sealing of court cases from public view.

- Find out what types of cases must stay in the court system and which settlements must be carefully approved by a judicial officer.

- Talk with a local judge about the views of court personnel toward mediation and ensuring equal access to both private and public justice.

- Reflect on your own fees. Are they so high that many people cannot afford to use your mediation services? Do you have sliding scales or make special payment terms (see Chapter Twelve)?

Mediation and the Process of Court and Law Reform

Legislators and judges are looking to mediation for principles and processes to make the justice system more responsive to the needs of citizens. Oregon reformed its state family law system from top to bottom using the mediation principles of self-determination and empowerment of diverse stakeholders and by providing nonjudgmental and safe places to have discussions to explore options in steps. Other jurisdictions are now also looking to mediation as a model for this important reform work.[2]

Generic Mediation Advertising

Think about the impact that the American Dental Association has had on dental hygiene with its advertisements promoting fluoride and semiannual checkups. Can anyone ever forget the antitobacco ads featuring an elderly woman patient, a lifetime smoker, lying in a hospital bed speaking through a hole in her trachea?

Generic advertising about mediation is in its infancy. There are some excellent videotapes on mediation, but they are generally limited to viewing in a few courthouses, mediation centers, or law offices. Some community and local governmental mediation programs have developed public service announcements that local television and radio stations air, usually late at night or on Sundays. That's about it.

What if President Jimmy Carter or Michael Jordan endorsed mediation in professionally produced advertising spots aired during prime time? In addition to

Judge Judy or Ally McBeal, the impact of a television series on mediation and conflict resolution could burn this alternative into the minds of citizens worldwide. As mediation continues to grab the attention of policymakers and legislators, mass media's recognition and support of mediation may not be far behind, particularly as school mediation programs continue to flourish, in the process educating future voters about the benefits of mediation.

As in all other public awareness advertising, funding must come from the government and corporate sectors. No single mediator or even any single mediation firm can afford to educate the public about the concept of mediation. During the 1992 presidential election, Vice President Dan Quayle's campaign against litigation and support for ADR was subsidized by federal campaign funds, but the important message got lost in the other issues and politics of the presidential race. Future opportunities for public discussions and promotion of mediation are not far away, particularly with the merger of major mediation organizations into the Association for Conflict Resolution (ACR) in Washington, D.C., with increased funding and political clout.

ᘒ Practice Tip ᘒ

- Work within your local mediation organization, bar association, or the ACR to develop concepts and production plans for generic advertising on mediation.

- Check with local mediation groups about the presence of advertising in your locale. Work with them collaboratively to contact local media to air advertisements off the shelf, develop new advertisements, or even just copy for station announcers to read.

- Contact nonprofit funding sources and local governmental agencies with pro-mediation policy to allocate monies for mediation advertising and programs.

Remember: If generic advertising expands the market for mediation services, your own career will benefit.

Turf Wars

Now that mediation is on the rise, some conflicts are emerging within the profession and between mediation and other professions. These conflicts are having a major impact on the quality, accessibility, and development of the profession and the ability to offer conflict resolution help to those who need it.

Struggles Within the Mediation Field. In an article published several years ago, "Our Communication Is Important Too," Jeffrey Kichaven and I expressed concern that mediators were often in conflict with each other over issues big and small: policy issues regarding professional standards and certification, funding from the government and foundations, appointments on key committees, who will be included on a conference program—and on and on.[3] I personally have been invited to travel to several communities throughout the United States to mediate disputes between mediators.

In some way, such conflict is to be expected. Mediators are human beings, not saints. Just as the shoemaker's children may do without shoes, conflict among mediators in this new and robust field may be expected. Many practicing mediators chose this line of work due to their own horror stories as litigants in their own conflicts. Finally, psychoanalysts may have deeper explanations for the motivations of many mediators entering the field, such as an effort to resolve our own inner conflicts and troubles with others.

Whatever our backgrounds or our motivations, walking the walk starts with the way we handle our own trouble within our professional family. Jeff and I summed up our thoughts:

> When we act as if we have better insights or answers than lawyers or we treat others as adversaries we are neither building own practices, nor building the field. To broaden the scope of mediation at large, it is essential to model mediative behavior within and without the mediation community. That is the only way to gain the confidence of those we are seeking to serve.[4]

Struggles with Related Professions. As a profession, we must remember that for the past twenty-five years, mediators have been on a campaign to inform lawyers and other helping professionals about the benefits of mediation. Maybe we should have been careful what we wished for, because today many believe that lawyers are trying to take over the mediation profession. It seems as if every bar association has a mediation committee or task force. Many mediation programs require a law license to offer services (even on a voluntary basis). Mediation standards and training programs are being evaluated for their compatibility to existing lawyer roles and ethical rules. Lawyers have now gotten the message so well that they see mediation as a key career enhancement for the next decade, a way to regain market share lost to nonlawyers and self-representers, and a public relations coup to improve the reputation and integrity of the profession.

Professional mediators are also looking over our shoulders and speculating on the impact of this profound interest of lawyers. At the 1999 Annual Conference of the Academy of Family Mediators (AFM) in Chicago, one workshop was entitled, "Is Mediation Becoming a Sub-Specialty of the Legal Profession?" Two past AFM presidents, Lynn Jacob (a mediator from Chicago with a background as a social worker) and Steve Erikson (a mediator from Minneapolis with a background as a lawyer), and I discussed this issue.[5] One of the reasons for the formation of ACR was to provide a less unequal balance of power between mediators and lawyers in shaping the future of mediation in this country.

As with our internal struggles within our profession, the way mediators approach this issue may affect the outcome. It is very satisfying to witness a lowering of adversarial tension between mediators and lawyers over the past two decades. I can recall when many mediators saw lawyers as the devil incarnate; they blamed the legal profession and the court system for exacerbating the pain of people in conflict rather than viewed them as collaborative allies with whom mediators can work to improve the system. Unfortunately, lawyers contributed to this struggle by ignoring the public's growing demand for mediation or, worse, actively opposing it.

As more lawyers are being exposed to the effective work of mediators and receiving mediation training themselves, the intense debate between lawyers and mediators is evolving into more constructive dialogue. The we-versus-them mentality is giving way to a common approach to helping the public.

ISSUES FOR YOUR PRACTICE

It is not uncommon for the work and even understanding of issues facing the mediation profession to be left to those few mediators with the interest and energy to make a public contribution. Although these profession-wide issues affect your practice, you may be more concerned with trends that more directly affect the way you practice. Some of these trends follow here.

Confidentiality

One of mediation's great benefits to participants is its privacy. The issue of confidentiality, and admissibility in court of mediation communications, is dealt with in statutes, court rulings, cases, professional standards, professional ethics opinions, and the mediation literature. There is a growing movement for national standards to guide the promulgation of confidentiality standards on the state and local levels (take a careful look at the Uniform Mediation Act draft in Appendix Two). With the growth of court mediation, litigants, lawyers, and mediators are facing the tension between the expectation of confidentiality and the court's need for efficiency and gaining compliance of court-ordered mediation. Because more mediators are getting their professional start as volunteers in court programs or receiving paid referrals from judges, this tension between court rules and best mediation practices is a fact of life. You can use your court mediation work to build your reputation with judges, lawyers, and others in your community—but only if you are fully conversant with the nuances of confidentiality.

Co-Mediation

Co-mediation is used in a variety of ways. Mediators team up, combining different genders, backgrounds, levels of experience, and styles. Some mediation programs require co-mediation to benefit parties with a breadth of perspective and as a teaching tool for beginning mediators. Some co-mediators in private practice reduce their combined fee; others charge their ordinary fees.

Those who co-mediate often report increased efficiency by sharing areas of expertise and having two problem solvers in the room. Positive communication between co-mediators can model collaborative behavior for participants. While one mediator handles the communication and negotiation dynamics, the other can record progress on the flip chart and observe and monitor what is working and what needs to be changed.

Because consumers and professionals are accustomed to mediators working alone, many are not willing to pay for an extra mediator to be in the room. Many bar associations and other professional groups have restrictions against multidisciplinary practices or fee sharing, inhibiting this form of practice. Many who have tried co-mediation express concerns about incompatibility or control struggles with their co-mediator that adds to rather than reduces conflict in the mediation room.

Find out the rules for confidentiality in your state:

- Do you have an omnibus mediation confidentiality statute, or do you have to search cases, statutes, court rules, and other sources to figure out what to do?

- Make sure your practice complies with the requirements for confidentiality. Is your written mediation contract in compliance with your state law and professional standards of mediator organizations? Do you give proper notice of limitations of confidentiality?

- Draft your mediated settlement agreement to be enforceable in court if there is noncompliance of the parties, or do rules of confidentiality handcuff the parties from using a settlement to enforce the agreement? Learn what the limits of confidentiality are in your state. For example, can you promise confidentiality if the parties are later involved in a criminal or administrative case, a federal or tax action, or other limitation?

- Look up the Uniform Mediation Act and National Standards for mediation confidentiality to get a broader perspective on how other jurisdictions treat confidentiality.

- Determine how you will handle disclosures of confidential information by the parties themselves. May they talk about mediation communications to the press, family members, consulting professionals such as lawyers or therapists, clergy, or others in the community?

Transformative Versus Evaluative Mediation Styles

Attend any mediation conference, and you will probably find a workshop discussing the virtues and problems with the transformational approach pioneered by Robert Baruch Bush and Joseph Folger in their groundbreaking book, *The Promise of Mediation: Responding to Conflict Through Empowerment and Recognition.*[6] Bush and Folger define true mediation as the growth of the participants rather than the reaching of a settlement. They endorse a facilitative approach to resolving conflict in mainly joint sessions, where the parties can communicate directly and learn from each other.

On the other end, judges, lawyers, and many consumers want mediators to be evaluative in their process and to use their experience (mainly as litigators and judges) to tell the parties the strengths and weaknesses in their case. *Settlement* is not considered a dirty word; in fact, pressure and muscle are fully expected to be employed in mainly a caucus-style format in which the parties are separated and the mediator shuttles back and forth.

Both the facilitative and evaluative approaches to mediating conflict exist. There are many mediators who fit in between these polar extremes using different approaches for different situations—the tool box school of mediation. While mediators throughout the spectrum have much more to share than to contest, the communication between the schools unfortunately is often more of a debate than a dialogue.[8]

Use of Experts in Mediation

Experienced lawyers know that factual disputes make it difficult to predict the outcome of a case in court. These differences often bring parties to the edge of impasse in mediation since neither side is prepared to accept the other's perspective of how much an asset is worth, the value of damages, the impact of a particular custody plan on the children, or other areas of factual disagreement.

Regardless of whether you practice within the facilitative or evaluative school, alone or with a co-mediator, you might consider involving neutral experts in your mediations. Most parties would rather debate facts within the mediation room rather than spend the money for two dueling experts who trot out their competing reports (replete with bells and whistles) and no one knows what will ultimately happen.

You can involve experts in numerous ways. The emerging models of mediated case management and expert models (see Chapter Seven) are being used more frequently in both court-ordered mediations and those starting voluntarily in the private sector.

- Assemble a list of local experts available for consultation and evaluation within your mediations.
- Find out their experience and commitment to being neutrals, as well as the extent of their own mediation training.
- Attend conferences and training sessions for experts to learn how they are being educated and trained to perform in mediations. There are local meetings of accountants, business and real estate appraisers, child custody evaluators, and others in your own community.
- Put on a presentation with your favorite expert, or coauthor an article. You will both learn how each other works, and get out the word about your availability to offer this expert option within your mediations.

Prevention and Avoidance of Conflict

In your role as peacemaker, when does the prevention and avoidance of conflict enter your career and practice? Is your job done when you have mediated a resolution to a current dispute but the parties have other sources of conflict raging in their lives, ready to erupt? Are you just a negotiation facilitator, or can you be a true healer of conflict to help parties around your table lead more satisfying lives?

In his powerful autobiography, *Lawyering Through Life,* the late Louis M. Brown dreamed of the day when the United States would have a department of legal health to study the causes of legal disease and discover cures and ways to prevent legal trouble.[10] As mediators, we have that opportunity daily, but we have to widen our lenses as to what we see and what we can do.

Appendix Eight presents a sample Conflict Wellness and Legal Health Checkup that is being studied and used in many forms throughout the world. What if such a conflict diagnosis were provided every time we renewed our driver's license, in public libraries, and in professional offices that dealt with the symptoms of conflict? If mediators are steadily replacing litigators as the consumers' first stop in times of conflict, you need to learn about conflict prevention as well as conflict resolution, and use it daily with your clients.

- Take the Conflict Wellness and Legal Health Checkup in Appendix Eight. How is your own legal health? Share your experience with other mediators. Give them a copy of the check-up and discuss their results.

- Find a way to give the check up to clients when they first come to you and again when you have resolved their presenting conflict.

- Set up office procedures to monitor your clients' conflict wellness. Schedule follow-up compliance meetings for the agreements you mediate, as well as asymptomatic life cycle (marriage, birth of a child, college age, retirement) consultations to discuss how disputes can be prevented.

- Think about ways to offer dispute resolution design and audit services to prevent disputes in businesses and other organizations.

FUTURE OF THE MEDIATION PROFESSION

In Chapter One, I noted that if I were investing in the future, I'd put my money on the future of mediation. After fourteen chapters, I hope you now share this bullish view.

If you still have lingering doubts, let me share some reality, circa 2001. The *Los Angeles Daily Journal* is the largest daily legal newspaper in the world. Each Wednesday, it has a "Verdicts and Settlements" supplement that features and reports on recent cases. The readership is primarily litigators who want to see what's going on in the courthouses and mediation tables around the state. Three display ads for mediators ran on one page alone of the February 14, 2001, issue:

Mediation will continue to grow in use and job opportunities for the following reasons:

- Many people cannot afford lawyers' fees. And many who can afford them do not want to pay them.

- More lawyers are referring clients to mediation because clients are demanding it and lawyers know mediation works.

- Courts are overcrowded, and budget increases are not on the horizon.
- People are becoming better consumers and like the choices that mediation offers.
- In a world where privacy and control over one's life are in short supply, mediation offers people in conflict these benefits.
- Mediators are becoming even more consumer friendly in the services and intangible benefits that they provide.
- As demand increases for mediation, more and more talented peacemakers are entering the field, giving clients wider choices.
- Students who have learned about mediation firsthand in school peer mediation programs are both recommending mediation to their parents and others, as well as entering the field itself.
- As major companies and government agencies use mediation to solve their institutional disputes and those external to the organizations, mediation is becoming part of the workplace culture that filters into personal lives.
- Marketing of mediation services is driving down the prices of dispute resolution services for both mediation and other professions.
- National mediation organizations such as ACR will wield more political clout, putting mediation on the policy and funding radar screens.
- National attention to legislation and other mediation policy issues will both institutionalize mediation and increase its professionalism.
- As mediation matures into a profession, it will not seem so risky for consumers to give it a try. Experience will produce more procedural and ethical protections for the public as well for mediators, lawyers, and other professionals.
- Mediation education and training will develop further to refine teaching techniques, curriculum, and relevance in the workplace.
- Since user satisfaction is so high, the cumulative population of satisfied users will provide a steady and growing base of referral sources so that mediation will be used more frequently and earlier in the conflict process.

Research is needed to study and validate these and many other trends that I believe will make mediation much more established in the coming years.

CONCLUSION

These trends and issues are only the tip of the iceberg. The rapid growth of mediation is being catalyzed by a rapidly developing literature. Your career as a practitioner is linked to the theoretical development of mediation. Your daily peacemaking work plays a symbiotic role with the growth of the field. As mediation grows, so does the expanded need for your services. And as your career grows, you can share your experience to help researchers learn what is really happening around the mediation table. In this way, theory, training, and practice materials can be adapted and enriched to meet your needs and those of your clients better.

Peacemaking is truly an exciting and challenging journey, one baby step at a time.

APPENDIX ONE: MEDIATOR SELF-SURVEY

Current Marketing Practices

1. What services do I offer as a private mediator?

2. What is the target market for my services?

3. How do I communicate the availability and nature of my services to my target market?

4. How do my services provide improvement or diversity from other mediators in the same market?

5. What is my involvement with organized professional associations in my trained profession?

6. What is my ongoing involvement with other mediators? How is such involvement cost-effective?

7. To which professional journal subscriptions and software do I subscribe?

8. What is my involvement with statewide and national mediator organizations?

   a. How is this involvement cost-effective?

9. What is the extent of my volunteer work for the community?

10. How do I help other mediators and professionals develop their professional craft or practices?

Financial Investment and Performance of the Practice

11. What out-of-pocket capital have I invested to develop my mediation business?

12. How much is budgeted for the next twelve months in direct capital outlay?

13. How much professional time have I invested to develop my mediation business?

14. What is the value of that time in foregone income?

15. What is my budget for professional time in the next twelve months?

16. What is the rate of economic return on my capital and professional time investment?

Fee Charging and Collection Practices

17. What is my record for being paid fairly, adequately, and on time for my mediation services?

18. How do I collect my unpaid fees?

19. What is the rate and timing of collection?

20. Am I willing to arbitrate or litigate to collect fees?

   What are my criteria for arbitrating or litigating fee collection?

   If I do not arbitrate or litigate, what corrective steps am I making to reduce unpaid fees?

   What are my criteria for writing off a fee?

21. What is contained in my written mission statement about my mediation practice?

22. What is contained in my written business plan to financially develop my mediation practice?

Management of Practice

23. Do I want to have a mediator partner or steady co-mediator? If so, why? If not, why not?

24. What is my contribution to the growth of mediation through training?

25. What is my contribution to the growth of mediation through articles?

26. What is my contribution to the growth of mediation through development of materials?

27. How do I work with the following experts:

   Forensic accountants?

   Actuaries?

   Real estate appraisers?

Business appraisers?

"Industry" specialists?

Child development experts?

Children and extended family members?

28. How does my mediation contract inform and educate clients as to my:

Services?

Rules of my practice?

Financial requirements?

29. How does my contract protect me:

Financially?

From malpractice claims?

30. What do I or my staff do to educate clients about mediation?

31. What procedures have I developed in the office for:

Mailing?

Display of consumer-friendly information about mediation?

Showing videos about mediation?

Helping clients prepare and succeed at mediation?

32. What is my policy in helping spouses locate consulting counsel?

33. Will I mediate by conference call? If so, what is my procedure?

34. How do I communicate outside of session with:

Parties?

Counsel?

Experts?

35. What role do I play in:

Mediation session summary letters?

Drafting agreements?

Interim court orders?

Filing legal documents?

36. Do I permit counsel to attend sessions?

37. What role will counsel play?

38. How are their procedures set up?

39. Once the presenting problem is resolved, what preventive planning do I conduct for the spouses?

40. What follow-up do I perform in monitoring compliance with mediated agreements?

41. What type of tickle system have I set up to keep mediators on track and to follow up on future developments?

42. How do I stay in contact with mediation clients?

43. What procedures do I have for initiating annual mediation wellness check-ups?

44. How do I engage in preventive mediation?

Training

45. What are my goals for training?

46. What skills do I wish to focus on in training?

  What role will I play in training?

  What role will the supervisor play in training?

47. What areas of economic practice development do I wish to focus on in training?

48. What training format do I believe will most help me?

49. What obstacles do I believe will hinder my training?

  What will I do to overcome these obstacles?

  What do I want the supervisor to do in helping me overcome obstacles?

50. What issues or techniques do you wish to focus on in my training?

51. What type of supervisory style would be most effective in my training?

52. What type of supervision format would be most effective in my training?

THE MODEL STANDARDS OF CONDUCT FOR MEDIATORS

The Model Standards have been approved by the American Arbitration Association, the Litigation Section and the Dispute Resolution Section of the American Bar Association, and the Society of Professionals in Dispute Resolution.

Introductory Note

The initiative for these standards came from three professional groups: The American Arbitration Association, the American Bar Association, and the Society of Professionals in Dispute Resolution.

The purpose of this initiative was to develop a set of standards to serve as a general framework for the practice of mediation. The effort is a step in the development of the field and a tool to assist practitioners in it—a beginning, not an end. The model standards are intended to apply to all types of mediation. It is recognized, however, that in some cases the application of these standards may be affected by laws or contractual agreements.

Preface

The model standards of conduct for mediators are intended to perform three major functions: to serve as a guide for the conduct of mediators; to inform the mediating parties; and to promote public confidence in mediation as a process for resolving disputes. The standards draw on existing codes of conduct for mediators and take into account issues and problems that have surfaced in mediation practice.

They are offered in the hope that they will serve an educational function and provide assistance to individuals, organizations, and institutions involved in mediation.

I. *Self-Determination:* A Mediator Shall Recognize That Mediation Is Based on the Principle of Self-Determination by the Parties.

Self-determination is the fundamental principle of mediation. It requires that the mediation process rely upon the ability of the parties to reach a voluntary, uncoerced agreement. Any party may withdraw from mediation at any time.

II. *Impartiality:* A Mediator Shall Conduct the Mediation in an Impartial Manner.

The concept of mediator impartiality is central to the mediation process. A mediator shall mediate only those matters in which she or he can remain impartial and evenhanded. If at any time the mediator is unable to conduct the process in an impartial manner, the mediator is obligated to withdraw.

III. *Conflicts of Interest:* A Mediator Shall Disclose All Actual and Potential Conflicts of Interest Reasonably Known to the Mediator. After Disclosure, the Mediator Shall Decline to Mediate Unless All Parties Choose to Retain the Mediator. The Need to Protect Against Conflicts of Interest Also Governs Conduct That Occurs During and After the Mediation.

A conflict of interest is a dealing or relationship that might create an impression of possible bias. The basic approach to questions of conflict of interest is consistent with the concept of self-determination. The mediator has a responsibility to disclose all actual and potential conflicts that are reasonably known to the mediator and could reasonably be seen as raising a question about impartiality. If all parties agree to mediate after being informed of conflicts, the mediator may proceed with the mediation. If, however, the conflict of interest casts serious doubt on the integrity of the process, the mediator shall decline to proceed.

A mediator must avoid the appearance of conflict of interest both during and after the mediation. Without the consent of all parties, a mediator shall not subsequently establish a professional relationship with one of the parties in a related matter, or in an unrelated matter under circumstances which would raise legitimate questions about the integrity of the mediation process.

IV. *Competence:* A Mediator Shall Mediate Only When the Mediator Has the Necessary Qualifications to Satisfy the Reasonable Expectations of the Parties.

Any person may be selected as a mediator, provided that the parties are satisfied with the mediator's qualifications. Training and experience in mediation, however, are often necessary for effective mediation. A person who offers herself or himself as available to serve as a mediator gives parties and the public the expectation that she or he has the competency to mediate effectively. In court-connected or other forms of mandated mediation, it is essential that mediators assigned to the parties have the requisite training and experience.

V. *Confidentiality:* A Mediator Shall Maintain the Reasonable Expectations of the Parties with Regard to Confidentiality.

The reasonable expectations of the parties with regard to confidentiality shall be met by the mediator. The parties' expectations of confidentiality depend on the circumstances of the mediation and any agreements they may make. The mediator shall not disclose any matter that a party expects to be confidential unless given permission by all parties or unless required by law or other public policy.

VI. *Quality of the Process:* A Mediator Shall Conduct the Mediation Fairly, Diligently, and in a Manner Consistent with the Principle of Self-Determination by the Parties.

A mediator shall work to ensure a quality process and to encourage mutual respect among the parties. A quality process requires a commitment by the mediator to diligence and procedural fairness. There should be adequate opportunity for each party in the mediation to participate in the discussions. The parties decide when they will reach an agreement or terminate a mediation.

VII. *Advertising and Solicitation:* A Mediator Shall Be Truthful in Advertising and Solicitation for Mediation.

Advertising or any other communication with the public concerning services offered or regarding the education, training, and expertise of the mediator shall be truthful. Mediators shall refrain from promises and guarantees of results.

VIII. *Fees:* A Mediator Shall Fully Disclose and Explain the Basis of Compensation, Fees, and Charges to the Parties.

The parties should be provided sufficient information about fees at the outset of a mediation to determine if they wish to retain the services of a mediator. If a mediator charges fees, the fees shall be reasonable, considering among other things, the mediation service, the type and complexity of the matter, the expertise of the mediator, the time required, and the rates customary in the community. The better practice in reaching an understanding about fees is to set down the arrangements in a written agreement.

IX. *Obligations to the Mediation Process:* Mediators Have a Duty to Improve the Practice of Mediation.

Copies of the Model Standards of Conduct for Mediators are available from the offices of the participating organizations. The addresses are listed below.

American Bar Association
Section on Dispute Resolution
740–15th Street, N.W.
Washington, D.C. 20005–1009
(202)622–1681; fax: (202) 662–1683; www.abanet.org/dispute

Association for Conflict Resolution
1527 New Hampshire Avenue, N.W., Third Floor
Washington, D.C. 20036
(202)667–9700; fax: (202)265–1968; e-mail: spidr@spidr.org

American Arbitration Association
335 Madison Avenue, Floor 10
New York, N.Y. 10017–4605
(212)716–5800; fax: (212)716–5905; customer service: (800)778–7879;
www.adr.org

MODEL STANDARDS OF PRACTICE
FOR FAMILY AND DIVORCE MEDIATION

After years of robust discussion and involvement of over ninety mediation organizations, the following standards are state of the art for the mediation profession. The value of the process in reaching consensus and actual substance of these standards are applicable to fields of mediation practice beyond family and divorce conflicts.

The official Reporter, Professor Andrew Schepard of Hofstra University, has been a national leader in family law mediation and is Editor of the *Family Court Review,* and the profession owes him and the prestigious steering committee a debt of gratitude for their historical work. See 39, *Family Court Review* (January 2001) or www.afcc.org for the complete Standards and comments. The Standards have been passed by the American Bar Association (February 2001) and by the Association of Family and Conciliation Courts as official policy of these organizations.

Convening Organizations

- The Association of Family and Conciliation Courts
- The Family Law Section of the American Bar Association
- National Council of Dispute Resolution Organizations (NCDRO) which includes:

    The Academy of Family Mediators

    The American Bar Association Section of Dispute Resolution

    The Association of Family and Conciliation Courts

- Conflict Resolution Education Network
- The National Association for Community Mediation
- The National Conference on Peacemaking and Conflict Resolution
- The Society of Professionals in Dispute Resolution

Overview and Definitions

Family and divorce mediation ("family mediation" or "mediation") is a process in which a mediator, an impartial third party, facilitates the resolution of family disputes by promoting the participants' voluntary agreement. The family mediator assists communication, encourages understanding, and focuses the participants on their individual and common interests. The family mediator works with the participants to explore options, make decisions, and reach their own agreements.

Family mediation is not a substitute for the need for family members to obtain independent legal advice or counseling or therapy. Nor is it appropriate for all families. However, experience has established that family mediation is a valuable option for many families because it can:

1. increase the self-determination of participants and their ability to communicate;

2. promote the best interests of children; and

3. reduce the economic and emotional costs associated with the resolution of family disputes.

Effective mediation requires that the family mediator be qualified by training, experience, and temperament; that the mediator be impartial; that the participants reach their decisions voluntarily; that their decisions be based on sufficient factual data; that the mediator be aware of the impact of culture and diversity; and that the best interests of children be taken into account. Further, the mediator should also be prepared to identify families whose history includes domestic abuse or child abuse.

These Model Standards of Practice for Family and Divorce Mediation ("Model Standards") aim to perform three major functions:

1. to serve as a guide for the conduct of family mediators;

2. to inform the mediating participants of what they can expect; and

3. to promote public confidence in mediation as a process for resolving family disputes.

The Model Standards are aspirational in character. They describe good practices for family mediators. They are not intended to create legal rules or standards of liability.

The Model Standards include different levels of guidance:

1. Use of the term "may" in a Standard is the lowest strength of guidance and indicates a practice that the family mediator should consider adopting but which can be deviated from in the exercise of good professional judgment.

2. Most of the Standards employ the term "should," which indicates that the practice described in the Standard is highly desirable and should be departed from only with very strong reason.

3. The rarer use of the term "shall" in a Standard is a higher level of guidance to the family mediator, indicating that the mediator should not have discretion to depart from the practice described.

Standard I

A family mediator shall recognize that mediation is based on the principle of self-determination by the participants.

Standard II

A family mediator shall be qualified by education and training to undertake the mediation.

Standard III

A family mediator shall facilitate the participants' understanding of what mediation is and assess their capacity to mediate before the participants reach an agreement to mediate.

Standard IV

A family mediator shall conduct the mediation process in an impartial manner. A family mediator shall disclose all actual and potential grounds of bias and conflicts of interest reasonably known to the mediator. The participants shall be free to retain the mediator by an informed, written waiver of the conflict of interest. However, if a bias or conflict of interest clearly impairs a mediator's impartiality, the mediator shall withdraw regardless of the express agreement of the participants.

Standard V

A family mediator shall fully disclose and explain the basis of any compensation, fees, and charges to the participants.

Standard VI

A family mediator shall structure the mediation process so that the participants make decisions based on sufficient information and knowledge.

Standard VII

A family mediator shall maintain the confidentiality of all information acquired in the mediation process, unless the mediator is permitted or required to reveal the information by law or agreement of the participants.

Standard VIII

A family mediator shall assist participants in determining how to promote the best interests of children.

Standard IX

A family mediator shall recognize a family situation involving child abuse or neglect and take appropriate steps to shape the mediation process accordingly.

Standard X

A family mediator shall recognize a family situation involving domestic abuse and take appropriate steps to shape the mediation process accordingly.

Standard XI

A family mediator shall suspend or terminate the mediation process when the mediator reasonably believes that a participant is unable to effectively participate or for other compelling reasons.

Standard XII

A family mediator shall be truthful in the advertisement and solicitation for mediation.

Standard XIII

A family mediator shall acquire and maintain professional competence in mediation.

Association of Family and Conciliation Courts
6515 Grand Teton Plaza, Suite 210
Madison, WI 53719–1048
(608)664–3750; fax: (608)664–3751; e-mail: afcc@afccnet.org

INTRODUCTION TO UNIFORM MEDIATION ACT

A signpost of mediation's development is the Uniform Mediation Act (UMA). After many years of discussion, the act is set for a vote by the delegates of each state at the National Conference of Commissioners in the summer of 2001. If adopted, states can begin introducing legislation based on the UMA.

The members of the drafting committees of the National Conference of Commissioners on Uniform State Law (NCCUSL) and the American Bar Association (ABA) included judges, bar leaders, professors, and professionals with expertise in law reform and alternative dispute resolution. Nancy Rogers of Ohio State University was the coordinator of the ABA efforts, and Richard Reuben of the University of Missouri served as the reporter.

If you are interested in innovative career models, Ron Kelly, commercial and real estate mediator, broke the mold. Passionate and well versed in the issues surrounding mediator confidentiality and the author of California's groundbreaking legislation on the subject, Kelly has served as an official observer of the UMA process and operates a Web site (www.ronkelly.com) covering updates on this important development of mediation.

The proposed Uniform Mediation Act (UMA) covers many of the most important issues facing mediation. You should read and study the entire act as well as many of the eloquent articles written about individual provision. Some of the key issues covered by the act are:

- The key values and policy goals of the mediation process
- Definitions for commonly used terms and concepts in mediation
- A careful discussion of what types of mediations are not covered by the UMA
- The scope of confidentiality of communications in mediation and conditions in which confidentiality can be waived
- Acknowledgment that parties may have lawyers or other representatives at mediation sessions
- Use of electronic signatures
- Enforcement of mediated agreements

PROFESSIONAL MEDIATION TRAINING PROGRAMS

You can begin your mediation training at any time. The following list is a sample of some training available in the United States. Contact each training provider directly for information on scheduled courses, instructor backgrounds, fees, accreditations, and course content.

For a more comprehensive list of training programs, see the following Web sites, which have graciously granted permission to reprint resources found on those sites.

The Alternative Newsletter: www.mediate.com/tan
The Conflict Resolution Info Source: www.crinfo.org
Professional Mediation Training Programs:

AA White Dispute Resolution Institute, University of Houston
325 Melcher Hall, College of Business Administration
Houston, TX 77204-6283
(713)743-4933; fax: (713)743-4934

American West Institute for Conflict Resolution
48212 Clear Creek Road
Halfway, OR 97834
(541)742-6790 or (800)742-4090; fax: (541)742-5175;
e-mail: bphillips@mediate.com; Web site: www.mediate.com/baphillips

CDR Associates—Collaborative Decision Resources
100 Arapahoe Avenue, Suite 12
Boulder, CO 80302
(303)442-7367; fax: 303-442-7442, e-mail: cdr@mediate.org;
Web site: www.mediate.org

Center for Dispute Settlement
Web site: www.cdsusa.org/

Commercial Mediation Training
700 Larkspur Landing Circle, Suite 199
Larkspur, CA 94939
(415)464-4888; fax: (415)454-2004; e-mail: ebarker7@aol.com;
Web site: www.members.aol.com/ebarker7/training.html

Conflict Management Institute
2800 Williams Way
Santa Barbara, CA 93105
(805)569-2747; fax: 805-569-2758; e-mail: jmediate@silcom.com;
Web site: www.mediate.com/rubenstein

Conflict Resolution and Mediation Training
128 James Street, Second Floor
Geneva, IL 60134
(630)232-1886; fax: (630)232-1890

Erickson Mediation Institute
3800 West 80th Street, Suite 850
Minneapolis, MN 55431
(612)835-3688

40-Hour Family Mediation Training Institute
3117-B Edgewater Drive
Orlando, FL 32804
(407)650-8900; fax: (407)650-8811; e-mail: wpalmer7@aol.com

Dorothy J. Della Noce Mediation
3618 Golfview Drive
Mechanicsburg, PA 17055
(717)728-1206; fax: (717)728-0248; e-mail: dellanoce@ezonline.com;
Web site: www.mediate.com/dellanoce

Harvard Law School—Program on Negotiation
Center for Management Research
55 William Sreet
Wellesley, MA 02181
(617)239-1111

i-CASE: Interactive Case Studies
Web site: www.i-case.com/newweb/index.htm

J&L Human Systems
570 East Quail Run Road
Rockwall, TX 75087-7321
(972)771-9985; fax: (972)772-3669; e-mail: lynelley@cs.com

Karrass Programs
133 Stanford Street
Santa Monica, CA 90404-4164
(310)453-1806; fax: (800)232-8000

Key Bridge Foundation Center for Mediation
5335 Wisconsin Avenue, N.W., Suite 440
Washington, D.C. 20015
(202)274-1823 or (800)346-7643; e-mail@ keybridge.org;
Web site: www.keybridge.org

Mediation Center
P.O. Box 51119
Eugene, OR 97405
(503)345-1456, (800)JDAGREE; fax: (503)345-4024;
e-mail: jmelamed@mediate.com; Web site: www.to-agree.com

Mediation Consultants
55 Pine Street, Fourth Floor
Providence, RI 02903
(401)272-5300; e-mail: Kathybiffa@ids.net;
Web site: www.mediationconsultants.com

Mediation and Conflict Management Services
8000 Boxhomme, Suite 201
St. Louis, MO 63105
(314)721-4333; e-mail: rbenjamin@mediate.com;
Web site: www.mediate.com/benjamin

Mediation First, LLC
15600 Northeast Eighth Street, M.S. B1-133
Bellevue, WA 98008-3900
(425)562-9821; fax: (425)562-1194

Mediation Matters
1500 Highland Drive
Silver Spring, MD 20910-1526
(301)565-8284 or (800)905-2221; fax: (301)565-8285;
e-mail: cdschneider@conflictnet.org; Web site: www.mediation-matters.com

Mediation Training and Consultation Institute
e-mail: mtci@igc.org; Web site:www.aamediationcenter.com

Mediation Training and Consultation Institute
330 East Liberty, Suite 3A
Ann Arbor, MI 48104
(800)535-1155 or (734)663-1155; fax: (734)663-0524;
e-mail:info@learn2mediate.com; Web site: www.learn2mediate.com/

Mediation Training Institute International
Web site: www.mediationworks.com/mti/

Mosten Mediation Training
11661 San Vicente Boulevard, Penthouse Suite 1010
Los Angeles, CA 90049-5118
(310)571-3255 or (310)473-7611; fax: (310)820-1594 or (310)473-7422;
e-mail: mosten@mediate.com; Web site: www.MostenMediation.com

National Institute for Dispute Resolution
e-mail:margebaker@crenet.org

Northern California Mediation Center
100 Tamal Plaza, Suite 175
Corte Madera, CA 94925
(415)927-1422; fax: (415)927-1477; e-mail:ncmc@ncmc-mediate.org;
Web site: www.ncmc-mediate.org

Northern Virginia Mediation Service (NVMS)
Web site: www.gmu.edu/departments/nvms/

Nova Southeastern University
3301 College Avenue
Fort Lauderdale, FL 33314-7721
(954)262-3055; fax: (954)262-3968; e-mail: itkin@nsu.acast.nova.edu;
Web site: www.nova.edu/mediation

One Accord
Web site: www.oneaccordinc.com/

Pacific Family Mediation Institute
12025 Bel-Red Road, Suite 21
Bellevue, WA 98005
(425)451-7940; e-mail: sdearborn@seanet.com

Pepperdine University School of Law
Straus Institute for Dispute Resolution
Malibu, CA 90263
(310)456-4655; fax: (310)456-4437

San Diego Mediation Center
625 Broadway, Suite 1221
San Diego, CA 92101
(619)238-2400, fax: 619-238-8041; e-mail: sdmc@mediate.com;
Web site: www.mediate.com/sdmc

EDUCATIONAL PROGRAMS IN MEDIATION, CONFLICT RESOLUTION, AND PEACE STUDIES

In exploring your opportunities to obtain a degree or certificate, or just to take individual training courses, following is a sample of programs throughout the United States. For a more comprehensive list and descriptions and those programs outside the United States, see the following Web sites:

The Alternative Newsletter: www.mediate.com/tan
The Conflict Resolution Info Source: www.crinfo.org

Undergraduate Programs

Alma College
Undergraduate Minor in Peacemaking and Conflict Resolution
14 West Superior Street
Alma, MI 48801-1599
(517)463-7111; Web site: www.alma.edu/academics/peaceconflict/index.htm

Antioch College
Undergraduate Concentration in Peace Studies
795 Livermore Street
Yellow Springs, OH 45387
(937)767-7331; Web site: www.antioch-college.edu/Catalog/html/peacestudies.html

Associated Mennonite Biblical Seminary
Peace Studies Program
3003 Benham Avenue
Elkhart, IN 46517
(219)295-3726 or (800)964-2627; fax: (219)295-0092;
e-mail: admissions@ambs.edu; Web site: www.ambs.edu/MAPS.htm

Ball State University
Center for Peace Studies and Conflict Resolution
Muncie, IN 47306
(765)285-8739
e-mail: ASKBSU@ bsu.edu; Web site: www.bsu.edu/csh/history/program/id1.htm

Berkshire Community College
Undergraduate Concentration in Peace and World Order Studies
Pittsfield and Great Barrington, MA
Web site: cc.berkshire.org/perl-cgi/showPage.cgi?deptData+peace

Bowie State University
Center for Alternative Dispute Resolution
14000 Jericho Park Road
Bowie, MD 20715-9465
(301)464-3000; fax: (301)464-7521; e-mail: center_for_adr@bowiestate.edu

Brandeis University
Undergraduate Program in Peace and Conflict Studies
415 South Street
Waltham, MA 02454-9110
(781)736-2000; Web site: http://kutz60.kutz.brandeis.edu/AutoCat/
PAX-provisional.html

Brenau University
Conflict Resolution and Legal Studies Program
One Centennial Circle
Gainesville, GA 30501
(770)534-6297; Web site: www.brenau.edu/humanities/frank

California State University, Fresno
Peace and Conflict Studies Program
5150 North Maple Avenue
Fresno, CA 93740-8026
(559)278-4240

Clark University
Peace Studies Program
950 Main Street, Worcester, MA 01610
(508)793-7431 or (800)GO-CLARK, fax: (508)793-8821;
e-mail: admissions@clarku.edu;
Web site: copace.clarku.edu/programs/cagsinconflict.htm

Clarke College
Justice and Peace Studies Program
1550 Clarke Drive
Dubuque, IA 52001
(319)588-6300 or (800)383-2345; Web site: www.clarke.edu/academics/
departments/justice&peacestudies/index.htm

Colgate University
Peace Studies Program
13 Oak Drive
Hamilton, NY 13346
(315)228-7806; fax: (315)228-7121; e-mail: peace@mail.colgate.edu;
web site: departments.colgate.edu/peacestudies/default.htm

College of the Holy Cross
Peace and Conflict Studies
One College Street
Worcester, MA 01610-2395
http://sterling.holycross.edu/departments/CISS/website/homepage/Peace.html

College of Saint Benedict (CSB)/Saint John's University (SJU)
Department of Peace Studies
CSB: (320)363-5248, SJU: (320)363-2770; fax: CSB: (320)363-6099,
SJU: (320)363-3300/3298; e-mail: janderson@csbsju.edu;
Web site:www.csbsju.edu/peacestudies

Cornell University
Peace Studies Program
130 Uris Hall, Tower Road
Ithaca, NY 14853
(607)255-6484; fax: (607)254-5000; e-mail: psp@admin.is.cornell.edu;
Web sites: www.einaudi.cornell.edu/PeaceProgram,
www.einaudi.cornell.edu/Peace Program/minor.html

Eastern Mennonite University
Conflict Transformation Program, and Justice, Peace and Conflict Studies
1200 Park Road
Harrisonburg, VA 22802-2462
(540)432-4400; Web sites: www.emu.edu/ctp/ctp.htm,
www.emu.edu/ug_dean/catalog/jpcs/intro.htm

Fairfield University
Program in Peace and Justice Studies
1073 North Benson Road
Fairfield, CT 06430
(203)254-4000; Web site: www.fairfield.edu/ academic/artsci/majors/faith/
ugfphome.htm

Georgetown University
Program on Justice and Peace
324 New North
Washington, D.C. 20057-1131
(202)687-7647; fax: (202)687-5445; e-mail: jups@georgetown.edu;
Web Site: www.georgetown.edu/departments/pjp/

Goshen College
Peace Studies
1700 South Main Street
Goshen, IN 46526
(219)535-7000; Web site: www.goshen.edu/catalog/peace.html

Haverford College
Peace and Conflict Studies
370 Lancaster Avenue
Haverford, PA 19041-1392
(610)896-1000; e-mail: dallen@haverford.edu;
Web site: www.haverford.edu/pols/hcpeace/hcpeace.html

Humboldt State University
Institute for Study of ADR
University Annex 109
Arcata, CA 95521
(707)826-4750; fax: (707)826-5450; e-mail: isadr@axe.humboldt.edu;
Web site: www.humboldt.edu/~isadr

Iliff School of Theology
Justice and Peace Studies Program
2201 South University Boulevard
Denver, CO 80210
(303)744-1287; fax: (303)777-3387; Web site: www.iliff.edu/about_iliff/
special_programs.htm#justice_peace

Indiana State University
Conflict Resolution Programs
Terre Haute, IN 47809
(812)237-6311; Web site: homeroom.indstate.edu/crp/

James Madison University
Conflict and Mediation Studies
800 South Main Street
Harrisonburg, VA 22807
(540)568-6211; Web site: falcon.jmu.edu/~kimseywd/conflict/

Juniata College
Peace and Conflict Studies
1700 Moore Street
Huntingdon, PA 16652
(814)641-3000; fax: (814)641-3199; e-mail: info@juniata.edu;
Web site: departments.juniata.edu/pacs

Manchester College
Peace Studies Program
604 East College Avenue, North
Manchester, IN 46962
(219)982-5000; Web site: www.manchester.edu/academic/peace.html

Manhattan College
Peace Studies
Manhattan College Parkway
Riverdale, NY 10471
(718)862-7943; fax: (718)862-8044; e-mail: mgroarke@manhattan._edu;
Web site: www.manhattan.edu/arts/peace/peace.html

Nova Southeastern University
Department of Dispute Resolution, School of Social and Systemic Studies
3301 College Avenue
Fort Lauderdale, FL 33314
(954)262-3000 or (800)262-7978; fax: (954)262-3968;
e-mail: ssss@nova.edu; Web site: www.nova.edu/ssss/DR

Rockford College
Peace and Conflict Studies
5050 East State Street
Rockford, IL 61108
(815)226-4050 or (800)892-2984; fax: 815-226-4119;
Web site: www.rockford.edu/academic/catalog/peace/_peace.htm

San Diego State University
Undergraduate Major in International Security and Conflict Resolution
Nasatir Hall, Room 121
(619)594-2778; fax: (619)594-7302; Web site: http://www.sdsu.edu/
academicprog/_iscor.html

San Francisco State University
Global Peace, Human Rights, and Justice Studies
College of Humanities, International Relations, HSS384
1600 Holloway Avenue
San Francisco, CA 94132
(415)338-1448; Web Site: www.sfsu.edu/~bulletin/current/programs/global.htm

Siena College
Peace Studies Program
515 Loudon Road
Loudonville, NY 12211-1462
(518)783-2300; Web site: http://www.siena.edu/catalog/
PEACE_STUDIES_PROGRAM.htm

Swarthmore College
Peace and Conflict Studies
500 College Avenue
Swarthmore, PA 19081-1390
(610-328-8000; Web site: www.swarthmore.edu/Home/Academic/catalog/
dept/peace.html

Tufts University
Peace and Justice Studies Undergraduate Major or Certificate Program
113 Eaton Hall
Medford, MA 02155
(617)627-2470; e-mail: pjoseph1@emerald.tufts.edu;
Web site: ase.tufts.edu/pjs/

University of Idaho
Martin Institute for Peace and Conflict Research
1 Continuing Education Building
Moscow, ID 83844-3229
(208)885-6527; Web site: www.uidaho.edu/catalog/5mrtn.html

University of Minnesota
Center for Restorative Justice and Peacemaking
School of Social Work
1404 Gortner Avenue, 105 Peters Hall
St. Paul, MN 55108-6160
(612)624-4923; fax: (612)625-8224; e-mail: rjp@tlcmail.che.umn. edu;
Web site: ssw.che.umn.edu/rjp

Wayne State University
Center for Peace and Conflict Studies
2320 Faculty/Administration Building
Detroit, MI 48202
(313)577-3453; fax: (313)577-8269; e-mail: marie.olson@wayne.edu;
Web site: www.pcs.wayne.edu

Woodbury College
Mediation/Conflict Management
660 Elm Street
Montpellier, VT 05602
(802)229-0516 or (800)639-6039; fax: (802)229-2141;
e-mail: admiss@woodbury-college.edu;
Web site: www.woodbury-college.edu/public/Academics/mcm.html

Graduate Programs

Antioch University—McGregor School
M.A. Program in Conflict Resolution
Office of Admissions
800 Livermore Street
Yellow Springs, OH 45387
(937)767-6325; e-mail: admiss@ mcgregor.edu;
Web site: www.mcgregor. edu/imacr.html

Arcadia University
M.A. in International Peace and Conflict Resolution
450 S. Easton Road
Glenside, PA 19038
(215)572-2900; e-mail: admiss@arcadia.edu; Web site: www.arcadia.edu

Arizona State University
M.S. and Ph.D. in Justice Studies with a concentration in Dispute Resolution
School of Justice Studies
P.O. Box 870403
Tempe, AZ 85287-0403
(480)965-7682; fax: (480)965-9199;
Web site: www.asu.edu/copp/justice/home.htm

Bethany Theological Seminary
Master of Divinity or Master of Arts in Theology with an emphasis in Peace Studies
Graduate Peace Studies Program
615 National Road West
Richmond, IN 47374
(765)983-1800 or (800)BTS-8822; fax: (765)983-1840;
e-mail: bethanysem@aol.com; Web site: www.brethren.org/bethany/peace.htm

California State University, Dominguez Hills
Behavioral Science M.A. in Negotiation and Conflict Management
e-mail: midl@csudh.edu; Web site: www.csudh.edu/dominguezonline/BEH.htm

Columbia College of Columbia, South Carolina
M.A. in Conflict Resolution
Certificate of Advanced Graduate Studies in Conflict Resolution
Graduate Program in Conflict Resolution
1301 Columbia College Drive
Columbia, SC 29203
(803)786-3180 or (800)277-1301;
Web site: www.columbiacollegesc.edu/grad-conflict.html

Columbia University, Teachers College
M. A. and Ph.D. Social-Organizational Psychology with concentration in Conflict Resolution
International Center for Cooperation and Conflict Resolution
http://www.tc.columbia.edu/admissions/catalog/4programs/ITS/compare.htm
288 Grace Dodge, Box 171
525 West 120th Street
New York, NY 10027
(212)678-3972

Dallas Baptist University
M.A. in Organizational Management with a Concentration in Conflict Resolution Management
3000 Mountain Creek Parkway
Dallas, TX 75211
Web site: www.dbu.edu/graduate/maom_concentrations.html

Duquesne University
M.A. in Social and Public Policy with a Concentration and Certificate Program in
Conflict Resolution and Peace Studies
McAnulty Graduate School of Liberal Arts
215 College Hall
Pittsburgh, PA
(412)396-6400; fax: (412)396-5265; e-mail: socialpolicy@duq.edu;
Web sites: www.duq.edu/liberalarts/gradsocial/program.html,
www.duq.edu/liberalarts/ gradsocial/certificate.html

Fordham University
M. A, M. S, in Religion/Religious Education, Social Ministry/Education for Peace
and Justice
Graduate School of Religion and Religious Education
East Fordham Road (East 190th Street)
Bronx, NY 10458-5163
Web site: www.fordham.edu/gsre/grrb.html

George Mason University
Institute for Conflict Analysis and Resolution
4400 University Drive
Fairfax, VA 22030-4444
(703)993-1300; fax: (703)993-1302; e-mail:icarinfo@osf1.gmu.edu;
Web site: www.gmu.edu/departments/ICAR

Harvard University
Program for Health Care Negotiation and Conflict Resolution
Harvard School of Public Health, Division of Public Health Practice
1552 Tremont Street
Boston, MA 02120
(617)495-4000; fax: (617)495-8543; e-mail: jguzman@hsph.harvard.edu;
Web site: www.hsph.harvard.edu/php/PHCNCR/phcncr.html

John F. Kennedy University
M.A. in Counseling Psychology with a Specialization in Conflict Resolution
Graduate School of Professional Psychology
12 Altarinda Road
Orinda, CA 94563-2603
(925)254-0200; Web site: www.jfku.edu/psych/mac-overview.html

Leslie College
Master of Education Curriculum and Instruction Program, with a Specialization in Conflict Resolution and Peaceable Schools; Graduate Certificate in Conflict Resolution and Peaceable Schools; and M.A. or Graduate Certificate in Intercultural Relations, either with a Specialization in Intercultural Conflict Management
29 Everett Street
Cambridge, MA 02138-1790
(800)999-1959; Web sites: www.lesley.edu/soc/86curriculum. Html#peaceable, www.lesley.edu/soc/advanced_cert_html, www.lesley.edu/gsass/65irp.html

Marquette University
Center for Dispute Resolution Education
P.O. Box 1881
Wehr Physics, Room 107
Milwaukee, WI 53201-1881
(414)288-5535; Web site: www.marquette.edu/ disputeres

Montclair State University
M.A. in Legal Studies, Concentration in Dispute Resolution
Dickson Hall-Room 348
Upper Montclair, NJ 07043
(973)655-4152; fax: (973)655-7951;
Web site: www.chss. Montclair.edu/leclair/LS/dr.html

New York University
Robert F. Wagner Graduate School of Public Service
Program on Negotiation and Conflict Resolution
4 Washington Square North
New York, NY 10003
(212)998-7400; Web site: http://www.nyu.edu/wagner/research1e.html

Northwestern University
Dispute Resolution Research Center
Kellogg Graduate School of Management
386 Leverone Hall, 2001 Sheridan Road
Evanston, IL 60208-2011
(847)491-8068; fax: (847)491-8896; e-mail: drrc@.kellogg.nwu.edu;
Web site: www.kellogg.northwestern.edu/research/disp_res

Portland Community College
M. A. and M. S. in Conflict Resolution
Graduate Studies in Conflict Resolution/Philosophy Dept.
Portland State University
P.O. Box 751
Portland, OR 97207
(503)725-3000; Web site: www.conflictresolution.pdx.edu

Rutgers University
Center for Negotiation and Conflict Resolution
Bloustein School of Planning and Public Policy
33 Livingston Avenue, Suite 104
New Brunswick, NJ 098901-1985
(732)932-2487; fax: (732)932-2493; e-mail: cncr@rci.rutgers.edu;
Web site: policy.rutgers.edu/CNCR

Southern Methodist University
Graduate Certificate in Dispute Resolution
Extended and Continuing Studies
5236 Tennyson Parkway
Plano, TX 75024-3544
(972)473-3437; Web site: www.smu.edu/~dess/Dispute_Resolution/index2.html

Syracuse University
Program in Nonviolent Conflict and Change
410 Maxwell Hall
Syracuse, NY 13244
(315)443-2367; fax: (315) 443-3818;
Web site: www.maxwell.syr.edu/parc/pncc.htm

Trinity College and Seminary
Ph.D. in Conflict Management, Doctor of Ministry in Conflict Management, M.A.
in Conflict Management, and Certification Programs as Christian Conciliator or
Conflict Consultant

Trinity Theological Seminary
4233 Medwel Drive, P.O. Box 717
Newburgh, IN 47629-0717
(812)853-0611; e-mail: 75413.22@compuserve.com;
Web site: www.trinitysem.edu/tccm.

University of Baltimore
M.S. in Negotiations and Conflict Management
Center for Negotiations and Conflict Management
1420 North Charles Street
Baltimore, MD 21201-5779
(410)837-6566; e-mail: dmulcabev@ubmail.ubalt.edu;
Web site: www.ubalt.edu/cncm/

University of Massachusetts, Boston
M. A. in Dispute Resolution
Graduate Certificate Program in Dispute Resolution
Graduate Program in Dispute Resolution Law Center-Downtown Campus
100 Morrissey Blvd.
Boston, MA 02125
(617)287-7421; e-mail: disres@umb.edu;
Web site: http://www.umb.edu/academic_programs/graduate/cpcs/
dispute_resolution/

University of Minnesota
Conflict and Change Center
252 Hubert H. Humphrey Institute of Public Affairs
301 Nineteenth Avenue South
Minneapolis, MN 55455
(612)626-8910; fax: (612)625-3513; e-mail: admissions@hhh.umn.edu;
Web site: http://www.hhh.umn.edu/centers/conflict-change/

University of Missouri, St. Louis
Dispute Resolution Program
Department of Sociology, 362 SSB Building
8801 Natural Bridge Road
St. Louis, MO 63121
(314)516-6050; fax: (314)553-5268; e-mail: sgjmcca@umslvma.umsl.edu

Law School Programs
Capital University Law School
Center for Dispute Resolution
303 East Broad Street
Columbus, OH 43215-3200
(614)236-6310; fax: (614)236-6972;
Web site: www.law.capital.edu/ disputeresolution

Faulkner University Jones School of Law
Institute for Dispute Resolution
Admissions Office
5345 Atlanta Highway
Montgomery, AL 36109
(334)260-6210;
Web site: www.faulkner.edu/jonesschooloflaw/dispute_resolution/default.cfm

Franklin Pierce Law Center
Dispute Resolution Institute
2 White Street
Concord, NH 03301
(603)228-1541; Web site: www.fplc.edu/dri.htm

George Washington University Law School
LL.M. in Litigation and Dispute Resolution
2000 H Street, N.W.
Washington, D.C. 20052
(202)994-6260; e-mail: ils@main.nlc.gwu.edu (for graduates of foreign law schools) or grad@main. nlc.gwu.edu (for graduates of U.S. law schools); Web site: www.law.gwu.edu/acad/ litig.htm

Ohio State University College of Law
J.D. with Certificate in Dispute Resolution
Dispute Resolution Program
55 West Twelfth Avenue
Columbus, OH 43210
(614)292-2631; Web site:www.osu.edu/units/law/ADRbrochure.pdf

Pepperdine University School of Law
M.A. and Certificate in Dispute Resolution
Straus Institute for Dispute Resolution
Malibu, CA 90265
(310)456-4655; fax: (310)456-4437; Web site: law-www.pepperdine.edu/straus/

Southwest Texas State University
M.A. in Legal Studies with a concentration in Alternative Dispute Resolution
601 University Drive
San Marcos, TX 78666
(512)245-2111;
Web site: www.gradcollege.swt.edu/98-99MCatalog/
deptpoliticalsci.html#Legal_Studies

Stanford University Law School
Center on Conflict and Negotiation
Crown Quadrangle
Stanford, CA 94305
(650)723-2574; fax: (650)723-9421;
e-mail: bland@leland.stanford.edu;
Web site: www.stanford.edu/group/sccn

University of Wisconsin-Madison Law School
Disputes Processing Research Program
975 Bascom Mall
Madison, WI 53706
(608)262-2244; fax: (608)262-5486;
e-mail: galanger@law.wisc.edu;
Web site: www.law.wisc.edu/ILS/disputes.htm

Certificate Programs

Boise State University
Dispute Resolution Certificate Program
University Drive
Boise, ID 83725
(208)426-1011; Web site: www.idbsu.
edu/conted/Fall98/DisputeResolution_FA98.html

Bryn Mawr College Graduate School of Social Work and Social Research
Certificate Program in Conflict Resolution
101 North Merion Avenue
Bryn Mawr, PA 19010-2899
(610)526-5000; Web site: www.brynmawr.edu/gsswsr/conflict. html

California State University, Hayward
Communication and Conflict Resolution Certificate
Extended and Continuing Education Office
25800 Carlos Bee Boulevard, Warren Hall, Room 851
Hayward, CA 94542
(510)885-3605; fax: (510)885-4817; e-mail: std_ext@csuhayward.edu;
Web site: www.extension.csuhayward.edu/html/ccr.htm

City University of New York
John Jay College of Criminal Justice
Dispute Resolution Certificate
445 West 59th Street
New York, NY 10019
(212)237-8693; fax: (212)237-8742;
e-mail: dispute@jjay.cuny. edu, dispute@faculty.jjay.cuny.edu:
Web site: web.jjay.cuny.edu/~dispute

Clark University
College of Professional and Continuing Education
Certificate of Advanced Graduate Study in Conflict Management
950 Main Street
Worcester, MA 01610
(508)793-7217; e-mail: Jparent@ClarkU.edu;
Web site: copace.clarku.edu/programs/cagsinconflict.htm

Florida Atlantic University
Peace Studies Certificate
Web site: www.fau.edu/divdept/hist/PeaceStudies.htm

Golden Gate University
Graduate Certificate in Conflict Resolution
Department of Psychology
536 Mission Street
San Francisco, CA 94105-2968
(800)GGU-4YOU; fax: (415)442-7807; e-mail: kcarman@ggu.edu or info@ggu.edu;
Web site: www.ggu.edu/schools/ls%26pa/psychology/ma_a_psy.html#Anchor-3800

Indiana University
Certificate in Conflict Management
School of Public and Environmental Affairs
315 East Tenth Street
Bloomington, IN 47405
Web site: ww.indiana.edu/~speaweb/academics/certificates.html

Kennesaw State University
Alternative Dispute Resolution Certificate Program
College of Humanities and Social Sciences, Political Science and International Affairs
1000 Chastian Road
Kennesaw, GA 30144-5591
Web site: www/.Kennesaw.edu/pols/adr/index.htm

Long Island University
Conflict Resolution/Mediation Certificate Program
Brooklyn Campus School of Continuing Studies
1 University Plaza, Brooklyn, NY 11201-8423
e-mail: Info-scs@brooklyn.liu.edu; Web site:
www.brooklyn.liunet.edu/cwis/bklyn/bbut05/sprbul99/counsel/conflict.html

New Hampshire Technical Institute
Certificate in Conflict Resolution and Mediation
11 Institute Drive, Concord, NH 03301-7412
603-271-6951; e-mail:
epederson@tec.nh.us; Web site: www.conc.tec.nh.us/frames_CnflctRes.htm

Oregon State University
Certificate Program in Peace Studies
c/o Speech Communication, 204 Shepard Hall
Corvallis, OR 97331-6199
(541)737-2461; Web site: osu.orst.edu/dept/gencat/coldep/libarts/peace/peace.htm

Saint Xavier University
Certificate Program through the Center for Conflict Resolution
3700 West 103rd Street
Chicago, IL 60655
(773)298-3000, ext. 3555; fax: (773)298-3314; e-mail: Cooper@sxu.edu

Sonoma State University
Conflict Resolution Certificate Program
1801 East Cotati Avenue
Rohnert Park, CA 94928
(707)664-2880;
Web site: www.sonoma.edu/ExEd/CertificateProgram/cnflprog1.html

Tufts University
Peace and Justice Studies
113 Eaton Hall
Medford, MA 02155
(617)627-2470; e-mail: pjoseph1@emerald.tufts.edu; Web site: ase.tufts.edu/pjs/

University of Akron
Center for Conflict Management
Certificate Program
Leigh Hall 201
Akron, OH 44325-6234
(330)972-7008; fax: (330)972-5263; e-mail: conmang@nakron.edu;
Web site: //gozips.nakron.edu/~conmang/

Graduate Certificate in Divorce Mediation
302 East Butchell Mall
Akron, OH 44325
web site: www.nakron.edu/gradsch/gradbull.html

MEDIATION WEB SITES

You can learn about the field of mediation and career opportunities by checking out a number of Web sites on mediation generally and sites that promote mediation services, training, and related issues and programs. Because Web sites change constantly, contact the following resources for more comprehensive listings, and do your own up-to-date search on the Web:

Academy of Family Mediators, www.mediators.org

The Alternative Newsletter, www.mediate.com/tan

The Conflict Resolution Info Source, www.crinfo.org

Mediation Information and Resource Center, www.mediate.com

Mediation On-Line Newsletter, adrr.com/adr9/mediation.htm (provides links to ADR Web sites)

Mosten Mediation—Books, www.MostenMediation.com

National Center for State Courts, www.nscs.dni.us/library

Online Mediation Resources, www.firstmediation.com

Readings in Dispute Resolution: A Selected Bibliography by Catherine Morris, www.peacemakers.ca/bibliography/bibintro99.html

Resolution Bookshop, www.resolutionbookshop.com

The Resolution Bookstore, www.mediate.com/resource/

Society Of Professionals in Dispute Resolution, www.spidr.org

BOOKS ON MEDIATION THEORY AND PRACTICE

Acland, A. *A Sudden Outbreak of Common Sense: Managing Conflict Through Mediation.* London: Hutchinson, 1990.

Bennett, M. D., and Hermann, M.S.G. *The Art of Mediation.* Notre Dame, Ind.: National Institute of Trial Advocacy, 1996.

Bodine, R., and Crawford, D. *The Handbook of Conflict Resolution Education.* San Francisco: Jossey-Bass, 1997.

Boulle, L. *Mediation: Principles, Process, and Practice.* Charlottesville, Va.: Butterworths, 1997.

Brown, H., and Marriott, A. *ADR Principles and Practice.* London: Sweet and Maxwell, 1993.

Brown, L. M. *Lawyering Through Life.* Littleton, Colo.: Rothman and Company, 1986.

Brunet, E., and Craver, C. B. *Alternative Dispute Resolution: The Advocate's Perspective.* Charlottesville, Va.: Michie, 1997.

Burne, S. *Flipchart Power.* San Francisco: Jossey-Bass.

Burton, J. W. *Resolving Deep Rooted Conflict: A Handbook.* Lanham, Md.: University Press of America, 1987.

Burton, J., and Dukes, F. (eds.). *Conflict: Readings in Management and Resolution.* New York: St. Mary's Press, 1990.

Bush, R. B., and Folger, J. P. *The Promise of Mediation: Responding to Conflict Through Empowerment and Recognition.* San Francisco: Jossey-Bass, 1994.

Charlton, R., and Dewdney, M. *The Mediation Handbook.* Holmes Beach, Fla.: Wm. W. Grant and Sons, 1995.

Cloke, K. *Revenge and the Magic of Forgiveness.* Santa Monica, Calif.: Center for Dispute Resolution, 1990.

Cloke, K. *Mediating Dangerously.* San Francisco: Jossey-Bass, 2000.

Cloke, K., and Goldsmith, J. *Resolving Personal and Organizational Conflict.* San Francisco: Jossey-Bass, 2000.

Deutsch, M., and Coleman, P. *The Handbook of Conflict Resolution: Theory and Practice.* San Francisco: Jossey-Bass, 2000.

Dingwell, R., and Eckelaar, J. (eds.). *Divorce Mediation and the Legal Process.* Oxford: Clarendon Press, 1988.

Edelman, J., and Crain, M. B. *The Tao of Negotiation.* New York: Oxford University Press, 1993.

Erickson, S. K., and McKnight, M. S. *The Practitioner's Guide to Mediation: A Client Centered Approach.* New York: Wiley, 2000.

Folberg, J., and Milne, A. (eds.). *Divorce Mediation: Theory and Practice.* New York: Guilford Press, 1988.

Folberg, J., and Taylor, A. *Mediation: A Comprehensive Guide to Resolving Conflicts Without Litigation.* San Francisco: Jossey-Bass, 1984.

Freeman, M. *Alternative Dispute Resolution.* New York: New York University Press, 1995.

Friedman, G. J. *A Guide to Divorce Mediation: How to Reach a Fair, Legal Settlement at a Fraction of the Cost.* New York: Workman, 1993.

Galton, E. *Representing Clients in Mediation.* Dallas: American Lawyer Media, 1994.

Golan, D. *Mediating Legal Disputes: Effective Strategies for Lawyers and Mediators.* New York: Little, Brown, 1996.

Goldberg, S., Sander, F., and Rogers, N. (eds.). *Dispute Resolution: Negotiation, Mediation and Other Processes* (2nd ed.). New York: Little, Brown, 1992.

Haynes, J. M. *The Fundamentals of Family Mediation.* Albany, N.Y.: State University of New York Press, 1996.

Kovach, K. K. *Mediation: Principles and Practice.* St. Paul: West, 2000.

Kressel, K., and Pruitt, D. (eds.). *Mediation Research: The Process and Effectiveness of Third Party Intervention.* San Francisco: Jossey-Bass, 1989.

Lang, M., and Taylor, A. *The Making of a Mediator.* San Francisco: Jossey-Bass, 2000.

Lederach, J. P. *The Journey Toward Reconciliation.* Scottdale, Penn.: Herald Press, 1999.

Levine, S. *Getting to Resolution: Turning Conflict into Collaboration.* San Francisco: Berrett-Koehler, 2000.

Levinson J. C., Smith, M.S.A., Wilson, O. R. *Guerrilla Negotiating: Unconventional Weapons and Tactics to Get What You Want.* New York: Wiley, 1999.

Leviton, S. C., and Greenstone, J. L. *Elements of Mediation.* Pacific Grove, Calif.: Brooks/Cole, 1997.

Mackie, K. (ed.). *A Handbook on Dispute Resolution: ADR in Action.* New York: Routledge, 1991.

Maggiola, W. *Techniques of Mediation.* Dobbs Ferry, N.Y.: Oceana, 1985.

Mayer, B. *The Dynamics of Conflict Resolution.* San Francisco: Jossey-Bass, 2000.

McFarlane, J. *Rethinking Disputes: The Mediation Alternative.* London: Cavendish, 1997.

McFarlane, J. *Dispute Resolution Readings and Case Studies.* Toronto: Edmond Montgomery Publications, 1999.

Mnookin, R. H., Peppet, S. R., Tulumello, A. S. *Beyond Winning: Negotiating to Create Value in Deals and Disputes,* Cambridge, Mass.: Belknap Press, 2000.

Moore, C. *The Mediation Process: Practical Strategies for Resolving Conflict,* San Francisco: Jossey-Bass, 1996.

Mosten, F. S. *The Complete Guide to Mediation.* Chicago: American Bar Association, 1997.

Mosten, F. S. *Unbundling Legal Services.* Chicago: American Bar Association, 2000.

Murray, J., Rau, A., and Sherman, E. *Process of Dispute Resolution: The Role of Lawyers.* Westbury, N.Y.: Foundation Press, 1989.

Noble, C. *Family Mediation: A Guide for Lawyers.* Canada Law Book, 1999.

Parkinson, L. *Family Mediation.* London: Sweet and Maxwell, 1999.

Riskin, L. L., and Westbrook, J. E. *Dispute Resolution and Lawyers* (2nd ed.). St. Paul: Minn.: West Group, 1998.

Rogers, N. H., and McEwen, C. A. *Mediation: Law, Policy and Practice.* (2nd ed.) Deerfield, Ill.: Clark Boardman Callaghan, 1994.

Rogers, N. H., and Salem, R. *A Student's Guide to Mediation and the Law.* New York: Matthew Bender, 1987.

Rothman, J. D. *A Lawyer's Practical Guide to Mediation.* Kearney, Neb.: Morris Pub., 1995

Saposnek, D. *Mediating Child Custody Disputes.* (Rev. ed.) San Francisco: Jossey-Bass, 1998.

Sarat, A., and Felstiner, W. *Divorce Lawyers and Their Clients.* New York: Oxford University Press, 1995.

Schön, D. *The Reflective Practitioner.* San Francisco: Jossey-Bass, 1987.

Shaffer, T. *Client Interviewing and Counseling in a Nutshell.* St. Paul, Minn.: West, 1987.

Slalkeu, K. A. *When Push Comes to Shove: A Practical Guide to Mediating Disputes.* San Francisco: Jossey-Bass, 1996.

Sochynsky, Y., and Baird, M. (eds.). *California ADR Practice Guide.* (4th ed.) New York: McGraw-Hill, 1995.

Ury, W. *The Third Side: Why We Fight and How We Can Stop.* Penguin Books, 1999.

Windslade, J., and Monk, G. *Narrative Mediation: A New Approach to Conflict Resolution.* San Francisco: Jossey-Bass, 2000.

Wisconsin Association of Mediators. *Self-Assessment Tool for Mediators.* 1998.

Yarn, D. H. *The Dictionary of Conflict Resolution.* San Francisco: Jossey-Bass, 1999.

CLIENT GUIDES TO MEDIATION

Bienenfeld, F. *Do-It-Yourself Conflict Resolution for Couples : Dynamic New Ways for Couples to Heal Their Own Relationships.* Franklin Lakes, N.J.: Career Press, 2000.

Bolton, R. *People Skills: How to Assert Yourself, Listen to Others and Resolve Conflicts.* New York: Simon & Schuster, 1987.

Butler, C. A., and Walker, D. D. *The Divorce Mediation Answer Book.* New York: Kodansha International, 1999.

Crowley, T. E. *Settle It out of Court: How to Resolve Business and Personal Disputes Using Mediation, Arbitration, and Negotiation.* New York: Wiley, 1994.

Fisher, R., Ury, W., and Patton, J. *Getting to Yes.* New York: Penguin Books, 1996.

Goodpaster, G. *A Guide to Negotiation and Mediation.* Irvington-on-Hudson, N.Y.: Transnational, 1997.

Levine, S. *Getting to Resolution: Turning Conflict into Collaboration.* San Francisco: Berrett-Koehler, 1998.

Potter, B. *From Conflict to Cooperation: How to Mediate a Dispute.* Berkeley, Calif.: Ronin, 1996.

Stoner, K. *Using Divorce Mediation: Save Your Money and Your Sanity.* Berkeley, Calif.: Nolo Press, 1999.

Talia, M. S. *A Client's Guide to Limited Legal Services.* San Ramon, Calif.: Nexus Publishing Co., 1997.

BOOKS ON MEDIATION PRACTICE
MARKETING AND MANAGEMENT

Abrams, R. M. *The Successful Business Plan: Secrets and Strategies.* Grants Pass, Ore.: Oasis Press, 1993.

Adams, J. L. *Conceptual Blockbusting: A Guide to Better Ideas.* Perseus Press, 1990.

Alfini, J. J., and Galton, E. R. *ADR Personalities and Practice Tips.* Chicago: American Bar Association, 1998.

Anderson, A. *Marketing Your Practice.* Chicago: American Bar Association Section of Law Practice Management, 1987.

Bergman, P., and Berman-Barrett, S. J. *Represent Yourself in Court: How to Prepare and Try a Winning Case.* Berkeley, Calif.: Nolo Press, 1993.

Berry, L. L., and Parasuraman, A. *Marketing Services: Competing Through Quality.* New York: Free Press, 1991.

Binder, D., Bergman, P., and Price, S. *Lawyers as Counselors: A Client-Centered Approach.* St. Paul, Minn.: West Publishing Co., 1991.

Crandall, R. *Marketing Your Services for People Who Hate to Sell.* Lincolnwood, Ill.: Contemporary Books, 1996.

Crandall, R. *1001 Ways to Market Your Services.* Lincolnwood, Ill.: Contemporary Books, 1997.

Davidson, J. *Avoiding the Pitfalls of Starting Your Own Business.* New York: Walker, 1988.

Denny, R., and James, C. S. *Action Steps to Marketing Success.* Chicago: American Bar Association Section of Law Practice Management, 1992.

Foonberg, J. *How to Start and Build a Law Practice.* Chicago: American Bar Association Section of Law Practice Management, 1998.

Goldblatt M. *Writing Your Law Firm Newsletter.* Chicago: American Bar Association, 1987.

Harper, S. *The McGraw-Hill Guide to Starting Your Own Business.* New York: McGraw-Hill, 1991.

Holland, P. *The Entrepreneur's Guide: How to Start and Succeed in Your Own Business.* New York: Putnam, 1984.

Hornsby, W. E. *Marketing and Legal Ethics.* Chicago: American Bar Association, 2000.

James, P. *Marketing and Maintaining a Family Law Mediation Practice.* American Lawyer Media, 1994.

Karlson, D. *Marketing Your Consulting or Professional Services.* Menlo Park, Calif.: Crisp Publications, 1988.

Kishel, G., and Kishel, P. G. *How to Start, Run, and Stay in Business.* New York: Wiley, 1981.

Kolb, D. M. *The Mediators.* Cambridge, Mass.: MIT Press, 1983.

Kolb, D. *When Talk Works: Profiles of Mediators.* San Francisco: Jossey-Bass, 1997.

Lawson, J. *The Complete Internet Handbook for Lawyers.* Chicago: American Bar Association, 1999.

Levinson, J. C. *Guerilla Marketing.* Boston: Houghton Mifflin, 1984.

Levinson, J. C. *Attack.* Boston: Houghton Mifflin, 1989.

Levinson, J. C. *Guerilla Marketing Excellence.* Boston: Houghton Mifflin, 1993.

Leza, R., and Placencia, J. *Develop Your Business Plan.* Grants Pass, Ore.: Oasis Press, 1982.

Mancuso, A. *Nolo's Quick LLC.* Berkeley, Calif.: Nolo Press, 2000.

Mancuzo, J. *How to Start, Finance, and Manage Your Own Small Business.* Upper Saddle River, N.J.: Prentice Hall, 1984.

McDonald, M.H.B., and Payne, A. *Marketing Planning for Services.* Boston: Butterworth-Heinemann, 1997.

McKeefer, M. *Small Business Start Up: How to Write a Business Plan.* Berkeley, Calif.: Nolo Press, 1988.

Mosten, F. S. *Operating a Profitable Mediation Practice.* Los Angeles: Mosten Mediation Training, 1998.

Munneke, G. A., and MacNaughton, A. L. *Multidisciplinary Practice: Staying Competitive and Adapting to Change.* Chicago: American Bar Association, 2000.

Paine, A. *The Essence of Services Marketing.* Upper Saddle River, N.J.: Prentice Hall, 1993.

Peters, T. *Thriving on Chaos.* New York: HarperCollins, 1987.

Peters, T. *The Circle of Innovation.* New York: Knopf, 1997.

Phillips, M., and Rasberry, S. *Marketing Without Advertising.* Berkeley, Calif.: Nolo Press, 1998.

Putman, A. O. *Marketing Your Services.* New York: Wiley, 1990.

Raridon, S. *Basics for Writing Your Law Firm Brochure.* Chicago: American Bar Association Section of Law Practice Management, 1987.

Reed, R. *Beyond the Billable Hour.* Chicago: American Bar Association Section of Law Practice Management, 1989.

Ross, M., and Ross, T. *Big Ideas for a Small Service Business: How to Successfully Advertise, Publicize, and Maximize Your Business or Professional Practice.* Buena Vista, Colo.: Communicating Creativity, 1994.

Schmidt, S. J. *Marketing the Law Firm: Business Development Techniques.* New York: Law Journal Seminars Press, 1991.

Steingold, F. S. *Legal Guide for Starting and Running a Small Business.* Berkeley, Calif.: Nolo Press, 2001.

Steingold, F., and Portman, J. *Leasing Space for Your Small Business.* Berkeley, Calif.: Nolo Press, 2001.

Susskind, R. *The Future of Law: Facing the Challenges of Information Technology.* New York: Oxford University Press, 1996.

Wert, R. C., and Hatoff, H. I. *Law Office Policy and Procedures Manual.* (4th ed.) Chicago: American Bar Association, 1996.

Following is a sample of mediation organizations. Contact them directly to find out about their conferences, educational programs, newsletters policy initiatives, membership requirements, publications, staff and volunteer leadership, and costs.

If you want to find out about many more organizations in the mediation and conflict resolution field in the United States and in other countries, check out the following Web sites:

The Conflict Resolution Info Source, www.crinfo.org

The Alternative Newsletter, www.mediate.com/tan

Mediation And Information Resource Center, www.mediate.com

MEMBERSHIP ORGANIZATIONS

Association for Conflict Resolution, www.acr.org

Association of Family and Conciliation Courts, afcc@afccnet.org, www.afccnet.org

Australian Family Mediation Association, dawnr@vla.vic.gov.au

Canadian Bar Association—ADR Section, www.cba.org/Sect_template.asp?Section=ADR

Center for Conflict Resolution, www.chicagobar.org/attorney/cbf/volunteer.html

Connecticut Bar Association, Alternative Dispute Resolution Section, www.ctbar.org

Costa Rican ADR Association, jlopezd@sol.racsa.co.cr

Family Mediation Canada/Médiation Familiale Canada, fmc@fmc.ca, www.fmc.ca

Family Mediators Association, info@familymediators.co.uk; Web site: www.familymediators.co.uk

International Alliance of Holistic Lawyers, info@iahl.org, www.iahl.org

International Bar Association, confs@int-bar.org, www.ibanet.org

Maine Association of Dispute Resolution Professionals, www.madrp.org

Maine State Bar Association (ADR Section), www.mainebar.org/pages/section-15.html

Mediation Network of North Carolina, mnnc@mnnc.org, www.mnnc.org

Mediation UK mediationuk, @cix.compTXink.co.uk

National Association for Community Mediation, nafcm@nafcm.org, www.nafcm.org

National Conference on Peacemaking and Conflict Resolution, ncpcr@apeacemaker.org, www.apeacemaker.org

New England SPIDR, ChuckDoran@MWI.org, www.igc.org/nespidr/ne03000.htm

New Jersey Association of Professional Mediators, info@njapm.org, www.njapm.org

New Jersey State Bar Association Dispute Resolution Section, info@njsba.com, www.njsba.com

New York State Dispute Resolution Association, Inc., nysdra@nysdra.org, www.nysdra.org

Quaker Peace Centre, qpc@wn.apc.org, www.quaker.org/capetown

San Diego Mediation Center, sdmc@mediate.com, www.mediate.com/sdmc

Society of Professionals in Dispute Resolution, spidr@spidr.org, www.spidr.org

South Australia Dispute Resolution Association, david.baker@unisa.edu.au, www.ausdispute.unisa.edu.au/SADRA.htm

South Dakota Mediation Association, dspader@usd.edu, www.usd.edu/sdma

Southern California Mediation Association, www.scmediation.org

State Bar of Michigan ADR Section, Sartinian@Dykema.com, www.michbar.org/sections/adrs

State Bar of Texas Alternative Dispute Resolution Section, www.texasadr.org

Victim Offender Mediation Association, voma@voma.org, www.voma.org

Victoria Association for Dispute Resolution, www.ausdispute.unisa.edu.au

MEDIATION SERVICES PROVIDERS

Asheville Mediation Center, tmc@buncombe.main.nc.us, www.main.nc.us/tmc/training/training.html

Bond University Dispute Resolution Centre, DRC@bond.edu.au, www.bond.edu.au/law/centres/index.htm

Cambridge Dispute Settlement Center, Inc., www.cambridgedispute.org

Center for Conflict Resolution at Salisbury State University, mamccormick@ssu.edu, http://campus-ministry.org/ccr

Center for Dispute Resolution at Capital University Law School, dispute-resolution@law.capital.edu, www.law.capital.edu/news/index.htm

Center for Dispute Resolution at the University of New Haven, boardman@cahrger.newhaven.edu, www.newhaven.edu

Centre for Dispute Resolution, mediate@cedr.co.uk, www.cedr.co.uk

Conflict Resolution Center at the University of North Dakota, udcrc@badlands.nodak.edu, www.und.nodak.edu/dept/crc

CPR Institute for Dispute Resolution, info@cpradr.org, www.cpradr.org

Cybersettle, support@cybersettle.com, www.csdocket.com

Danish Centre for Conflict Resolution, ceko@post3.tele.dk, www.cfk.sutie.dk

Dispute Management, Inc., office@dispute-management.com, www.dispute-management.com

Erickson Mediation Institute, emi@ericksonmediation.com, www.ericksonmediation.com

Federal Mediation and Conciliation Service, publicinformation, @fmcs.gov, www.fmcs.gov

Florida Dispute Resolution Center, burlisod@flcourts.org

Institute for International Mediation and Conflict Resolution, info@iimcr.org, www.iimcr.org

Institute for Organizational and Personal Transformation, Inc., pkestner@igc.apc.org or www.i-opt.com

JAMS: The Resolution Experts, www.jamsadr.com

Key Bridge Foundation for Education and Research, mail@keybridge.org, www.keybridge.org

Lancaster Mediation Center, lancmed@ptdprolog.net

Mediation Center, agree@conflictnet.org, www.to-agree.com

Mennonite Conciliation Service, mcs@mccus.org

Montgomery County Mediation Center, mcmpeace@aol.com

Mosten Mediation Centers, www.MostenMediation.com

National Network of Violence Prevention Practitioners, NNVPP@edc.org, www.edc.org/HHD/NNVPP

New Jersey Society of Professionals in Dispute Resolution, bginnj@aol.com

New Zealand Institute for Dispute Resolution, Ian.Macduff@vuw.ac.nz, www.vuw.ac.nz/nzidr

Northern Virginia Mediation Service, www.gmu.edu/departments/nvms/training.htm

Technology Mediation Services, ssellers@technologymediation.com, www.technologymediation.com

Utah State Courts Mediation Program, patrm@email.utcourts.gov, courtlink.utcourts.gov/mediation

Victim Offender Reconciliation Program, vorp@fresno.edu, vorp.org

West Virginia Center for Dispute Resolution, wvcdr@sbccom.com

West Virginia State Bar Mediation Referral Service and Alternative Dispute Resolution Committee, pettyc@wvbar.org, www.wvbar.org/barinfo/fyi/medref.htm

PUBLIC INTEREST ORGANIZATIONS

Arkansas Alternative Dispute Resolution Commission, courts.state.ar.us/adr/index.html

Australian Dispute Resolution Directory, www.ausdispute.unisa.edu.au

Austrian Study Center for Peace and Conflict Resolution, aspr@aspr.ac.at, www.aspr.ac.at

California Center for Public Dispute Resolution, sacjean@saclink.csus.edu, www.csus.edu/ccpdr

California Dispute Resolution Institute, www.cdrc.net/cdri_index.htm

Campus Mediation Resources, w.warters@wayne.edu, www.mtds.wayne.edu/campus.html

Cardozo Online Journal of Conflict Resolution, www.cardozo.yu.edu/cojcr/index.html

Carter Center, scallah@emory.edu, www.cartercenter.org

CDR Associates, cdr@mediate.org, www.mediate.org

Center for African Peace and Conflict Resolution/California State University, uwazieee@csus.edu, www.csus.edu/org/afpeace/capcr3.html

Center for Alternative Dispute Resolution, The Judiciary, State of Hawaii, ekent@hawaii.edu, www.hawaii.gov/jud

Center for Applied Conflict Management, jmaxwell@kent.edu, www.kent.edu/cacm

Center for Conflict Resolution at Loyola University School of Law, www.lls.edu

Center for Information Technology and Dispute Resolution at the University of Massachusetts, katsh@legal.umass.edu, www.umass.edu/dispute

Center for International Development and Conflict Management at the University of Maryland, ewilson@bss2.umd.edu, www.bsos.umd.edu/cidcm

Center for Peace Research and Strategic Studies, luc.reychler@soc.kTXeuven.ac.be, www.kTXeuven.ac.be/facdep/social/pol/cvo/cvo.htm

Center for Peacemaking and Conflict Studies at Fresno Pacific University, rlclaass@fresno.edu, www.fresno.edu/pacs

Center for the Prevention of School Violence at North Carolina State University, pamela_riley@ncsu.edu, www.ncsu.edu/cpsv

Center for Public Policy Dispute Resolution/University of Texas School of Law, jsummer@mail.law.utexas.edu, www.utexas.edu/law/admissions/addprograms.html#cppdr

Center for Restorative Justice & Peacemaking at the University of Minnesota rjp@tlcmail.che.umn.edu, http://ssw.che.umn.edu/rjp

Center for the Study of Dispute Resolution at the University of Missouri School of Law, umclawcdr@missouri.edu, www.law.missouri.edu/csdr

Center for the Study and Prevention of Violence/Institute of Behavioral Science/University of Colorado, cspv@colorado.edu, www.colorado.edu/cspv

Children's Creative Response to Conflict, prisjudcrc@aol.com, http://eric-web.tc.columbia.edu/directories/ anti-bias/ccrc.html

City University of New York Dispute Resolution Consortium dispute, @jjay.cuny.edu, web.jjay.cuny.edu/~dispute

Colorado Office of Dispute Resolution, cynthia.savage@judicial.state.co.us

Conflict Analysis and Management Division of Royal Roads University, rruconflict@royalroads.ca, www.royalroads.ca/macam

Conflict Analysis and Transformation Program at Eastern Mennonite University, zimmermr@emu.edu

Conflict Management Research Group of the University of South Australia, dale.bagshaw@unisa.edu.au, www.ausdispute.unisa.edu.au

Conflict Research Consortium at the University of Colorado, crc@colorado.edu, www.colorado.edu/conflict

Conflict Resolution Education Network, crenet@crenet.org, www.crenet.org

Conflict Resolution Information Source, www.crinfo.org

Conflict Resolution Network, crn@crnhq.org, www.crnhq.org

Conflict Resolution Resource Center, www.conflict-resolution.net

Consensus Building Institute, cconsensus@igc.org, www.cbi-web.org

Consortium on Peace Research Education and Development at George Mason University, copred@gmu.edu, www.gmu.edu/departments/ICAR/copred

Cornell PERC Institute on Conflict Resolution, DBL4@cornell.edu, www.ilr.cornell.edu/depts/ICR

Department of Dispute Resolution Services, Office of the Executive Secretary, Supreme Court of Virginia, www.courts.state.va.us

Dispute Resolution Services, chris.honeyman@ibm.net, www.convenor.com

Disputes Processing Research Program at the Institute for Legal Studies, University of Wisconsin Law School, www.law.wisc.edu

Eastern Mennonite University Conflict Transformation Program, jantziv@emu.edu, www.emu.edu/ctp/ctp.htm

Educators for Social Responsibility, www.esrnational.org

European Platform for Conflict Prevention and Transformation, uconflict@euconflict.org, www.euconflict.org

Florida Conflict Resolution Consortium, flacrc@mailer.fsu.edu, http://consensus.fsu.edu

Florida Growth Management Conflict Resolution Consortium, http://consensus.fsu.edu

Georgia Office of Dispute Resolution, bartona@mindspring.com, www.agree.org/state/georgia.html

Hawaii State Judiciary's Center for Alternative Dispute Resolution, ekent@shawaii.edu, www.hawaii.gov/jud

Illinois Institute for Dispute Resolution/National Center for Conflict Resolution Education/National Peaceable School Project, info@nccre.org, www.nccre.org

Indiana Conflict Resolution Institute at Indiana University, lbingham@indiana.edu, www.spea.indiana.edu/icri

Initiative on Conflict Resolution and Ethnicity, incore@incore.TXst.ac.uk, www.incore.TXst.ac.uk

Institute for MTXti-Track Diplomacy, imtd@imtd.org, www.imtd.org

Interconflict Center for Conflict Information contact@conflict.com, www.conflict.com/Interconflict.htm

International ADR info@internationalADR.com, www.internationaladr.com/ab.htm

International Association for Conflict Management, Conflict and Change Center, at the University of Minnesota, iacm@gold.tc.umn.edu, www.oneworld.org/euconflict/guides/orgs/am_n/229.htm

International Association for Public Participation, iap2hq@pin.org

International Center for Cooperation and Conflict Resolution at Columbia University, ldm15@columbia.edu or dbwl18@columbia.edu, www.tc.columbia.edu/~icccr

International Conflict Resolution Centre at the University of Melbourne, icrc@psych.unimelb.edu.au, www.psych.unimelb.edu.au/icrc/index.html

International Ombudsman Institute, dcallan@law.ualberta.ca, www.law.ualberta.ca/centres/ioi

International Peace Research Association, bmoeller@copri.dk, www.copri.dk/ipra/ipra.html

Joan B. Kroc Institute for International Peace Studies at the University of Notre Dame, krocinst@nd.edu, http://www3.nd.edu/~krocinst

Lombard Mennonite Peace Center, admin@lmpeacecenter.org

Massachusetts Office of Dispute Resolution, fredie.kay@state.ma.us, www.state.ma.us/modr

Mediation Information and Resource Center, mediate@mediate.com, www.mediate.com

Mediation Law Project, clement.1@osu.edu, www.stanford.edu/group/sccn/mediation

National Peace Council, peace2@sri.lanka.net, www.peace-srilanka.org

New Jersey Council for Children's Rights, Info@NJCCR.org, www.njccr.org

New York State ADR Office, www.courts.state.ny.us/adr

New York State Forum on Conflict and Consensus, ajz1@is3.nyu.edu, www.capital.net/~jerryn

North Carolina Dispute Resolution Commission, leslie.ratliff@aoc.state.nc.us, www.aoc.state.nc.us/www/drc

Ohio Commission of Dispute Resolution and Conflict Management, www.state.oh.us/cdr

Oregon Dispute Resolution Commission, odrc.mail@state.or.us, www.odrc.state.or.us

Peace Games, eric@peacegames.org, www.peacegames.org

Peace Watch,usip_requests@usip.org, www.usip.org

Public Disputes Resolution Program and Institute of Government at the University of North Carolina, Chapel Hill, stephens@iogmail.iog.unc.edu, http://ncinfo.iog.unc.edu/dispute

Refugee Conflict Management Project, www.fresno.edu/pacs/refugee

Research Annual on Dispute Resolution, s-nagel@uiuc.edu

Royal Roads University Conflict Analysis and Management Program, jbayer@royalroads.ca, www.royalroads.ca

Stanford Center on Conflict and Negotiation at Stanford University School of Law, byron.bland@stanford.edu, www.stanford.edu/group/sccn

Syracuse University Program on the Analysis and Resolution of Conflicts, alhusen@mailbox.syr.edu, www.maxwell.syr.edu/parc/parcmain.htm

United States Institute for Environmental Conflict Resolution, palmer@ecr.gov, www.ecr.gov

United States–México Conflict Resolution Center at New Mexico State University, CRC@crc.nmsu.edu, http://crc.nmsu.edu

University of New Hampshire Program on Consensus and Conflict Resolution, jsv@christa.unh.edu, www.agree.org/state/new+hampshire.html

Wayne State University Program in Mediating Theory, ac7085@wayne.edu

Western Justice Center, info@westernjustice.org, www.westernjustice.org

Wi'am Center/Palestinian Conflict Resolution Center, alaslah@planet.edu, www.planet.edu/~alaslah

Willamette Law Online, www.willamette.edu/law/wlo/dis-res

APPENDIX SIX:
SAMPLE OPPORTUNITIES
IN CONFLICT RESOLUTION

Following is a listing of some of the opportunities available to conflict resolution professionals as reported by the three leading Web sites:

Alternative Newsletter, July 2000, www.mediate.com/tan

www.CRINFO.com, March 2001

www.Mediate.com, March 2001

The announcements that follow are no longer current. They are listed for illustrative purposes only. Check the listed Web sites for updated and full announcements for employment, panels, fellowships and grants, prizes and awards, and other opportunities.

EMPLOYMENT OPPORTUNITIES

- The Consortium on Negotiation and Conflict Resolution at a law school seeking a Research Project Director to develop and coordinate research efforts associated with existing programs.

- The Alternative Dispute Resolution Division of a Federal Agency has a part-time position available to help with developing a computer tracking system for ADR cases and to develop policy documents.

- Peace Games is seeking a Boston Executive Director/New England Regional Director responsible for supervising the senior staff as they implement aspects of Peace Games work in Boston area school communities.

- A Washington, D.C.–based consulting firm seeks senior and mid-level individuals with recent experience in peace-keeping operations, conflict resolution strategies, and other related experience in designing transition interventions to establish or reenergize democratic institutions.

- The United Nations Centre for Human Settlements (Habitat) Housing and Property Directorate and Housing and Property Claims Commission are internationally supervised bodies mandated by the UN Secretary General to regularize housing and property rights in Kosovo until such a time as local courts and governmental institutions are able to operate effectively and impartially.

- A New Mexico Center for Dispute Resolution, an agency with national leadership in conflict resolution and mediation, is seeking an Executive Director.

- A Community Dispute Resolution Center, Inc., a full-service community mediation center, seeks two members for a new management team to work closely with the founding Executive Director.

- A Director of Dispute Resolution Services for an industry-leading processor of electronic payments transactions is being sought.

- An interdisciplinary, non-profit institute, is seeking an individual with expertise and substantial experience in the fields of conflict prevention, resolution, and negotiations to be an Associate Director of its Conflict Resolution Program.

- A religious Conflict Resolution Program is seeking a Coordinator for their Peacebuilding and Demilitarization Program.

OTHER OPPORTUNITIES

- Mediators, facilitators, consensus builders, dispute systems designers, neutral evaluators, settlement judges, and conflict assessors can apply for listing on a National Roster of Environmental Conflict Resolution and Consensus Building Professionals.

- An International Organization is gathering a list of names for panels of dispute resolution professionals to resolve international trade disputes under the General Agreement on Trade in Service (GATS).

FELLOWSHIPS AND GRANTS

- A Program for International Peace invites applications for Dissertation Fellowships for projects addressing international peace and conflict resolution.

PRIZES AND AWARDS

- The American Bar Association Section of Dispute Resolution and the Society of Professionals in Dispute Resolution (SPIDR) have jointly announced the James Boskey ADR Writing Competition.

- The University of Toronto School of Continuing Studies has announced a new award in dispute resolution to be given annually to recognize the creative application of dispute resolution, and to expand the dispute resolution body of knowledge through critical commentary and examination.

- The Office of Personnel Management in the Federal Government has established an OPM Director's Award for Outstanding Alternative Dispute Resolution (ADR) Programs.

MARKETING BUDGET FOR THE FIRST YEAR IN PRACTICE

Strategy	Capital	Staff Cost	My Time
Mission statement			
Business plan			
Meetings of board of directors			
Public relations consultant			
Marketing consultant			
Seminars			
Books and videotapes			
Brochures			
Business cards			
Announcements			
Stationery			
Travel			
Entertainment/meals			
Attend conferences and programs			
Host open house			

Strategy	Capital	Staff Cost	My Time
Computer software			
Press releases			
Marketing packet folders			
Duplication of materials			
Assembling packets			
Resume			
Training			
Direct mail			
Database			
Listing in professional directories			
Membership dues			
Yellow Page Ads			
Web listing			
Web site			
Web links			
Web ads			
Print ads: Consumer			
Print ads: Trade			
Teaching materials			
Write articles			
Charity and public interest donations and volunteering			
Volunteer mediation			
Total			

SAMPLE OFFICE EXPENSES FORM

Ordinary Income/Expenses
   Income
      Fee Income   _____
         Client   _____
         Consulting   _____
         Fee Income—other   _____
      Total fee income   _____
      Total income   _____

Expenses
   Advertising
      Internet   _____
      Marketing brochures   _____
      National Yellow Pages   _____
      Print   _____
      Television   _____
      Yellow pages   _____
      Advertising—other   _____
   Total advertising   _____

   Automobile expense
      Mileage   _____
      Automobile expense—
      other   _____
   Total automobile expense   _____

   Bank service charges   _____
   Business development
      Contractor   _____
      Promotional material   _____
      Travel   _____
      Business
         development—other   _____
   Total business development   _____

Compensation
    Salaries   _____
    Training   _____
    Payroll taxes   _____
    Health insurance   _____
    Disability insurance   _____
    Compensation—other _____
Total compensation   _____

Computer equipment   _____
Computers
    Data system   _____
    Equipment   _____
    Repairs   _____
    Web site development _____
    Computers—other   _____
Total computers   _____

Conference marketing _____
Continuing legal
    education   _____
Contributions   _____
Court fees   _____
Credit card processing fee _____
Depreciation expense _____
Dues and subscriptions _____
Education   _____
Entertainment
promotions   _____
Equipment rental   _____
Filing fees   _____
Firm meetings   _____
Gifts   _____
Insurance
    Key executive   _____
    Liability insurance   _____

Malpractice	_____	
Workers compensation	_____	
Insurance—other	_____	
Total insurance		_____
Interest expense	_____	
Legal library	_____	
Licenses and permits	_____	
Marketing expenses		
Marketing	_____	
Promotional materials	_____	
Marketing expenses—other	_____	
Total marketing expenses		_____
Office	_____	
Total office		_____
Office expense	_____	
Office furniture and equipment	_____	
Parking	_____	
Postage and delivery	_____	
Professional fees		
Accounting	_____	
Bookkeeping	_____	
Consulting	_____	
Legal fees	_____	
Mediation	_____	
Professional fees—other	_____	
Total professional fees		_____
Professional membership	_____	
Public relations	_____	
Publications	_____	
Reference materials	_____	
Rent	_____	

Repairs
    Building repairs   _____
    Computer repairs   _____
    Copier   _____
    Dictation equipment   _____
    Equipment repairs   _____
    Repairs-other   _____
Total repairs   _____

Storage   _____
Supplies
    Marketing   _____
    Office   _____
    Supplies—other   _____
Total supplies   _____

Taxes
    Federal   _____
    Local   _____
    Property   _____
    State   _____
    Taxes—other   _____
Total taxes   _____

Telephone
    Cellular   _____
    DSL line   _____
    Local calls   _____
    Long distance   _____
    Telephone equipment   _____
    Toll free   _____
    Telephone—other   _____
Total telephone   _____

Travel and entertainment
    Accommodations   _____

Entertainment	_____	
Meals	_____	
Travel	_____	
Travel and entertainment—other	_____	
Total travel and entertainment		_____
Utilities		
Gas and electric	_____	
Water	_____	
Utilities—other	_____	
Total utilities		_____
Total expense		_____
Net ordinary income	_____	
Other income/expense		
Other income	_____	
Other receipts	_____	
Total other income		_____
Other expense		
Other expenses	_____	
Total other expenses		_____
Net other income		_____
Net income		_____

AGREEMENT TO MEDIATE

I have read the attached Mediation Agreement completely and understand its contents. I have initialed each page to indicate my understanding and agreement of the terms.

This is an agreement between:

_____ ,

hereinafter "parties," and

_____ ,

hereinafter "mediator," to enter into mediation with the intent of resolving issues related to:

_____

_____

$ _____

HOURLY RATE PER PARTY

_____   _____
Dated   MEDIATOR

_____   _____
Dated   PARTY #1

_____   _____
Dated   PARTY #2

| Party #1 _____ |
| Party #2 _____ |

MEDIATION AGREEMENT

The parties and the mediator understand and agree as follows:

1. ESTABLISHMENT OF MEDIATION RELATIONSHIP

The undersigned wish to retain the services of MEDIATOR to mediate disputed issues.

All references to "mediator" apply to any person designated by the mediator to assist in the mediation process, such as the Dispute Resolution Associate.

2. NATURE OF MEDIATION

The parties understand that mediation is an agreement-reaching process in which the mediator assists parties to reach agreement in a collaborative, consensual and informed manner. It is understood that the mediator has no power to decide disputed issues for the parties. The parties understand that the mediator's objective is to facilitate the parties themselves reaching their most constructive and fairest agreement.

3. RIGHT OF CONSULTATION WITH LAWYER

During the mediation, the parties are each encouraged to consult or be represented by a lawyer at any time, especially before signing the final settlement agreement. Parties are entitled to the confidentiality of any communication with their attorney(s).

4. MEDIATOR REPRESENTS NEITHER PARTY

The parties acknowledge that the mediator does not represent the interests of either party and is not acting as an attorney. The parties acknowledge that the purpose of mediation is to facilitate the ultimate resolution and agreement between the parties regarding the issues, problems, and disputes presented in mediation and that the mediator does not act as an advocate, representative, fiduciary, lawyer, or therapist for either party.

5. IMPARTIALITY OF MEDIATOR

The parties acknowledge that, although the mediator will be impartial and that the mediator does not favor either party, there may be issues in which one party may be reasonable and the other may not be reasonable. The mediator has a duty to assure a balanced dialogue and to diffuse any manipulative or intimidating tactics.

> **Party #1** _____
> **Party #2** _____

6. CONFIDENTIALITY

It is understood between the parties and the mediator that the mediation will be strictly confidential. Mediation discussions, written and oral communications, any draft resolutions, and any unsigned mediated agreements shall not be admissible in any court proceedings. Only a mediated agreement, signed by the parties, may be so admissible. The parties further agree not to call the mediator to testify concerning the mediation or to provide any materials from the mediation in any court proceeding between the parties. The mediation is considered by the parties and the mediator as settlement negotiations. The parties understand the mediator has an ethical responsibility to break confidentiality if he or she suspects another person may be in danger of harm. The only other exceptions to this confidentiality of the mediation are with regard to the mediator's duty to report reasonable suspicion of child abuse and domestic violence; the mediator's ability to defend himself or herself in any legal action; in the event of a joint written waiver of confidentiality by the parties; or otherwise as may be required by law.

7. RIGHT OF MEDIATOR TO WITHDRAW

The mediator will attempt to resolve any outstanding disputes among the parties as long as both parties make a good-faith effort to reach an agreement based on fairness to both parties. Parties must be willing and able to participate in the process. The mediated agreement requires compromise, and parties agree to attempt to be flexible and open to new possibilities for a resolution of the dispute. If the mediator, in his or her professional judgment, concludes that agreement is not possible or that continuation of the mediation process would harm or prejudice one or all of the participants, the mediator shall withdraw and the mediation conclude.

8. TERMINATION OF MEDIATION WITHOUT CAUSE

The mediation may be terminated without cause by any party at any time. No reason must be given, either to the other parties or to the mediator. A decision to terminate mediation must be made in writing. Mediation may not resume following said notification, unless expressly authorized in writing by all parties.

Upon termination of mediation for any reason, the mediator agrees not to counsel either party or represent any party against any other party, in any court proceeding, adversary negotiation, or for any other reason involving a dispute between the parties.

Party #1 _____
Party #2 _____

9. VOLUNTARY DISCLOSURE OF POSSIBLE PREJUDICIAL INFORMATION

The parties agree that, while mediation is in progress, full disclosure of all information is essential to a successful resolution of the issues. Since the court process may not be used to compel information, any agreement made through mediation may be rescinded in whole or in part if one party fails to disclose relevant information during the mediation process. Since the voluntary disclosure of this information may give one party an advantage that may not have been obtained through the traditional adversarial process, the parties agree to release and hold harmless the mediator from any liability or damages caused by voluntary disclosure of prejudicial information in the mediation process that may be used in subsequent negotiations or court proceedings. The mediator has no power to bind third parties not to disclose information furnished during mediation.

10. THE MEDIATOR DOES NOT PROMISE RESULTS

Each party acknowledges that, since mediation is a process of compromise, it is possible that any party might agree to settle on terms that might be considered to be less favorable in comparison to what the party might have received from a Judge after a contested court hearing, or through negotiation in which one or all of the parties have retained legal counsel. The mediator makes no representations that the ultimate result would be the same in kind or degree as might be concluded through negotiation or a contested trial on one or all of the issues. Any questions concerning fairness should be addressed to the mediator as they occur. In addition, parties should consult with independent legal counsel to review compromises made during the course of mediation, and all provisions of a final agreement prior to executing any court documents.

11. FILING OF COURT DOCUMENTS

Once an agreement is reached, in whole or in part, or at any time the parties desire to file any court documents to confirm the agreement and to obtain court order or judgment based thereon, the parties understand that the mediator may not represent either party in a court of law. However, the parties agree that if the parties are represented by counsel, or act as their own attorney(s) In Pro Per, the parties may authorize MEDIATOR to contract with a law firm to neutrally prepare court papers and to monitor all paperwork through the court system. In

Party #1 _____
Party #2 _____

performing such work, MEDIATOR is performing its neutral mediator function and will take no action without the mutual agreement and authorization of all parties.

12. MEDIATION FEES

The parties agree that the administrative start-up fee is $_____ per party (flat fee). Payment is due upon signing of this agreement.

The parties agree that if they need assistance in gathering the necessary information in preparation for the mediation and need assistance in filling out the necessary paperwork, they will schedule an Orientation with the Dispute Resolution Assistant for $_____ per hour. All parties understand that this is optional.

The client(s) agree that the fee for contacting and attempting to convene necessary parties to the mediation is $_____ per each party you wish for us to contact.

The parties and the mediator agree that the fee for the mediator shall be $_____ per hour, per party for time spent with the parties and for time to study documents, research issues, correspond, telephone call, prepare draft and final agreements, and do such other things as may be reasonably necessary to facilitate the parties' reaching full agreement. Payments of fees are due prior to each mediation session based on the mediator's hourly rate and expected length of session.

The clients and the DRA agree that the fee for the Dispute Resolution Assistant shall be $_____ per hour for time spent in addition to the orientation.

Inter-session letters (optional) will be charged for one half hour of the mediator's hourly rate (flat fee). Payment is due upon request for the letters. One inter-session telephone call between the Dispute Resolution Assistant and the party(ies) is free of charge. However, if more than one telephone call is made, the fee is 20 percent of the Dispute Resolution Assistant's hourly rate. Payment is due at the next session. Telephone calls between the mediator and clients are charged at the mediator's hourly rate in increments of 0.2 of an hour.

The parties shall be jointly and severally liable for the mediator's fees and expenses.

Should payment not be timely made, MEDIATOR may stop all work on behalf of the parties, including the drafting and/or distribution of the parties' agreement, and withdraw from the mediation. If collection or court action is taken by the me-

Party #1 _____
Party #2 _____

diator to collect fees and/or expenses under this agreement, the prevailing party in any such action and upon any appeal therefrom shall be entitled to attorney fees and costs therein incurred.

13. MEDIATION

If there is a dispute over fees, Parties and Mediator shall engage in Mediation for a minimum of 2 hours (unless agreement is reached earlier) with a mutually agreed upon mediator or a mediator selected by _____ . All costs shall be shared 50% by the mediator and 50% apportioned equally between the parties.

14. BINDING ARBITRATION

All disputes between the parties and the mediator regarding any aspect of our professional relationship will be resolved by binding arbitration administered through the County Bar Association and not by litigation in court. By this provision, the parties and mediator are both giving up the right to have any such dispute decided by a judge or a jury and we are each giving up the right of appeal. All costs shall be shared 50% by the mediator and 50% apportioned equally between the parties.

The prevailing party in any arbitration between us will be entitled to reasonable attorney's fees and costs. Any litigation or arbitration between us will take place in _____ County and State law will apply.

It is important for you to know that under current California law a mediator has complete immunity from suits regarding negligence or malpractice or any other cause of action. This means that you cannot sue our mediators for any damage to you arising out of the mediation relationship.

Before signing this agreement, you have a right to consult your own attorney about the legal consequences to you of signing this agreement and specifically waiving the right to use the courts in any fee dispute and using arbitration instead.

15. MEDIATOR'S FEES

Should it be necessary to institute any legal action or arbitration for the enforcement of this agreement, the prevailing party shall be entitled to receive all court costs and reasonable attorneys fees incurred in such action from the other party.

16. EXECUTION OF MEDIATION AGREEMENT

By signing this Mediation Agreement, each party agrees that he or she has carefully read and considered each and every provision of this Agreement and agrees to each provision of this agreement without reservation.

Party #1 _____
Party #2 _____

CONFLICT WELLNESS AND LEGAL HEALTH CHECKUP

We are dedicated to not only solving your disputes, but also ensuring your ongoing legal health and conflict wellness. Like a legal thermometer, this checkup helps you assess your current legal health so that we can work as a team to prevent or minimize trouble in your life. Please take a few minutes to complete this confidential checkup.

Date: _____ Name: _____

1. Do you have a will that has been revised within the past three years?
   Yes ☐ No ☐

2. Do you currently have any concerns about your job or business?
   Yes ☐ No ☐

3. Do you have adequate life insurance protection? Yes ☐ No ☐

4. Do you have adequate medical insurance? Yes ☐ No ☐

5. Do you have a written and current listing of all important future dates concerning your legal and financial matters? Yes ☐ No ☐

6. Do you have a file, stored in a secure and fireproof location, containing all important documents (for example, wills, titles, securities, contracts, marriage, divorce papers, deeds, pension plans, profit-sharing plans)?
   Yes ☐ No ☐

7. Within the past three years, have you reviewed the beneficiary designations on insurance policies, pension plans, bank accounts, and other important documents? Yes ☐ No ☐

8. Do you have a complete and current personal financial statement that lists in detail all of your personal assets and liabilities? Yes ☐ No ☐

9. Do you currently have a monthly budget that details your current income and all expenses? Yes ☐ No ☐

10. Do you have any concerns about your debts? Yes ☐ No ☐

11. Do you have a complete and current inventory of all your physical possessions sufficient to support a claim in the event of a loss? Yes ☐ No ☐

12. Do you have concerns about the academic, emotional, or social development of your child(ren)? Yes ☐ No ☐

13. Are there currently extraordinary emotional pressures and stresses in your life? Yes ☐   No ☐

14. After reviewing these questions, are there any matters or issues that you believe should be updated, reconsidered, or brought to the attention of your mediator? Please explain below. Yes ☐   No ☐

15. Have any of these questions caused you to consider taking some action or making some further review? Please explain below. Yes ☐   No ☐

16. Is there any other legal, financial, or personal concern that you believe should be brought to the attention of your mediator? Please explain below. Yes ☐   No ☐

On the lines below, please expand on any answers that you believe would give your mediator a better picture of your current legal health.

_____

_____

_____

_____

_____

_____

Mediator's Notes: _____

_____

_____

_____

_____

_____

_____

_____

CLIENT EVALUATION FORM

1. NAME OF PARTY: _____

2. ATTORNEY: _____

3. MEDIATOR: _____

4. DATE OF MEDIATION: _____

5. LOCATION: _____

6. NATURE OF CASE: _____

7. SETTLEMENT REACHED? _____

Please use the following rating scale to determine an overall rating under each category. Below each heading are listed several factors to consider in making a rating. Under the "Comments" section, discuss specifically the areas of strength and those areas needing improvement.

5 – Excellent   3 – Satisfactory   1 – Unsatisfactory
4 – Highly competent   2 – Needs improvement   0 – Not applicable

Overall Rating

1. Orientation with dispute resolution associate _____

_____ Provided information packets

_____ Provided welcome and opening comments

_____ Explained mediation process

_____ Clarified role of participants

_____ Provided a selection of mediators

_____ Established ground rules

_____ Covered mediation agreement

Comments:

_____

_____

_____

_____

_____

2. Location/mediation setting _____

_____ Location

_____ Convenient to all parties

_____ Provided comfortable mediation room

_____ Provided necessary equipment (flip chart, computer, calculator)

_____ Comfortable and safe setting

Comments:

_____

_____

_____

_____

3. Mediator's performance _____

_____ Provided information sharing between the parties

_____ Understood and clarified issues

_____ Accurately and briefly summarized information and concerns

_____ Balanced time and focus between clients

_____ Identified common ground

_____ Generated options

_____ Facilitated negotiation and bargaining

_____ Discussed options for noncompliance or resolving future conflict

_____ Worked effectively with attorneys (if applicable)

_____ Drafted agreement that addressed all issues (if applicable)

Comments:

_____

_____

_____

_____

_____

4. Do you have any ideas or suggestions for improvement?

_____

_____

_____

_____

Thank you for taking the time to help us improve.
[Names of principal mediators]

PEACEMAKER PLEDGE

I will *think* about peace, why peace is important and how it works.

I will actively *use* my peacemaker efforts to help people in conflict:

In my family

In my [school] [work]

In my community

I will *be* a *Rodef Shalom*—an active pursuer of peace.

Date: _____   By: _____

DIRECTIONS: Place the signed Peacemaker Pledge into a sealed envelope. Put the envelope into a safe place. On the one-year anniversary of your pledge, open the envelope, take out your signed pledge, think about your last year's peacemaking efforts, and then re-pledge for another year.

NOTES

Chapter One

1. You can read a summary of the research at www.to-agree.com/advres.htm and the full report at www.virginia.law.com/matreas/adrcomm.htm.
2. Rand Corporation. *An Evaluation of Mediation and Neutral Evaluation Under the Civil Justice Reform Act.* Rand Institute for Civil Justice (www.rand.org).
3. Ury, W. *The Third Side: Why We Fight and How We Can Stop It.* New York: Viking Press, 2000.
4. Fisher, R., Patton, S., and Ury, W. *Getting to Yes.* New York, Penguin, 1991.
5. Schön, D. *Reflective Practitioner.* New York: Basic Books, 1983.
6. Lang, M., and Taylor, A. *The Making of a Mediator.* San Francisco: Jossey-Bass, 2000.

Chapter Two

1. Lederach, J. P. *Academy of Family Mediators News,* Summer 2000.
2. Maggiolo, W. *Techniques of Mediation.* Dobbs Ferry, N.Y.: Oceana, 1971.

Chapter Three

1. I learned this from Rabbi Jeffrey Marx of Los Angeles, who is also a trained professional mediator. See the Peacemaker Pledge in Appendix Nine.
2. Mosten, F. "Mediation and the Process of Family Law Reform." *Family Court Review,* November 1999.
3. See Robert Bush and Joseph Folger, *The Promise of Mediation.* San Francisco: Jossey-Bass, 1994.

Chapter Four

1. Send questions to John Windmueller at John@conflictresolver.com.

Chapter Five

1. See www.Financenet.gov/iadrwg.htm for information on the Interagency Alternative Dispute Resolution Working Group.
2. Marsh, S. "Five Paths to Teaching Dispute Resolution and Conflict Management." *ADR Newsletter, 38* (www.adrr.com).

Chapter Six

1. Moore, C. *Mediation Process.* (2nd ed.) San Francisco: Jossey-Bass, 1996.
2. Peters, T. *Thriving on Chaos.* New York: HarperCollins, 1987.
3. Senge, P. *The Fifth Discipline.* New York: Doubleday, 1990.
4. Peters, T. *Thriving on Chaos.* New York: HarperCollins, 1987, p. 486.
5. Peters. *Thriving on Chaos.*
6. Lang, M., and Taylor, A. *The Making of a Mediator.* San Francisco: Jossey-Bass, 2000.
7. n8 CalApp 4th 653; 92CalReptr2d 916 (2000). For articles on *Foxgate* and mediator confidentiality, see www.mediate.com article on Foxgate case.
8. Mayer, B. *Dynamics of Conflict Resolution.* San Francisco: Jossey-Bass, 2000.
9. Riskin, L. "Understanding Mediator Orientations, Strategies, and Techniques: A Grid for the Perplexed." *Harvard Negotiation Law Review,* 1996, *1.*
10. Krivis, J., and McAdoo, B. "A Style Index for Mediators." *Alternatives,* Dec. 1997. [www.mediate.com/articles/krivis2.cf].
11. Ury, W. *The Third Side.* New York: Viking, 2000, p. 114.
12. Cloke, K. *Resolving Personal and Organizational Conflict: Stories of Transformation and Forgiveness.* San Francisco: Jossey-Bass, 2000.

Chapter Seven

1. Mosten, F. S. *Unbundling Legal Services: A Guide to Delivering Legal Services à la Carte.* Chicago: American Bar Association, 2000.
2. New York State Bar Association. Ethics Opinion 736. Mar. 2001.
3. Brown, L. M. *Mediation, Arbitration, and Preventive Law.* Cambridge, Mass.: Harvard Law School, 1988. Videotape.

Chapter Eight

1. Rand Corporation. *An Evaluation of Mediation and Neutral Evaluation Under the Civil Justice Reform Act.* Rand Institute for Civil Justice (www.rand.org).
2. Peters, T. *Thriving on Chaos.* New York: HarperCollins, 1987.

Chapter Nine

1. Adapted from Mosten, F. S. *Unbundling Legal Services.* Chicago: American Bar Association, 2000.

Chapter Eleven

1. For further information on capital investment, see the following books: Mancuso, J. *How to Start, Finance, and Manage Your Own Small Business.* Upper Saddle River, N.J.: Prentice Hall, 1984. Kamoroff, B. *Small Time Operator: How to Start Your Own Small Business, Keep Your Books, Pay Your Taxes, and Stay Out of Trouble* (25th ed). Willits, Calif.: Bell Springs Publishing, 1988.
2. Abrams, R., and Kleiner, E. *The Successful Business Plan: Secrets and Strategies.* Central Point, Ore.: Oasis Press, 1993.
3. Steingold, F. *Legal Guide for Starting and Running a Small Business* (5th ed.). Berkeley, Calif.: Nolo Press, 2001.

Chapter Twelve

1. Peters, T. *Thriving on Chaos.* New York: HarperCollins, 1987.
2. Peters, *Thriving on Chaos.* p. 85.
3. Levitt, T., *Marketing Imagination.* New York: Free Press, 1986.

Chapter Thirteen

1. Mosten, F. S. *The Complete Guide to Mediation.* Chicago: American Bar Association, 1997.
2. Peters, T. *Thriving on Chaos.* New York: HarperCollins, 1987.
3. American Bar Association Commission on Advertising. *Yellow Pages Advertising: An Analysis of Effective Elements.* Chicago: American Bar Association, 1979.

Epilogue

1. Sander, F. *Varieties of Dispute Processing: Perspectives of Justice in the Future.* Chicago: American Bar Association, 1979.
2. See Mosten, F. S. "Mediation and the Process of Family Law Reform." *Family Courts Review,* October 1999, *37,* 429, for a proposed agenda for law reform.
3. Mosten, F. and Kichaven, J. "Our Communication Is Important Too." Southern California Mediation Association, November 1997.
4. Mosten and Kichaven, "Our Communication Is Important Too." p. 4.
5. Mosten, F., Jacob, L., and Erikson, S. "Is Mediation Becoming a Subspecialty of the Legal Profession?" Academy of Family Mediators 1999 Annual Conference.
6. Bush, R. B., and Folger, J. *The Promise of Mediation: Responding to Conflict Through Empowerment and Recognition.* San Francisco: Jossey-Bass, 1994.
7. For background, see the American Bar Association Commission on Multi-Disciplinary Practice (MDP). Munneke, G. A., and MacNaughton, A. L. *Multidisciplinary Practice: Staying Competitive and Adapting to Change.* Chicago: American Bar Association, 2000.

8. Ellinor, L., and Gerard, G. *Dialogue.* New York: Wiley, 1998.
9. Riskin, L. "Understanding Mediator Orientations, Strategies and Techniques: A Grid for the Perplexed." *Harvard Negotiation Law Review,* 1996, *1,* 7.
10. Brown, L. M. *Lawyering Through Life.* Littleton, Colo.: Rothman, 1986.

THE AUTHOR

Forrest S. (Woody) Mosten, a mediator since 1979, has been recognized for his pioneering work in mediation and expanding legal access by mediation organizations and bar associations throughout the United States.

An original partner in the groundbreaking firm of Jacoby and Meyers and president of Mosten Mediation Centers with offices nationwide, Mosten trains mediators worldwide and was the international convener and editor of the *Family Court Review*'s Millennium Special Issue (January 2000), *Training Mediators for the Twenty-First Century*. His prior books receiving critical acclaim are *The Complete Guide to Mediation, Unbundling Legal Services,* and *Operating a Profitable Mediation Practice.*

Mosten is passionate about encouraging mediators on all levels to make peacemaking their life's work and their day job. He practices and lives in Los Angeles and can be reached at www.MostenMediation.com.

INDEX